European Distance and E-Learning Network Annual Conference (EDEN 2022)

Shaping the Digital Transformation of the Education Ecosystem in Europe

Tallinn, Estonia
20-22 June 2022

Editors:

Josep M. Duart
Elena Trepule

ISBN: 978-1-7138-8972-4

Printed from e-media with permission by:

Curran Associates, Inc.
57 Morehouse Lane
Red Hook, NY 12571

Some format issues inherent in the e-media version may also appear in this print version.

Printed with permission by Curran Associates, Inc. (2024)

For permission requests, please contact European Distance and E-Learning Network (EDEN) at the address below.

European Distance and E-Learning Network (EDEN)
Budapest University of Technology & Economics
H-1111 Budapest, Egry J. u.1.
Hungary

Phone: +36 1 463 1628
Fax: +36 1 463 1858

secretariat@eden-online.org

Additional copies of this publication are available from:

Curran Associates, Inc.
57 Morehouse Lane
Red Hook, NY 12571 USA
Phone: 845-758-0400
Fax: 845-758-2633
Email: curran@proceedings.com
Web: www.proceedings.com

EDEN Conference Proceedings

Shaping the Digital Transformation of the Education Ecosystem in Europe

EDEN 2022 Annual Conference

hosted by

Tallinn University, Estonia

20-22 June 2022

Edited by
Josep M.Duart, Elena Trepule
on the behalf of EDEN Digital Learning Europe

EDEN Conference Proceedings

2022 Annual Conference | Tallinn, 20-22 June, 2022

ISSN: 2707-2819

Published by EDEN Digital learning Europe

Editors:

Josep M. Duart

Elena Trepule

Editorial co-ordination:

Gabija Kvieskaite

Carlos Madrid

EDEN DLE Secretariat

Roosikrantsi 2, 10119, Tallinn, Republic of Estonia

E-mail: secretariat@eden-europe.eu

https://eden-europe.eu/

Supported by the Erasmus+ Programme of the European Union

The publication reflects the authors' view, the EACEA and the European Commission are not responsible for any use that may be made of the information it contains.

Acknowledgement and thanks are given to the Programme and Evaluation Committee

Josep M. Duart, EDEN President, Professor at Open University of Catalonia (UOC), Spain

Mart Laanpere, Professor at Tallinn University, Estonia

Terje Väljataga, Senior Researcher at Tallinn University, Estonia

Airina Volungeviciene, former EDEN President, Director of Innovative Studies Institute, Vytautas Magnus University, Lithuania

Sandra Kučina Softić, former EDEN President, Assistant Director for Education and User Support at the Zagreb University Computing Centre, Croatia

Mark Brown, National Institute for Digital Learning, Dublin City University, Ireland

Helga Dorner, Central European University, Hungary

Timothy Read, Universidad Nacional de Educatión a Distancia, UNED, Spain

Denise Whitelock, The Open University, United Kingdom

Alfredo Soeiro, Universidade do Porto, Portugal

Vlad Mihaescu, Politehnica University of Timisoara, Romania

TABLE OF CONTENTS

ISSN: 2707-2819

DIGITAL ECOSYSTEM "UNIVERSITY" AS INNOVATION INCUBATOR FOR MERGING HYBRID AND AI-SUPPORTED HIGHER EDUCATION

Christian-Andreas Schumann, Frank Otto, Nico Kling, Claudia Tittmann and Anna-Maria Nitsche, West Saxon University of Zwickau

Abstract

Digitization is transforming education systems, including higher education, into digitalized ecosystems, because they integrate economic, environmental, and social processes into one specific system. The technical and technological aspects of system design are brought in through forms of digitalization and automation of educational, administrative, and service processes. The interplay of various factors in a digital ecosystem of higher education supports a modelling close to reality and the view of the theoretically based, practice-oriented use of educational processes in regional, national, and international higher education networks through the multidimensional and realistic approach. Taking a holistic view of the interplay of multiple factors in teaching, learning, and support processes provides new insights into knowledge transfer in higher education, which can better promote and generate innovation. It is therefore natural to consider digital ecosystems of higher education from the perspective of innovation incubators. Incubators have the property of providing increased support for processes or domains of special interest and significantly accelerating their development. The corresponding entry of additional resources and the focus on these special processes and domains, as well as the creation of framework conditions conducive to development, will also create better conditions for innovations to emerge, develop and be used. Organizational units or organizational forms of institutions serve as innovation incubators if they possess the corresponding innovation-promoting characteristics. Universities as organizational units of education generally have the capabilities to generate, develop and apply innovations. They can therefore take on the function of innovation incubators. Emerging technologies are, on the one hand, means to accelerate innovation and, on the other hand, are themselves objects of research and development in innovative processes, which is especially true for universities and non-university research institutions. Due to the potential for innovation, new educational technologies in higher education are gaining importance in the digital university ecosystem. However, they can only exploit their potential if they receive accelerated support and are fully integrated into the higher education system. Currently, outstanding emerging technologies are linked in the context of digitalization with hybrid approaches and AI applications. They serve as innovation drivers for the universities. Their integration into their digital ecosystems of higher education means that they need to be merged with all other components as well as with each other. Now that both emerging technologies have been given an extra push by the pandemic and are of such great importance for the advancement of education, the state of development is progressing rapidly. Their integration and merger are being planned and realized in ongoing university education projects.

Keywords: Digital ecosystem, Hybridization, AI Application, Innovation incubator, Higher Education

Introduction

As early as 1713, Hans Carl von Carlowitz, the Saxon chief miner of the Ore Mountains, developed the innovative concept of a sustainable economy, specifically related to the forestry industry of the time. His new approach to the management of resources, especially wood, in the context of mining was aimed at carrying out economy through careful management of the environment, with responsibility for future generations, for the common good. [1][2] It was not until the 20th century that this idea was expanded in the sense of a general welfare for mankind, whereby, however, the basic idea of a balance of economic interests, social justice and environmentally conscious action could be adopted. [3] In 1996, Moore looked at the interrelationship of economic, ecological, and social aspects in the context of biological systems and developed the concept of business ecosystems. [4]

The connection between economy, ecology and social issues is evident. If the whole is put into the system context, there is also a word equivalence between ecological system and economic system in the short form: ecosystem. The social component is inherent in any case since economy and ecology are related to human society and are influenced by people. Human impact on economy and ecology is nowadays always connected with technology. If the ecosystems are supplemented by digitalization, the technology aspect will also be further strengthened by ICT and expanded by information processing. Although organizations are forced to act sustainably under penalty of their demise, digital ecosystems are often reduced to business, technology, and organizational optimization.

However, it makes sense to understand digital ecosystems as a balance of economic, ecological, social, technological, and informal interests, as necessary for the well-being of human society. Since innovation means building on the tried and tested to create something new, the systemic approach is based on the proven economic, ecological, social, technological, and digital components and their relationships for innovations. Universities, as institutions of knowledge transfer and development, are per se focused on teaching how to generate innovations and on actively innovating in research. In this relatively protected and supported environment for research and teaching, ideas can be hatched as in an incubator. Funders, such as government institutions and private sector financiers, influence the focus of innovation. Therefore, it is important that universities have a pillar of independent funding to remain open to innovation in all directions and an incubator for new ideas.

Hybridization and AI as emerging technologies in higher education

Hybrid methods and systems are related to emerging technologies, as is artificial intelligence. Since both approaches are being massively pushed and promoted while advancing digitization, the question arises as to what significance they have in general and for higher education. Both hypes have already shown their usefulness in various fields of application in recent years, which is why every management in higher education must deal with the associated methods, technologies, and tools to maintain the competitiveness of their own organization in the future.

Reasons for hybridization of education [5]	Reasons for AI in higher education [6]
Designing new, hybrid forms of work and study	Better development of cognitive skills
More efficient design of organizational forms	Formation of metacognitive skills such as critical thinking
Optimizing collaboration in networks	Individually successful study through personalization
Adapting the interaction of stakeholders to networking	Improved prediction of study progress through pattern recognition
Upskilling of teaching staff, administration, and students.	Early detection of risks for students and personalized intervention
Increasing the diversity of intercultural cooperation	Shortening of study time or avoidance of dropouts
New opportunities for strategic alignment	Individualized feedback in problem-solving processes
Increasing flexibility and permeability	Support in reviewing and securing teaching strategies
More effective forms of performance generation and evidence.	Provision of analyses and recommendations for curricula
Strengthening interdisciplinary cooperation and innovation	Expansion of digital university teaching through new didactic approaches

Table 1. Aspect of hybridization of education and application of AI in higher education.

Since both hybridization and AI are emerging technologies that can improve the quality and quantity of knowledge transfer and competence development for the benefit of all stakeholders in higher education, they are essential for higher education planning and development in the future. The reasons for establishing hybrid IT [7] as a backbone system also apply to the applications of hybrid, AI-supported higher education and research that build on it, which include:

- Innovation through flexibilization in achieving various technological goals, including digital transformation goals, thereby promoting innovative organizational models through new ideas and services, and accelerating the pace of innovation.
- Improve services using hybrid and AI-powered systems, whereby platforms and functions can be better selected and combined with each other regardless of time and location.
- Organic growth through incremental development of education systems using maturity models that enables iterative penetration of AI while controlling growth by changing hybrid states
- Simplification and efficiency increase through the right mix of processes, functions, methods, and tools of higher education using multidimensional combination of hybrid expressions especially related to AI applications.
- Transformational governance by mastering and controlling transitional states of higher education processes, applications, platforms, and services by exploiting hybridization and AI support.
- Scalability of university education as a single organization or educational networks depending on the needs of employers, educational institutions, and students due to the changeability of organizations and their processes based on hybrid states and with the help of the use of AI.
- Security and compliance through adapted decisions on which particularly safety-relevant tasks, functions, and services are carried out under central control of the university or educational network or which can be decentralized in cooperation with external partners worldwide, for which hybrid systems as well as AI support are particularly suitable.
- Reliability and resilience by adapting the service in the context of hybrid states and the use of AI methods and tools to the needs and suitability for the current university educational missions.
- Preserving and embedding proven solutions that are indispensable into new concepts and models of higher education through hybrid transitions between legacy systems and new applications supported by AI.
- Target and cost control by adapting university strategies, concepts, and models of higher education, taking advantage of hybridization and the associated increase in the adaptability and flexibility of solutions, also taking advantage of the opportunities offered by AI.

Hybrid features and AI are not only emerging technologies that are having a systemic and lasting impact on higher education, but they are entering into a symbiotic relationship. The interplay between hybridization and AI expands their impact on higher education and potentiates their effects.

University digital ecosystem as innovation incubator for hybridization and AI

Universities combine economic, ecological, and social aspects with technical and, for some years now, digital developments, both in terms of their own organization and the content of their teaching and research. For this reason, they are per se digital ecosystems that also acquire, develop, network, publish, disseminate, and preserve knowledge about these systems. The growth of university ecosystems connects science as well as business and is under government oversight in the public context of academic degree recognition. University campuses are home to incubators, accelerators, and innovation facilitators taking the form of innovation hubs. [8]

While increasing digitization, a virtualization of previously predominantly physical systems can be seen, i.e., the campus is becoming just as virtual as innovation hubs, incubators as well as accelerators. The research on innovation hubs is related to considerations of innovative environments characterized by innovation, digital innovation, and hyper competition as well as regional development and clustering, and innovation hubs and network management. [9]

Incubation is a process focused on organizations that should be supported in their development. An incubator is a place where incubation activities are carried out and where stakeholders find a suitable place to satisfy their needs and develop their ideas, turning them into a sustainable reality. Innovation incubators are special types of incubators that support the further development of proven processes, products, services, tools, methods, etc. and take the form of corporate incubators, innovation accelerators, innovation labs and innovation cooperatives.

From the university perspective, there is a pre-university incubation stage, an academic incubation stage, and a post-university incubation stage. The pre-university stage offers services for establishing contact, for joint idea and project development. Expertise and facilities from the partnership of university and interested parties, who are to be supported in the development of their ideas and concepts, are used for incubation. The pure academic incubation stage is supported by the universities and their research, development, and transfer centers as well as incubation unites.

New ideas and concepts of employees, students or complex R&D activities are promoted and supported. In the post-university incubation stage, services are relevant for stabilizing innovations in the competitive environment, rolling out and further developing the solutions in the context of the university's social presence. Emergent technologies such as hybrid systems and applied AI therefore find an excellent breeding ground in the upstream, downstream and core processes of universities as incubators, particularly in relation to new education. Emergent technologies such as hybrid methods and applied AI therefore find an excellent breeding ground in the pre-, post and core processes of the "university" ecosystem as an incubator, particularly regarding education as one of the main tasks of the universities. (see Fig. 1)

Universities as digitized ecosystems thus per se offer all the necessary drivers to serve as incubators for innovations in the field of emerging technologies. That's why you also support and promote the application of hybrid systems and AI both in your own education and training and in educational research.

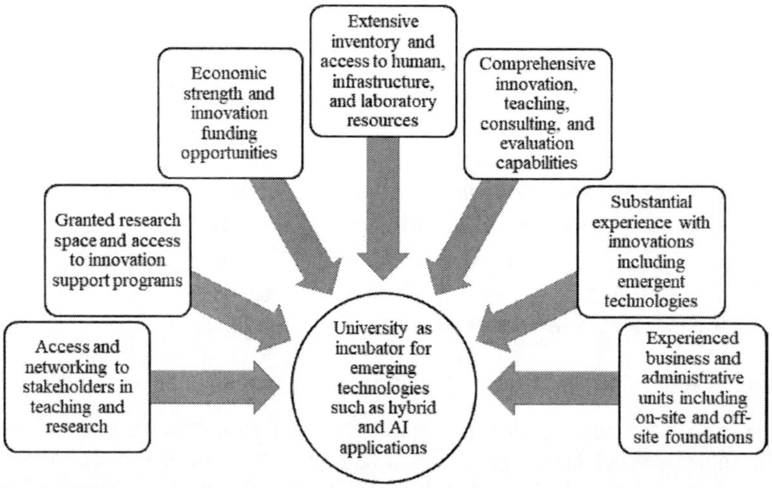

Fig. 1. University incubation drivers for emerging technologies as hybrid and AI applications.

Hybrid and AI-supported higher education in the form of products and services finds a wide field of application especially in the non-profit sector, but also in combination with commercial activities. (see Table 2 [10])

Motivation	Non-profit				Commercial
Potential size of opportunities	High Growth, Equity investible	Medium Growth, Self/debt funded	Small Scale, Self/debt funded	High Potential, Investible social enterprises	High Growth, Equity investible
Typical parent organisation	Academic institutions, Corporate houses	Academic institutions, Corporate houses	Academic institutions, Community associations	Non-profit, impact investors	Funding institutions

Table 2. Options for incubations for innovative, hybrid, and AI-supported higher education

In the context of these diverse applications emerging technologies are combined and merged. Since hybridization and AI are being pushed simultaneously and equally, especially by the pandemic wave of digitization, their parallel development and deployment inevitably leads to synchronization in the development and application teams and thus to crucial synergy effects in higher education.

Merger of hybridization and AI through innovation incubation process in higher education

Hybridization of education and AI applications in higher education are still at a very early stage of maturity across the broad spectrum, but in spots have reached the point where expansions are taking place. From the perspective of incubating the associated innovations, the entire breadth of the incubation process is used. (see Table 3)

Innovation launch Pre-incubation	Early stage Incubation	Expansion Post-incubation
Innovation assessments	Advanced project planning	Application development
Project plan elaboration	Coaching & Mentoring	Innovation validation
Educational and support process modelling	Networking & Hosting Project proposal & financing Pilot applications & training	Internationalisation
		Extension and business actions
Further education & training		Beginning of commercialisation
Emerging technologies: Hybridisation & AI application by digitalization		

Table 3. Emerging technologies hybridization and AI in the innovation incubator "University" [11]

The ecosystem of universities is thus available to push the incubation of emerging technologies, such as in this case of hybrid and AI-based application systems, in the context of digitization. Since there are both corresponding preliminary projects and their solutions for the hybridization of teaching and for AI use in research and education, there is now the task of merging both emerging technologies into a holistic approach as part of a new project for AI at universities. (see Table 4)

N dimensional hybrid concept in higher education				
	Expression X of dimension Y			
Dimension Y	Minimum X=0	Example intermediate state; more of the minimum side 0<X<0.5	Example intermediate state; more of the maximum side 1>X>0,5	Maximum X=1
Education section size	Micro certification	Certificate	Postgraduate course	Course
Digitization	No digitization	Low digitization	Medium digitization	Complete digitization
Technical networking	Single unit	Lan	MAN	WAN
Cooperation	Individual educational institution	Regional education network	International education network	Global education network
Networking of the students	No networking	Low connectivity	High networking	Complete networking
Connectivity	Offline	Predominantly offline	Predominantly online	Online
Teaching support	Unsupervised learning	Mainly unsupervised	Mainly supervised	Supervised learning
Presence	Distance learning	Milestone presence	Blended learning	Presence teaching
Location dependency	Stationary	Predominantly stationary	Predominantly mobile	Mobile
Learning centering	Interactivity	Predominantly instructive	Predominantly constructivist	Constructivist
AI based higher education in pre-study, study, and alumni phase				

Table 4. Merging hybrid learning systems and AI-based higher education in an innovation project

The theories of hybrid systems as well as methods and tools of AI are combined and realized in an integrated concept over several subprojects. The university's digital ecosystem serves as an innovation incubator by providing both the development resources and the application field.

Summary and Conclusions

Work in progress

References

1. Carlowitz, H.C.v.: Sylvicultura oeconomica. Published by Johann Friedrich Braun, Leipzig (1713).
2. Carlowitz, H.C.v.: "Sylvicultura oeconomica". In: Robin, L., Sörlin, S., Warde, P. (eds.) The Future of Nature: Documents of Global Change. pp. 67-77. New Haven: Yale University Press (2013).
3. United Nations: AGENDA 21. United Nations Conference on Environment & Development Rio de Janerio. United Nations Division for Sustainable Development, New York (1992).
4. Moore, J.F.: The Death of Competition: Leadership and Strategy in the Age of Business Ecosystems. Harper Business, New York (1996).
5. CIPD Homepage, https://www.cipd.co.uk/Images/hybrid-working-practical-guidance- 2021_tcm18-103709.pdf, last accessed 2022/03/28.
6. de Witt, C., Rampelt, F., Pinkwart, N. (Hrsg.) Künstliche Intelligenz in der Hochschulbildung. Whitepaper. KI-Campus, Berlin (2020).
7. Flexential Homepage, https://www.flexential.com/resources/blog/top-10-reasons-hybrid-it- solution, last accessed 2022/03/29.
8. European Institute of Innovation & Technology (EIT) Homepage, https://eit.europa.eu/ourcommunities/eit-innovation-communities/innovation-hubs, last accesses 2022/03/30.
9. Lantz, C.E., Wu, K.Y.: Building and managing an innovation hub: A case study of the challenges and opportunities faced by a Northern Swedish innovation hub, pp 3-8. UMEA Universitet, Umeå (2017).
10. NEN National Entrepreneurship Network: Guidelines Metrics & Milestones For Successful Incubator Development. Recommendation version 2.0 Made to Department of Science
11. & Technology, Govt. of India, pp. 13-17. Wadhwadi Foundation, Delhi (2013).
12. Vanrie, P., Dichter, G., Reis, G., Marchand, N.: The Smart Guide to Innovation-Based Incubators (IBI), pp. 5-7. European Union. Regional Policy, Brussels (2010).

Shaping the Digital Transformation of the Education Ecosystem in Europe
EDEN Digital Learning Europe Proceedings
2022 Annual Conference | Tallinn, 20-22 June, 2022
ISSN: 2707-2819

THE QUEST FOR QUALITY IN DIGITAL HIGHER EDUCATION: A CRITICAL ANALYSIS OF QA FRAMEWORKS

Mark Brown, Dublin City University

Abstract

This research is set against the backdrop of ongoing concerns about the quality of online education and renewed emphasis on hybrid and blended models of learning following the messy post-COVID return to campus. It explores the thorny question of how to define quality in the next normal of digital higher education and asks what does it looks like and who should get to judge it? What quality assurance (QA) standards and processes are required for online and blended learning? While this is not a new question do these QA standards need to be updated following the pandemic experience and should they differ from those already in place for more traditional delivery modes? To what extent is quality linked to the mode of delivery? Two recent studies frame the conversation around these questions. Firstly, the paper draws on a review of institutional self-assessment tools and instruments for digitally enhanced learning and teaching (DELT) undertaken as part of the Digi-HE project led by the European Universities Association (EUA). Secondly, it reports some of the findings from a critical analysis of QA frameworks from around the globe for online and blended delivery undertaken by the author as part of a major study for the Organisation for Economic Co-operation and Development (OECD). The full results of this study will be published later in 2022. In the meantime, the paper offers a critical synthesis of the published research in this area, noting key trends and significant gaps in the literature. It also offers a brief comparison of 12 different QA frameworks published to support digital higher education and identifies some of the new risks and emerging considerations from a multi-layered perspective. While there is no shortage of quality frameworks for online and blended learning, the research reveals that not all of them are created equal and there is a dearth of evidence on their in fostering cultures of continuous improvement.

Keywords: Quality, Quality Assurance, Digital Education, Online Learning, Blended Learning, Higher Education

Introduction

This research on the elusive question of quality in digital higher education is particularly timely given the importance of applying tangible lessons from the pandemic experience. In the Irish context, the study has even greater relevance as Quality and Qualifications Ireland (QQI), the national quality assurance (QA) agency, is currently developing new and revised Statutory Guidelines for Blended and Online Learning Programmes. Set against this backdrop, the intention of this paper is to promote critical discussion on the dynamic, multifaceted and multi-layered nature of quality in the context of new models of digital higher education. It invites debate on the meaning of quality in this context and the relationship between external QA measures and internal quality enhancement (QE) processes implemented by individual HEIs. The paper begins by establishing the relevance of this study in the post-pandemic higher education environment and then considers the nature of QA drawing on different viewpoints and the central role that institutions play in fostering a culture of continuous improvement. Three framing assumptions are then reported before providing a brief synthesis of the published academic literature. The remainder of the paper shares preliminary findings of a major analysis of QA frameworks from around the globe. Importantly, the study makes the case for an integrated, multifaceted, and multi-layered approach to QA and then identifies some of the gaps in current frameworks in terms of new risks and emerging issues for future consideration.

Why Quality Assurance?

Digital higher education has never been more in the spotlight. The COVID-19 crisis was a watershed moment for online learning and with the messy return to campus, hybrid and blended models of learning have never featured more prominently as a strategic priority for higher education institutions (HEIs). This claim is supported by the findings of a major European survey of 368 institutions from 48 countries administrated in 2020 during the pandemic (Gaebe, et al., 2021). Notably, 95% of responding institutions see digitalisation as a strategic priority over the next five years. The survey also found that three-quarters of the institutional respondents have concrete plans to boost digital capacity beyond the pandemic. In the European context, a renewed Digital Education Action Plan (2021–2027) also puts the spotlight on developing a high-performing digital education ecosystem (European Commission, 2020). One of the major initiatives arising from the Action Plan is the development of the new Digital Education Hub. It follows that quality considerations should be of central importance with this level of new investment in digital education.

While respondents to the above survey widely acknowledge that new models of digital education can enhance the student experience, the benefits bring additional risks. Moreover, the survey findings confirm that strategic investment and successful institution-wide implementation of digitalisation can be a real challenge. For example, when asked about internal QA, the picture is somewhat mixed with around half of the responding institutions not having specific processes in place. That said, a large minority (41%) are considering developing them, which reinforces the timeliness of revisiting the question of quality (Gaebe, et al., 2021). Indeed, in the Irish context, QQI is currently embarking on a project to develop new and revised Statutory QA Guidelines for Blended and Online Learning Programmes to respond to the rapid growth of fully online delivery. Of course, a plethora of quality rubrics, scorecards and benchmarking frameworks already exist to support the development online and blended delivery models. Despite these frameworks, however, only 12% of the responding European institutions reported that they had previously used or engaged in a self-assessment tool for digital education. This finding suggests there is a serious implementation gap between the development of such QA frameworks and their application in practice.

The above survey was undertaken as part of the Erasmus+ co-funded Digi-HE project, led by the European Universities Association (EUA). In 2021, the project team also published a substantial report reviewing 20 different quality tools and frameworks designed for digital higher education (Volungevičienė, et al., 2021). This analysis provides a strong knowledge base for the current research. A related lesson is that few of the 20 instruments reviewed in the EUA study make any effort or explicit attempt to integrate with existing forms of QA required by national agencies or regulatory bodies. This lack of integration is a serious shortcoming in terms of designing a strong quality digital education ecosystem, although Ireland stands out for its foresight in developing the original Statutory QA Guidelines for Blended Learning Programmes (QQI, 2018).

What is Quality Assurance?

It is important to acknowledge that "quality is an elusive term for which there is a wide variety of interpretations depending upon the views of different stakeholders" (Schindler, et al., 2015:

4). Indeed, there is no consensus or agreement as to a definition or single preferred QA model (Ryan, 2015). Depaul (2022) points out in the context of new models of online learning that who gets to judge what is quality is part of the debate. An important difference is often made between external QA for the purpose of accountability and QA for the purpose of improvement or quality enhancement (QE) (European Association for Quality Assurance in Higher Education, 2015). While there are a spectrum of views on the relationship between QA and QE, the basic premise underlying this study is that they are an integral part of the same process.

Importantly, HEIs must be at the centre of all QA processes if the goal is to develop a high-quality culture of continuous improvement. Therefore, any effort to develop national QA requirements must seek to actively engage a wide range of providers and related stakeholders, including students. As a general principle, fit-for-purpose QA guidelines need to be multifaced and multi-layered if they are to support local institutional contexts and the complexity of provision across different education sectors. In a similar vein, any such QA guidelines need to be widely owned, shared, and understood by stakeholders if they are to be impactful in terms of supporting a quality ecosystem. The key point is that efforts to support quality cultures need to embrace an educative approach working closely with the education sector in partnership rather than imposing QA standards and processes leading to a culture of compliance. Therefore, QA guidelines should avoid prescribing how HEIs are to operate and instead provide opportunities for local interpretations according to individual contexts. Put another way, institutions should be able to interpret and apply such guidelines to inform, adapt and enable their own QA processes in ways that are locally fit-for-purpose.

Three Underlying Assumptions

This section describes three important assumptions framing this study before then providing a synthesis of the published academic literature relevant to QA frameworks for online and blended learning.

Quality is not defined by delivery mode

Firstly, the QA of distance education has a long history and there is strong empirical evidence that:

Distance education, when properly planned, designed, and supported by the appropriate mix of technology and pedagogy, is equivalent to, or in certain scenarios more effective than, traditional face-to-face classroom instruction. (Joksimović, et al., 2015: p. 11)

The emergence of online and blended learning builds on this history and is supported by a solid body of empirical research. Despite the recent experience of "Emergency Remote Teaching" in response to the COVID-19 pandemic, which is not the same as well-designed online learning (Hodges, et al., 2020), there is convincing research evidence showing no significant differences in educational outcomes based solely on delivery mode (Nguyen, 2015; Siemens, et al., 2015). Thus, delivery mode is not a key factor by itself in determining the quality of the educational provision. Accordingly, in the academic literature online learning research has moved away from narrow comparative studies to better understanding the nuances and many different aspects that contribute to the design of quality online and blended learning (Florence, et al., 2020). There is little to be gained from sweeping generalisations, which treat online learning as a single monolith entity (Brown, 2021). The crucial point is that online learning has many different faces in the same way that blended and traditional face-to-face teaching models do not all follow the same delivery formula. It is also important to keep the following paradox in mind:

The overarching paradox is that online and distance education systems with their digital content and the persistent record of online transactions provide a rich source of evidence to enable quality assurance and audit processes. If open and distance learning were the current dominant mode of Higher Education and lecture-based education the innovation, the challenge would lie in how to quality assure a form of education in which interactions at the core of the system were ephemeral, highly dependent on personal interpretation by the teacher and student and seldom directly monitored (Ossiannilsson et al., 2015: p. 16).

An integrated approach to quality assurance

Secondly, there is a question of whether or not new online and blended delivery modes require separate QA processes to those already in place for more traditional forms of teaching, learning and assessment. While this is an important question, the framing assumption underpinning this study is that despite issues particular to these learning modes, existing QA processes should be adapted to accommodate them rather than looking to create new or parallel processes. This position is consistent with the considerations for QA of e-learning provision published by the ENQA (2018) where an embedded approach is seen as more desirable, especially if online and blended delivery is part of an institution's overall strategy for development. Similarly, the International Network of Quality Assurance Agencies in Higher Education (INQAAHE, 2018: p. 7) has taken an integrated approach, as evidenced by this statement in its Guidelines of Good Practice Procedural Manual 2018:

Standards or criteria take into consideration the specific aspects related to different modes of provision, such as transnational education, distance or online programmes or other non-traditional approaches to HE as relevant to the context in which they operate.

More recently, a strong commitment to a single integrated or embedded approach appears in the Global Convention on the Recognition of Qualifications Concerning Higher Education (UNESCO, 2019: p. 5), which state that qualifications "...subject to comparable quality assurance mechanisms... will be assessed... using the same criteria as those applied to similar qualifications acquired through traditional learning modes". Historically, distance education in most countries has been subject to specific laws, regulations, and practices imposed by national, regional, and/or international QA or accreditation agencies (Latchem, 2016). In some developing parts of the world, national QA agencies require online programmes to follow separate accreditation processes that place constraints and significant barriers on providers.

UK NARIC (2020) describe some of these more restrictive jurisdictions in a recent report reviewing recognition issues in relation to international distance learning in 15 countries. Despite this history, and misgivings about the quality of online learning in some parts of the world, this present study supports a more enabling and integrated approach to QA. This position is consistent with the new reality and a growing international trend to mainstream QA, which is further advocated by the Asia-Pacific Economic Cooperation (APEC, 2017, p. 21) in a recent discussion paper:

Taking an approach toward the quality assurance of online education, which is integrated within existing frameworks, ensures that standards and quality are equivalent for all modes of learning.

Having said that, APEC (2017, p. 22) recognises that an integrated approach to the quality assurance of online and blended learning "... may require specific assessment approaches, contextual interpretation of standards, and new indicators that ensure a standard is met". This point reflected in a follow-up toolkit (APEC, 2019) suggests that additional quality indicators or guidelines may be useful as long as they align with existing QA standards and processes. Importantly, the paper concludes:

The importance of agencies working together in this area cannot be underestimated. Government agencies seeking to quality assure higher education in all its modes of delivery can benefit from benchmarking their standards, aligning themselves with current practices and participating in inter-agency collaborations. (APEC, 2017: p. 34).

Linking to the wider European context

This last point helps to introduce the third underlying assumption. The above discussion raises the importance in the European context of the European Qualifications Framework (EQF). This overarching framework links the qualifications frameworks of different European countries together. It serves as a translation tool between different national qualifications frameworks in EU Member States. Within this wider context, any effort to develop quality guidelines for digital higher education needs to be cognisant of two European frameworks for QA: the European Standards and Guidelines (ESG) framework for higher education and the European Quality Assurance in Vocational Education and Training (EQAVET) framework. That said, on last count there are over 300 external QA activities on offer by agencies registered in the European Quality Assurance Register for Higher Education (EQAR) and so:

The evaluation instruments of quality assurance agencies and by extension the quality assurance systems where they operate, are more complex and diversified than ever. (European Commission/EACEA/Eurydice, 2020, p. 71)

Notwithstanding this diversity, the European Association for Quality Assurance in Higher Education (ENQA) plays an important role in developing a strong and coherent quality assurance ecosystem. As previously mentioned, ENQA (2018) supports an embedded approach to QA for what it calls e-learning as the most desirable option. In 2018, following the establishment of a working group on QA and e-learning, ENQA (2018) published a number of specific considerations for the QA (internal and external) of e-learning provision. The considerations map the applicability of European Standards and Guidelines (ESG) to e-learning programmes as well as institutional offerings of those programmes. For each ESG standard, specific elements of e-learning that should be considered are identified, with 48 indicators for fulfilling the standard.

Although not applicable to all providers, these e-learning considerations need to be taken into account within the wider European QA architecture. On a related note, in 2021 ENQA established a working group to discuss the QA considerations of micro-credentials, which by design appear to have a strong predisposition towards new models of online delivery. Moreover, MICROBOL (2022) recently published its final report with important QA considerations. The key point is that these wider European developments need to inform the development of specific QA guidelines for online and blended learning programmes.

Synthesis of the Academic Literature

This section provides a brief synthesis of key findings from the published academic and research literature focusing on QA and self-assessment frameworks for digital higher education. It is important to note that the literature in this area generally falls into three categories:

- Published academic literature
- Published frameworks and guidelines by QA agencies
- Published standalone frameworks specifically designed to promote QA and QE in online and blended learning.

In focusing initially on the first category, the literature was identified through a systematic search of key websites, publication databases and reports produced by professional bodies following the guideless of the Preferred Reporting Items for Systematic Review and Meta-Analysis (PRISMA) (Moher et al. 2009).

While the analysis of the literature is more extensive than what is reported in this paper, the following synthesis relies extensively on Esfijani's (2018) seminal meta-synthesis arising from a study of 112 publications between 2000 and 2017 on efforts to measure quality in online education. Even though the study focuses on online delivery, it found that a variety of terms were interchangeably used in the literature and therefore the research has wider applicability to blended learning and the broader field of digital education.

Firstly, Esfijani (2018) found there is a tendency to more readily focus on easily measurable aspects of quality that give attention to the inputs, processes and resources, rather than the outputs and outcomes. Few of the quality rubrics, scorecards or benchmarking frameworks that have been developed over more than a decade incorporate data or analytics reporting on the outcomes and significant achievements that result from new models of online and blended learning. Thus, the main shortcoming of these quality frameworks is that they fail to adequately consider digital higher education in its totality from all its stakeholders' perspectives, including employers and industry professional bodies. Of course, this is not a unique issue to just online and blended delivery modes.

The second trend Esfijani (2018) identifies is that most of the existing quality criteria for teaching and learning have general utility to online and blended forms of delivery. There are no exceptional aspects to QA that are not applicable to traditional delivery modes, except for the technology itself. On a related note, however, the issue of accessibility appears to warrant greater attention based on Lowenthal, et al. (2021) recent analysis of QA frameworks from this perspective. They note the risk that existing QA frameworks for online learning can "... reinforce the idea that accessibility is a set of boxes to check off some checklist" (Lowenthal, et al., 2021: p. 26). On the other hand, their analysis acknowledges that accessibility standards can be too technical for most educators and QA frameworks are primarily intended to provide succinct prompts of the essential components when designing blended and online courses.

Notwithstanding this point, the above utility finding adds further weight to the argument that there is no strong case for developing separate QA processes to those already in place for more traditional forms of delivery. Moreover, Esfijani's (2018) seminal meta-synthesis of the literature found considerable common ground among QA dimensions and indicators in those frameworks that have already been developed for online and blended learning. As Esfijani (2018, p. 69) notes:

The commonalities are mostly related to different aspects of an educational system such as course content, design and structure, different types of support, teaching and learning processes, and evaluation and assessment. The differences are mostly in the grouping of the criteria associated with these aspects.

Thirdly, given a plethora of different quality rubrics, scorecards, and benchmarking frameworks the development of common global standards for digital higher education may be beneficial. However, Esfijani (2018) cautions that any such global framework would need to be intentionally tailored to each provider's circumstances to reflect the educational context, which suggests a local focus is more likely to yield the greatest benefits. This point underscores yet again the importance of identifying the right fit-for-purpose approach to QA for the specific educational context and that providers need to be at the centre of all quality processes.

On a related point, however, Esfijani (2018) does not refer to any international organisations such as INQAAHE or national QA agencies in this major synthesis of the published literature. This important omission suggests there is a serious gap or disconnection between those groups primarily focused on promoting quality in online and blended delivery, and the global, national and discipline-specific QA communities. This disconnection runs both ways. For example, out of 14 articles appearing in a recent special issue of the journal Quality Assurance in Education on the theme of "quality assurance in an era of sudden online education", only one paper (Perrin & Wang, 2021) cites Esfijani's (2018) seminal meta-synthesis. This example highlights a crucial tension between QA agencies advocating for an integrated approach using existing quality standards and processes, and those dedicated professional bodies and online learning champions claiming to support integration.

While the latter group might argue for QA processes that are "not separate from the mainstream" (Tait, 2022: p. 9-10), active development continues around separate quality rubrics, scorecards, and benchmarks specific to online and blended delivery. For example a consortium of institutions and organisations are currently developing a new Benchmarking Framework for Online, Open, Smart, and Technology Enhanced Higher Education (Hassan 2022). Reconciling this tension and the relationship between different types of frameworks is a matter of priority.

Finally, Esfijani (2018) identifies a serious gap in the literature in terms of evidence of the impact of existing quality frameworks. A recent study by Simunich et al. (2022) is a notable exception. While the field does not lack frameworks, there is a dearth of research on their implementation and impact. This implementation gap at least in the research is particularly noteworthy given the diverse range of cultural, institutional, and organisational contexts for which HEIs can deploy quality frameworks to support online and blended forms of teaching, learning and assessment. Further research is needed to investigate to what extent the various quality frameworks are actually being implemented by institutions and the value they are having in enhancing practice. Such research may help to better identify their value in mainstream QA processes and key factors that contribute to their effective uptake by HEIs in promoting quality digital higher education. In summary, the literature reveals:

- There is already an abundance of QA frameworks
- Not all QA rubrics, scorecards, and frameworks are created equal
- Many common dimensions are shared across the different QA frameworks
- There are inherent tensions and contradictions in competing efforts to promote and help mainstream QA processes for online and blended learning
- Silos and disconnections exist across different groups, stakeholders and professional communities engaged in promoting QA
- There is evidence of existing QA principles and processes being adapted to incorporate new issues and dimensions arising from the growth of online and blended learning
- A lack of research exists on how HEIs are implementing QA frameworks and limited evidence is available on their impact on supporting cultures of continuous quality improvement.

Analysis of Quality Frameworks

This section reports a brief analysis and comparison of 12 quality frameworks purposively selected from a larger sample. The frameworks are chosen to amplify variations in the approaches taken to QA and to reiterate several gaps in their design and implementation, including the lack of supporting research. Table 2 illustrates that only one of the 12 profiled frameworks is designed to incorporate a nano-level through to macro-level dimension (i.e., the New Zeeland National eLearning Guidelines). This framework, first developed in 2005, through its multi-layered design, including an important focus on the learner (nano level), was intended to support a whole of system approach to the QA. Notably, the Irish Statutory Quality Assurance Guidelines for Providers of Blended Learning Programmes (QQI, 2018) also standouts for incorporating a multi-layered perspective. Following a sector-wide consultation process this framework adopts a multilevel structure based around three key contexts, including a learner focus. While the European Maturity Model for Blended Education (EMBED) is the only other framework intentionally designed to reflect multiple levels (course, programme and institution), the learner's role and the importance of providing adequate support for them is less obvious in this model.

Quality Framework	Latest Version	Quality Domains	No. of Indictors	Target Level	Includes Guide	Action Plan	Research On Use
ACODE TEL Benchmarks	2014	- Institution-wide policy and governance - Planning for institution-wide quality improvement - Information technology systems, services, and support - Application of technology enhanced learning services - Staff professional development - Staff support for the use of technology enhanced learning - Student training for the effective use of technology enhanced learning	64	Meso	Yes	No	No
APEC Online Learning Toolkit	2019	- Leadership and management - Staffing profile and professional development - Review and improvement - Resources - Student information and support - Student experience - Curriculum design - Assessment and integrity - Learning outcomes	42	Meso	No	No	No
Benchmarking Framework for Online, Open, Smart, and Technology Enhanced HE	2022	- Teaching and learning - Learner services - Technology environment - Outcome and impact on society - Diversity and inclusiveness - Organisational aspects	39	Meso	No	No	No
CoL TEL Benchmarks	2019	- Policy - Strategic plan - IT support - Technology applications - Content development - Documentation - Organisational culture - Leadership - Human resource training - TEL champions	44	Meso	Yes	Yes	No
DigCompOrg	2015	- Leadership and governance practices - Teaching and learning practices - Professional development - Assessment practices - Content and curricula - Collaboration and networking - infrastructure	74	Meso	No	No	No

EMBED	2020	- Institutional support - Institutional strategy - Sharing and openness - Professional development - Quality Assurance - Governance - Finance - Facilities	21	Micro Meso	Yes	No	No
E-xcellence	2016	- Strategic management - Curriculum design - Course design - Course delivery - Staff support - Student support	35	Meso	Yes	No	No
NZ eLearning Guidelines	2019	- The learner perspective - The teacher perspective - The manager perspective - The organisational leader perspective - The QA body perspective	124	Nano Micro Meso Macro	Yes	No	No
QQI Statutory Guidelines for Blended Learning	2018	- the organisational context - the programme context - the learner experience context	50	Nano Micro Meso	No	No	No
OLC Quality Scorecard for Blended Learning Programs	2015	- Institutional support - Technology support - Course development/instructional design - Course structure - Teaching and learning - Social and student engagement - Faculty support - Student support - Evaluation and assessment	70	Micro Meso	Yes	No	No
Quality Matters	2018	- Course Overview/Introduction - Learning objectives - Assessment and measurement - Instructional materials - Course activities and learner interaction - Course technology - Learner support - Accessibility and usability	42	Micro Meso	Yes	No	Yes
UNESCO Blended Learning Self-Assessment Tool	2019	- Vision and philosophy - Curriculum - Professional development - Learning support - Infrastructure - Facilities - Resources and support - Policy and institutional structure - Partnerships - Research and evaluation	17	Meso	No	No	No

Table 1: Overview of 12 Current QA Frameworks

From a synthesis of the 12 selected frameworks, 15 overarching quality themes emerge. In Figure 1, each of the individual framework domains are collapsed under one of these themes. This high-level representation of the data shows that "Learning design and course delivery" is the most frequently mentioned (n=15) quality consideration across the 12 frameworks. This theme is followed equally by "Infrastructure, finance and learning environment" and "Student support, development and experience" (n=12).

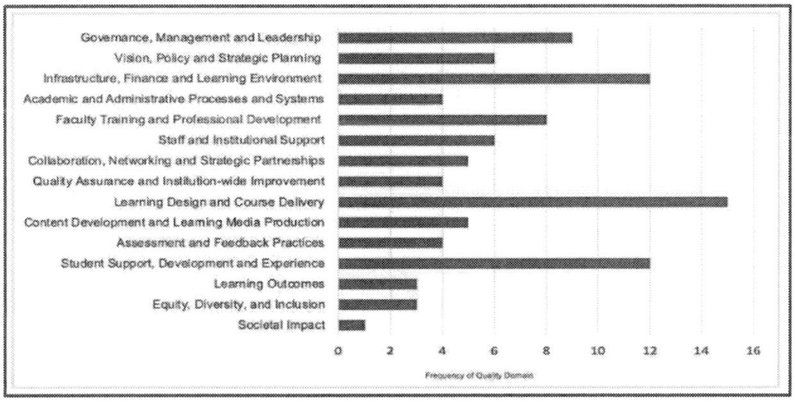

Figure 1: Aggregated summary of quality theme across frameworks

As some frameworks focus more on the Meso-level and others on the Micro-level, Table 2 provides a more detailed analysis of the most common domains by level and framework. The three contexts structure of the QQI framework is used to present these data.

At the Organisational Context, the data shows that "Infrastructure, finance and learning environment" is the most frequently mentioned domain (n=12), followed by "Governance, management and leadership" (n=9). Notably, only one framework refers explicitly to the importance of organisation culture and similarly the role of organisational structures is not identified as a crucial part of this domain. This absence is somewhat surprising as a EUA (2006: p. 16) report on building quality cultures from the bottom-up recognises "... the need for stable and durable organisational structures to assure quality". Where operational matters appear in a handful of frameworks, this quality indicator appears to be immature in terms of how it understands the balance between centralised and decentralised structures. It is recognised that while centralised structures can offer greater coherence and coordination across the institution, decentralised structures "... have the advantage of ensuring a greater sense of ownership locally and are more adapted to local circumstances (EUA, 2006: p. 17). The disadvantage from a QA perspective is they risk fragmentation and people working at cross-purposes in terms of the whole institution. The key point is that "since the hallmark of a stable quality culture is shared ownership by all, quality cannot and should not be confined to a unit alone" (EUA, 2006: p. 17). Given the "top-down", "middle-out" and "bottom-up" choices available to institutions, and the influence organisational structures have on their practices and ways of working; this appears to be an important gap in quality indicators for harnessing the transformative potential of digital higher education.

Context	Overarching theme	No.	Domain	Framework
Organisational context	Governance, management and leadership	9	Institution-wide policy and governance Management and operations Leadership and management Organisational culture Leadership Organisational aspects Strategic management Leadership and governance practices Governance	ACODE KVI APEC CoL CoL Global Consortium E-xcellence DigCompOrg EMBED

	Vision, policy and strategic planning	6	Vision and philosophy Policy and institutional structure Policy Strategic plan Institutional strategy Strategy and planning for blended learning	UNESCO UNESCO CoL CoL EMBED QQI
	Infrastructure, finance and learning environment	12	Technology support Information technology systems, services, and support Application of technology enhanced learning services Infrastructure and technological support Infrastructure Facilities Technology applications Technology environment Infrastructure Finance Facilities Infrastructure and resources	OLC Scorecard ACODE ACODE KIV UNESCO UNESCO CoL Global Consortium DigCompOrg EMBED EMBED QQI
	Academic regulations and administrative processes and systems	4	Academic administrative processes Documentation Published expectations on blended learning Approval and programme validation processes	KVI CoL QQI QQI
	Faculty training and professional development	8	Staff professional development Faculty experience and training Staffing profile and professional development Professional development Human resource training Technology-enabled learning champions Professional development Professional development	ACODE KVI APEC UNESCO CoL CoL DigCompOrg EMBED
	Staff and institutional support	6	Faculty support Institutional support Staff support for the use of technology enhanced learning IT support Staff support Institutional support	OLC Scorecard OLC Scorecard ACODE CoL E-xcellence EMBED
	Collaboration, networking and strategic partnerships	5	Partnerships Collaboration and networking Sharing and openness Learners outside Ireland Collaboration and other partners	UNESCO DigCompEd EMBED QQI QQI
	Quality assurance and institution-wide improvement	4	Planning for institution-wide quality improvement Review and improvement Research and evaluation Quality assurance	ACODE APEC UNESC O

Programme context	Learning design and course delivery	15	Course development / instructional design Course structure Teaching and learning Course activities and learner interaction Social and student engagement Course overview / introduction Learning objectives Course technology Curriculum design Curriculum Teaching and learning Curriculum design Course delivery Teaching and learning practices Content and curricula	OLC Scorecard OLC Scorecard OLC Scorecard OLC Scorecard OLC Scorecard Quality Matters Quality Matters Quality
	Content development and learning media production	5	Instructional materials Resources Resources and support Content development Learning resources, materials and delivery mechanisms	Quality Matters APEC UNESCO Co
	Assessment and feedback practices	4	Evaluation and assessment Assessment and measurement Assessment and integrity Assessment practices	OLC Scorecard Quality Matters APEC
Learner experience context	Student support, development and experience	12	Student support Learner support Student training for the effective use of TEL Student support technology enhanced learning Students Student access to university services Student information and support Student experience Learning support Learner services Student support Support available to learners	OLC Scorecard Quality Matters ACODE ACODE KVI KVI APE C APE C
	Learning outcomes	2	Learning outcomes Programme outcomes	APC QQI
	Equity, diversity, and inclusion	3	Accessibility and usability Diversity and inclusiveness Equality of opportunity	Quality Matters Global Consortium QQI

Table 2: Map of overarching quality themes by context, domain and framework

The need for "Vision, policy and strategic planning" is evident in half the frameworks and more likely to be found in those focusing on the Meso-level. Importantly, EUA (2006: p. 11) found that "a crucial factor and indeed the starting point of the development of quality culture is the mission of the institution". This point along with the role distributed leadership and strategic planning plays in shaping organisational culture is reiterated in EUA's (2022: p. 3) recent report on this topic:

...responsibility for shaping new learning cultures does not stop with senior management in the boardroom but requires a commitment to a more distributed approach to institutional leadership.

While not surprisingly, "Faculty training and professional development" was common to many frameworks (n=8), there is a basic failure to recognise that some types of professional learning are more effective and impactful than others. Few, if any, quality indicators focused on the outputs of this professional development. The importance of "Academic and administrative processes and systems", which include fit-for-purpose IT platforms such as the Student Information System (SIS), Timetabling System (TS) and is not frequently mentioned (n=4) and on a related note enterprise-wide support for the use of learning analytics does not receive attention. Only four framework domains explicitly refer to QA processes and planning for institution-wide quality improvement. Lastly, the role of "Collaboration, networks and strategic partnerships" is recognised by a handful of frameworks (n=5), but this theme has wider significance. There are several dimensions to consider under this theme, including QA provision for learners studying online from other countries and the types of agreements and arrangements HEIs have with third party suppliers, including Online Programme Management (OPM) providers and IT companies.

At the Programme Context, "learning design and course delivery" is the most common quality consideration (n=15), although the adoption of an explicit learning design model is not identified as a quality indicator. Notably, only a handful of frameworks specifically single out the role of "content development and learning media production" (n=5). With the rapid growth of educational video, lecture recording technology, and a proliferation of Open Educational Resources (OERs), this appears to be an important gap in existing frameworks. Surprisingly, even fewer frameworks give explicit consideration to "Assessment and feedback practices" (n=4), which is a notable weakness, especially given the contemporary literature in this area. More to the point, the type of Assessment a programme involves can fundamentally influence the student learning experience. It should be noted that "feedback" is not mentioned in any of the framework domains at this level. Similarly, "academic integrity" is only explicitly mentioned at the programme level by one framework.

At the Learner Experience Context, "Student support, development and experience" is the most common theme (n=12). This suggests a strong appreciation of the central role students can play in supporting a quality culture. However, there are important differences between "support", "development" and "experience" that are not fully articulated in the frameworks. For example, a focus on student support or services does not necessarily include a strong development perspective and only one framework placed a wider emphasis on the nature of the student experience. None of the frameworks consider the quality provision of external contracted student services such as writing development, careers guidance and online counselling that have become common in some institutions. Also, few of the quality frameworks include a quality indicator on whether students are actively involved in institutional decision-making bodies. Limited attention is placed on learning outcomes (n=2), which reflects a general focus on inputs, processes, and resources rather than quality outputs. Explicit acknowledge of quality indicators related to equity, diversity, and inclusion (n=3) are rare. The need to assess whether institutions have targeted initiatives to support indigenous, first nation and new migrant and refugee communities falls into this category, which is an area lacking in all frameworks.

Mapping the Gaps and Additional Considerations

This final section offers a preliminary map of the gaps and additional considerations that may need to be taken into consideration in the future from a QA perspective. Table 3 identifies some of these gaps for each of the three contexts. Further analysis of the literature along with wider stakeholder consultation is likely to help validate and identify additional quality considerations. Importantly, the intention of this exercise is not to add a long list of new quality requirements to current QA frameworks, thus making the elusive quest for quality even harder. Instead, the intention is to raise these as new and emerging areas for further discussion alongside the planning for a more integrated, fit-for-purpose and whole of institution approach to fostering a culture of continuous improvement.

Context	Overarching Themes	Additional Considerations
Organisational context	Governance, management and leadership	Organisational culture Organisational structures Leadership development
	Vision, policy and strategic planning	External stakeholder engagement Internal communication Micro-credentials Green technology Societal impact

	Infrastructure, finance and learning environment	Artificial intelligence Library access Digital video recording Virtual labs
	Academic and administrative processes and systems	Academic integrity Online proctoring Cheating Ethics and privacy
	Staff training and professional development	Performance appraisal Workload models Promotion criteria Capability framework alignment Staff recruitment Recognition and incentive schemes Scholarship of practice
	Collaboration, networking and strategic partnerships	Business models Procurement Practices
	Quality assurance and institution-wide improvement	Application of learning analytics Institutional self-assessment
Programme context	Learning design and course delivery	Learning design models Asynchronous forum engagement Synchronous online engagement
	Content development and learning media production	Use of OER Use of digital video
	Assessment and feedback practices	Cheating Plagiarism Online proctoring Assignment response time
Learner experience context	Student support, development and experience	Student readiness Digital literacy Data literacy Career services Counselling Writing support
	Learning outcomes	Student evaluations Student satisfaction Completion rates
	Equity, diversity, and inclusion	Universal design for learning Ethics and data protection New migrants and at risk learners Indigenous and first nations learners

Table 3: Gap Analysis of New and Emerging Quality Considerations

Conclusion

The elusive pursuit of quality is an enduring challenge and matter of contested debate in higher education - irrespective of the delivery mode. This paper has revisited this debate through a post-pandemic lens as HEIs and QA agencies respond to the continued growth in demand for new online and blended learning programmes. In asking what quality looks like in the context of the next normal of digital higher education, the paper has provided a synthesis of key lessons from an analysis of seminal literature and shown there are gaps and inherent contradictions in competing efforts to promote and help mainstream QA processes for online and blended learning. While a plethora of quality frameworks are available to HEIs, silos and disconnections exist across different groups, stakeholders and professional communities engaged in promoting quality. There remains a fundamental tension between separate and integrated QA processes, which in the European context needs to be resolved as a matter of priority. Moreover, the analysis reveals from a multi-layered perspective that not all quality frameworks for online and blended learning are created equal and quality is a dynamic concept as new and emerging issues continue to arise. Some of these additional quality considerations are identified but the importance of the local educational context and the central role institutions need to play in developing their own QA processes remains crucial, especially if we are to avoid the tap of using such frameworks to develop noting more than cultures of quality compliance.

References

1. Asia-Pacific Economic Cooperation. (APEC) (2019). Quality assurance of online learning toolkit. University of Melbourne. https://www.apec.org/Publications/2019/12/APEC- Quality-Assurance-of-Online-Learning-Toolkit
2. Asia-Pacific Economic Cooperation (APEC). (2017). Quality assurance of online learning: Discussion paper. https://tech.ed.gov/files/2018/11/APEC-Quality-Assurance-of-Online- Learning-Discussion-Paper-AUS-3.pdf
3. Brown, M. (2021). What are the main trends in online learning? A helicopter view of possible futures. Asian Journal of Distance Education, 16 (2), 118-143.
4. Depaul, K. (2022). The evolving conversation about quality in online learning. Inside Higher Ed NC SARA. https://www.insidehighered.com/content/evolving-conversation-about- quality-online-learning
5. Esfijani, A. (2018). Measuring quality in online education: A metasynthesis. American Journal of Distance Education, 32(1), pp. 57-73. DOI: 10.1080/08923647.2018.1417658
6. European Association for Quality Assurance in Higher Education. (2018). Considerations for quality assurance of e-learning provision. Report from the ENQA Working Group VIII on Quality Assurance and E-Learning, Occasional Papers 26. Brussels. http://www.enqa.eu/index.php/publications/papers-reports/occasional-papers
7. European Association for Quality Assurance in Higher Education et al. (2015), Standards and Guidelines for Quality Assurance in the European Higher Education Area (ESG), http://www.enqa.eu/wp-content/uploads/2015/11/ESG_2015.pdf.
8. European Commission (2020). Digital Education ActionPlan (2021–2027).
9. https://education.ec.europa.eu/focus-topics/digital/education-action-plan
10. European Commission/EACEA/Eurydice (2020). The European Higher Education Area in 2020: Bologna Process Implementation Report, Education, Luxembourg: Publications Office of the European Union. https://eacea.ec.europa.eu/national- policies/eurydice/sites/default/files/ehea_bologna_2020_chapter03.pdf
11. European Universities Association (2006). Quality Culture in European Universities: A Bottom-Up Approach. European Universities Association. Report on the Three Rounds of the Quality Culture Project 2002 – 2006, Brussels. https://eua.eu/downloads/publications/quality%20culture%20in%20european%20univ ersities%20a%20bottom-up%20approach.pdf
12. Florence, M., Ting S., & Westine, C. (2020)."A systematic review of online teaching and learning. Computers & Education, 159, pp. 1-17.
13. https://doi.org/10.1016/j.compedu.2020.104009
14. Gaebel, M., Zhang, T., Stoeber, H., & Morrisroe, A. (2021). Digitally enhanced learning and teaching in European higher education institutions. European University Association, Brussels. https://eua.eu/resources/publications/954:digitally-enhanced-learning-and- teaching-in-european-higher-education-institutions.html
15. Hassan, M. (2022), Middle East region: Benchmarking framework and data set for online, open, smart and technology-enhanced higher education (pp. 19-21), in A. Tait (ed.), Report from the ICDE quality network: Global quality perspectives on open, flexible and distance learning. International Council for Open and Distance Education. https://www.icde.org/knowledge-hub/icde-quality-network-report-2021
16. Hodges, C., Moore, S., Lockee, B., Trust, T., & Bond, A. (2020). The difference between emergency remote teaching and online learning. Educause Review, 27 March, https://er.educause.edu/articles/2020/3/the-difference-between-emergency-remote-teaching-and-online-learning
17. International Network of Quality Assurance Agencies in Higher Education. (2018). Guidelines of Good Practice Procedural Manual 2018. https://www.inqaahe.org/sites/default/files/GGP_ProceduresManual.pdf
18. Joksimović, S., Kovanović, V., Skrypnyk, O., Gašević, D., Dawson, S., & Siemens, G. (2015). The history and state of

online learning (pp. 95-131), in Siemens, et al. (Eds.), Preparing for the digital university: A review of the history and current state of distance, blended, and online learning. Edmonton, AB: Athabasca University Press. https://eddl.tru.ca/wp- content/uploads/2018/12/PreparingDigitalUniversity-George-Siemens.pdf

19. Lowenthal, P., Smith, C., Lomellini, A., & Greear, K. (2021). Accessible online learning: An analysis of online quality assurance frameworks. The Quarterly Review of Distance Education, 22(2), pp. 15–29.
20. MICROBOL. (2022). Common Framework for Micro-credentials in the EHEA. https://microcredentials.eu/wp-content/uploads/sites/20/2022/03/Micro- credentials_Framework_final-1.pdf
21. Moher, D., Liberati, A., Tetzlaff, J., & Altman, D. (2009). Preferred reporting items for systematic reviews and meta-analyses: the PRISMA statement. The BMJ, 339, 2-8. doi: 10.1136/bmj.b2535
22. Nguyen, T. (2015). The effectiveness of online learning: Beyond no significant difference and future horizons. MEROT Journal of Online Learning and Teaching, 11(2), pp. 309-319. https://jolt.merlot.org/Vol11no2/Nguyen_0615.pdf
23. Ossiannilsson, E., Williams, K., Camilleri, A., & Brown, M. (2015). Quality models in online and open education around the globe: State of the art and recommendations. International Council for Open and Distance Education, Oslo, Norway. https://files.eric.ed.gov/fulltext/ED557055.pdf
24. Perrin, S. & Wang, L. (2021). COVID-19 and rapid digitalization of learning and teaching: quality assurance issues and solutions in a Sino-foreign higher education institution. Quality in Education, 29(4), pp. 463-476. DOI 10.1108/QAE-12-2020-0167
25. Quality and Qualifications Ireland. (2018). Statutory quality assurance guidelines for providers of blended learning programmes. Dublin. https://www.qqi.ie/sites/default/files/media/file-uploads/Statutory%20QA%20Guidelines%20for%20Blended%20Learning%20Progra mmes.pdf
26. Ryan, P. (2015). Quality assurance in higher education: A review of literature. Higher Learning Research Communications, 5(4). https://doi.org/10.18870/hlrc.v5i4.257
27. Schindler, L., Puls-Elvidge, S., Welzant, H., & Crawford, L. (2015). Definitions of quality in higher education: A synthesis of the literature. Higher Learning Research Communications, 5(3), doi:10.18870/hlrc.v5i3.244
28. Siemens, G., Gasevic, D., & Dawson, S. (Eds.) (2015). Preparing for the digital university: A review of the history and current state of distance, blended, and online learning. https://www.pure.ed.ac.uk/ws/portalfiles/portal/21130003/PreparingDigitalUniversity.pd f
29. Simunich, B., McMahon, E., Hopf, L., Altman, B., & Zimmerman, W. A. (2021). Creating a culture of online quality: The people, policies, and processes that facilitate institutional change for online course quality assurance", American Journal of Distance Education, DOI: 10.1080/08923647.2021.2010021
30. Tait, A. (ed.) (2022). Report from the ICDE quality network: Global quality perspectives on open, flexible and distance learning. International Council for Open and Distance Education. https://www.icde.org/knowledge-hub/icde-quality-network-report-2021
31. UK NARIC. (2020). Guide to recognition issues in international distance learning (2nd Ed.), https://ecctis.com/documents/Guide%20to%20Recognition%20Issues%20in%20Intern ational%20Distance%20Learning%202nd%20edition.pdf
32. UNESCO. (2019). Global Convention on the Recognition of Qualifications Concerning Higher Education. https://unesdoc.unesco.org/ark:/48223/pf0000373602.locale=en
33. Volungevičienė, A., Brown, M., Greenspon, R., Gaebel, M., & Morrisroe, A. (2021), Developing a high-performance digital education system: Institutional self-assessment instruments. European University Association, Brussels. https://eua.eu/resources/publications/953:developing-a-high-performance-digital- education-ecosystem.html

ISSN: 2707-2819

A CRITICAL GOVERNANCE INFRASTRUCTURE FRAMEWORK AT ODL INSTITUTIONS AND BEST PRACTICES FOR ITS PROTECTION DURING AND BEYOND NEW NORMAL

Pankaj Khanna, Indira Gandhi National Open University (IGNOU)

Abstract

The outbreak of Covid-19 has forced us to extend distance education beyond territorial boundaries mainly due to limitations caused by pandemic conditions. A critical governance infrastructure (CGI) for open and distance learning (ODL) institutions is presented to manage the "new normal" institutional governance activities quite efficiently and effectively. The CGI is supplemented with control systems to efficiently monitor critical information and control critical parts of institutional prominent centres and associated services. Its vulnerabilities to basic attacks (such as cyber-attacks and physical attacks) have been analyzed. The emerging new challenges and risks for ODL governance, the cyber security crises along with its protection management are presented. Lastly, best practices for protecting and managing the CGI are recommended to achieve a safe, robust and resilient CGI for the ODL institutions. It is inferred that the incorporation of such a CGI into the institutional education system would play a prominent role for establishing an uninterrupted and efficient governance system that is necessary for sustainable development and growth of the ODL institution concerned during and beyond "new normal".

Keywords: Governance, Open and distance learning, Critical governance infrastructure, New normal, Pandemic, Cyber threats.

Introduction

The open and distance learning institutions have become quite popular after Covid-19 pandemic as they have made distance education open to many, irrespective of age, sex, place of learning or completion etc. As a result, distance education has been adopted by quite a significantly large number of people all over the world. For instance, in India alone, there are about 4.2 million learners receiving education through distance mode (AISHE, 2021). In recent times it is observed that management and governance of the ODL institutions is adversely affected by frequent cyber-attacks and physical attacks. As such it has become crucial to properly manage and govern the ODL institutions so that they can carry out their assigned functions quite effectively and efficiently. Kwikkers (2005) proposed that the quality of governance in an institution can be determined by scrutinizing as to how it is structured; how it build up its plans and policies; what is its administrative, legal and operational framework; and how it interacts with other external institutions. Thereby the quality of institutional Governance depends as to how the institution is externally and internally structured, creates its resources, builds up its policies, and translates them into action. This implies that quality of governance in an institution critically depends not only upon its governance infrastructure but also upon how it can be managed and protected against basic attacks. As the present study is concerned about critical governance infrastructure, it is worthwhile to first examine about the critical aspects of governance infrastructure.

The governance infrastructure and its critical aspects

The governance infrastructure in an educational organization is considered to consist of a collection of governing systems, structures, information communication technologies (ICT), regulatory frameworks, people, policies and practices that interact to support governing activities (Johnston, 2010; Johnston & Hansen, 2011). That is the components of governance infrastructure are actively integrated to support the various organizational governance activities. However, in such an integrated system each step in the integration process triggers some major unforeseen side-effects as risks; many of them may be serious and challenging. Further though the incorporation of ICT based systems and devices into the governance infrastructure enhances the overall performance of the institution's programs and services yet at the same time the increased reliance of the infrastructure on internet and computer networks makes it vulnerable to cyber-attacks. The cyber-criminals may gain access to infrastructure's components and networks, steal information and interrupt services. This disruption in normal operations and services makes the governance infrastructure critical.

It is realized that the components of the institutional governance infrastructure are critically connected to the educational system and at the same time are also found to be critically vulnerable to basic attacks. Under such circumstances the critical information and control systems pertaining to the infrastructure monitors and controls the institutional operations and services. Thereby such an institutional governance infrastructure is termed as Critical Governance Infrastructure or CGI.

The present study is concerned with the protection and management of CGI for ODL institutions. The CGI is considered to be mainly comprised of five basic components namely, organizational governing structures, governance network of people and regulatory framework, institutional operating systems, institutional support centers and services, instructional design systems and educational resources. The ICT based systems and devices have been used to intertwine these diverse components. With latest modern technologies, the ICT enabled infrastructure thus evolved has transformed the limits of Internet technology, be it through cutting-edge products, service transaction technologies, innovative automation concepts, devices, and networked gadgets. These are changing and revolutionizing the governance operating systems; intelligent networked information management as well as decision making systems. Though this is providing many new opportunities for the distance education systems involved while also raises a number of issues. The increased reliance of the governance infrastructure on Internet and computer networks increases its vulnerability to cyber-attacks. The risks, threats and challenges emerging from such attacks and the resulting CGI security crises have been discussed. The risk management and various measures for the protection and management of CGI are proposed. By adopting the cyber security strategies as suggested in this study the CGI will successfully overcome the challenges while improving the overall operational efficiency of the ODL institution concerned.

Lastly, best practices for protecting and managing the CGI are recommended so as to achieve a safe, robust and resilient CGI for the ODL institutions. Thus, to sum up it is envisaged that the incorporation of the CGI into the institutional education system would play an effective role for smooth uninterrupted operation and excellent management of the institution.

Literature review.

The concept of critical infrastructure is not quite old. It was conceived by Wenger, Metzger and Dunn in 2002, and later by G8 (G8, 2003) and the Organisation for Economic Co-operation and Development (OECD, 2007, OECD, 2008). African Union (2014) defines Critical cyber / ICT infrastructure as "The infrastructure, which is essential to vital services for public safety, economic stability, national security, international stability, sustainability and restoration of critical cyberspace." Critical information infrastructure (CII) as mentioned by UK Parliament (2011) refers it as the IT system that is essential to support vital services and assets as related to the national framework. Simon (2017) depicts the critical infrastructure systems as the assets and networks that decide about the safety, success and well-being of a country. In this regard, Internet of things (IoT) was put forward as an important concept that has intensified both opportunities and challenges for the critical infrastructure across the globe.

Rouse (2018) regards Critical infrastructure as a framework that is necessary to provide uninterrupted services as related to the national security, public's health, financials and safety. Various elements of IT infrastructure as suggested by Rouse (2018) include Infrastructure management tools and services; Servers; Data Storage Network; Routers; Firewalls and Load balancers. The data centre facility houses IT equipment and includes necessary power, cooling and security components.

Abhishta, Junger, Joosten, & Nieuwenhuis (2019) have conducted a study on the number of DDoS attacks that are targeting the infrastructures related to Dutch academic institutions. It was found that most of these attacks are not random and are initiated by someone who might be benefited by disrupting scheduled educational activities.

Kulkarni & Akhilesh (2020) have illustrated that online services in higher educational institutions have become frequent targets of cyber criminals in modern era. The cyber criminals hack the information assets related to the institutions while disrupting the online services. As such the various cyber security measures have been proposed that need to be implemented in these institutions for their proper functioning.

Humayun, Niazi, Jhanjhi, Alshayeb, & Mahmood (2020) provided a systematic mapping study of cyber security threats and vulnerabilities while reviewing 78 studies in this area. The purpose of this study was to identify and analyze common cyber security vulnerabilities (such as phishing, denial of services and malware) for targeted infrastructures. It was argued that cyber security measures so far adopted are not sufficient to protect the targeted infrastructures from ever increasing cyber-attacks. As such it was stressed to conduct a more rigorous analysis for the cyber security threats and vulnerabilities so as to find out more appropriate and better security measures while also implementing them more effectively.

Although many of the above-mentioned concepts about critical infrastructure have been presented in the national perspective yet they hold equally well in case of educational organisations and particularly more in case of ODL institutions since they are comparatively more dependent on ICT as compared to campus based educational organisations. It is observed that the ODL as well as campus-based institutions have become regular targets for cybercriminals. Biddle (2017) in her report stated that as compared to last half of the year 2016, the education sector accounted for 13 percent more of data breaches in the first half of 2017 that has resulted to compromise about 32 million records.

Higher education's vulnerability to cyber-attacks (Harris & Hammargren, 2016) reports that during (2005-15) time period ODL as well as campus based higher education institutions witnessed 539 breaches involving nearly 13 million records. However, ODL institutions are the one that are likely to be more frequently attacked organizations due to the critical nature of their network and extensive reliance on IT systems. That is why security needs to be a serious concern for ODL institutional management. Introducing innovative tools and technologies that facilitate to identify and mitigate threats quite efficiently have become the matter of utmost importance for ODL institutions.

Based on the above-mentioned literature on critical infrastructure and author's experience (Khanna, 2017, 2019) in governance systems, the following critical governance infrastructure has been contextualized for ODL institutions.

Critical governance infrastructure for ODL institutions.

A critical governance infrastructure is stated to be such a framework in which continued operation of its components is essential, whereas the disruption or destruction in any one of them would have serious consequences. The critical governance infrastructure for ODL institution is presented in Fig.1.

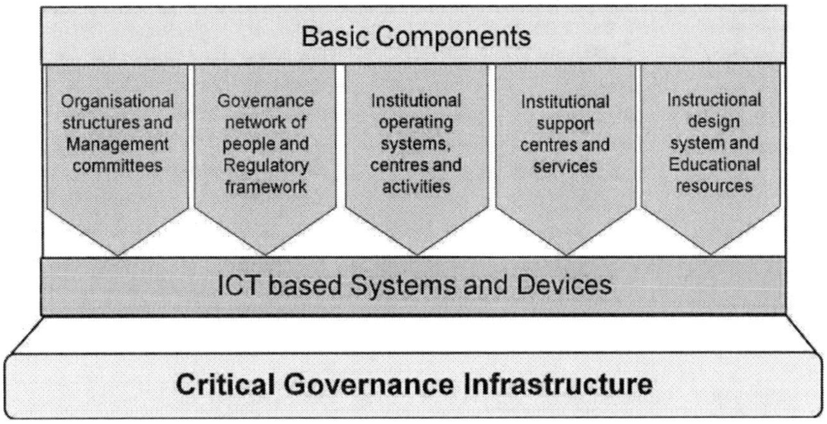

Fig.1. A Schematic Diagram of Critical Governance Infrastructure for ODL Institutions.

The CGI is proposed to be comprised of five basic components namely Organizational structures and Management committees; Governance network of people and Regulatory framework; Institutional operating systems, centres and activities; Institutional support centres and services; Instructional design system and educational resources. Each of the basic components is structured with various sub-components and a brief description of their involvement in different governance activities is given in Table 1.

Component	Sub- Component	Description
Organizational structures and Management committees	<u>*Organizational structures:*</u> Vice Chancellor office *(Planning and development management)* Registrar office *(Adminstrative Management)* Finance and account section IT Management and Organization Estate management *Management Commit-tees:*	• Delineates organisational structures, reporting lines and relationships as per act and statues of the institution concerned. • Outlines board and management committees' structures, policies, charter, membership and mandates. Establishes design and content of regulatory governance framework. • Aligns governance with operational and management responsibilities. <u>*Management Committees perform decision making and facilitates in:*</u> • Determining and executing the pro-
	Board of Management Executive Council Academic Council Finance committee	• Engagement of personnel (teachers, counsellors and other supporting staff); mobilization and deployment of institutional resources; including creation and maintenance of institutional infrastructure.

Governance network of people and Regulatory framework	Chancellor Vice Chancellor Directors Registrar Managers / Executives Teaching faculty and supporting staff	• All players of governance are required to discharge their respective roles and responsibilities with full loyalty and devotion while adopting good governance principles and best working practices as prescribed by the regulatory framework. • Vice chancellor, board members and senior Directors are liable to approve the decisions whereas others (such as managers) are required to execute the agreed decisions.
Institutional operating systems, Centers and Activities	Information management system Decision making system Management support system	• Facilitate to provide overall institution's operational information that is updated, factually correct and reliable. • Regulates flow of information and reporting lines all across the institution. • Perform decision making with full information advice and support.
Institutional support centers and services	*Support centres:* Regional services division Regional Centers Study Centers Work Centers *Institutional services:* Pre enrollment services Post enrollment services Admission and tutoring services Academic; administrative and finance support General institutional information	*Institutional Support centers:* • Study centres provide academic and administrative support to the learners whereas work centres support for practical / experimental work. • Regional centres coordinate and supervise work of study centres and work centres under their jurisdiction. *Institutional services:* • Admission of students and maintenance of their records. • Learning, counselling and tutoring. • Learner assessment and evaluation. • Finance and other services including helpdesk services.
	Helpdesk support	
Instructional design system and educational resources	*Instructional system:* Printing and Publication division Material distribution division Electronic media and production Centre *Educational resources:* Course / program content e-content Educational repositories OER architecture framework	• Development and maintenance of instructional system and mechanisms. • Preparation and production of study materials / learning packages including their storage and distribution. • Preparation of audio video cassettes and CDs for national broadcast and telecast. • Open /online content development and maintenance. • Creating educational resources and OER (open educational resources) architecture framework.

Table 1. Description of Five Basic Components.

The network of ICT based systems and devices are integrated with each of the CGI basic components. The ICT enabled infrastructure thus evolved would facilitate to provide a fully automated and highly efficient governance system. It provides good quality IT management tools and aligns technology with automation requirements to create integrated ICT based fully automated ODL institution. The computer division processes and maintains all the data relating to programs, courses and other governance activities. Thus, the organization of ICT enabled governance infrastructure in ODL institution would be able to provide a highly efficient platform for all the necessary institutional services, applications and functions to be performed by the institution.

The above-mentioned basic components of the governance infrastructure are critically connected with each other and also with the overall system involved. The critical information, communication and control system technologies are used across the institutional systems and processes. The various critical elements such as technical, educational, and logistic systems are increasingly inter-connected in collaboratively delivering critical end-to-end services.

At the heart of CGI is the network of control systems that can manage and regulate processes and control flows of information. The critical information and control systems monitor and control the critical components of CGI. The control systems comprising of software, sensors and control components are employed for running contemporary facilities and equipment quite efficiently.

Vulnerability to basic attacks

The critical governance infrastructure system is vulnerable to basic attacks that include cyber-attacks and physical attacks. A close view of the critical governance infrastructure as exhibited in Figure 1 reveal that ICT based systems and devices are integrated with all the CGI basic components so as to create a fully automated ODL institution. This reliance on computers and Internet makes the governance system highly prone to cyber-attacks. According to Simon (2017), Cyber-attacks have been identified to be of four types: hacktivism, cybercrime, cyber espionage, and cyberwar. In the context of critical governance infrastructure in ODL institutions, cyber espionage and cyberwar are considered to be more dangerous than hacktivism or cybercrime attacks, however, their frequency of occurrence is comparatively low (Morag, 2014). Some of the different kinds of threats that occur due to the above-mentioned basic attacks are Distributed denial of service (DDoS), Phishing, Ransomware; Inside misuse and unintentional actions; Legacy IT infrastructure and inadequate IT Resources; Mobile devices and Network access control (NAC).

Risks and challenges

Risks emerge when the institutional appliances including network of operating systems, control systems, remote facilities are subjected to cyber / physical attacks (Daugherty, Banerjee, Negm, & Alter, 2015). Some of the risks emerging in CGI are risk of mismanagement practices; risk of virus attacks; risk of network failure; risk of sabotage; and risk of mail transportation error. Numerous kinds of risks are also found to emerge in ODL institutions during breaches in IT systems including computers and other networks.

The impact of risks and challenges may be different at different level. It is desired that they should be identified and managed by traditional approaches like prototyping. Among the biggest cyber challenges facing the distance education sector is an increased number of cyber-attacks that aim to acquire individual personnel information, steal data for money and disrupt ODL institution's operations. Hayden, Assante and Conway (2014) have identified security vulnerabilities, research and development cost, and high initial cost as the main challenges that are to be taken care by the CGI management.

Security crises and protection management

The term CGI security is related to the security of the governance infrastructure systems, structures as well as users' assets and the protection management required to safeguard them. It is linked with the policy documents and action plans to be undertaken during the overall working of the ODL institution. However, there may exist benevolent individuals (called hackers) in and around the ODL institutions that intentionally try to breach infrastructures' security systems. Such breaches will occur and remain present if the owner is not fully alert or cautious.

There are numerous incidents of cyber-attacks and security breaches that have taken place in various institutional systems possessing critical infrastructure. It is realized that in addition to cyber-attacks, there is also an alarming danger of physical attacks (Johnson, 2008) to ODL institutions. As a result the traditional organizational perimeters start eroding while deteriorating the institutional performance. Under such circumstances, the security solutions like encryption and antivirus software remain the control keys for combating today's known attacks (EY, 2013). In addition, the premises accommodating governance infrastructure networks and systems are to be managed appropriately so as to make them secured by various measures, such as electronic key entry, physical token entry, human and video surveillance, fire-rated walls, controlled access to the server and storage space, and so on.

Best practices for protection of CGI.

Considering the existing literature (Biddle, 2017; Simon, 2017; Solomon, 2018; Luiijf, Schie, Ruijven & Huistra, 2016; Rouse, 2018) on critical infrastructures and author's experience in governance systems, a number of best practices are recommended for the protection and management of CGI during and beyond "new normal". The following are the best practices that are suggested to be adopted

Develop standard operating procedures

Repositories of standard operating procedures are required to be created to defy the occurrence of future malicious activities against the critical infrastructural system involved. It may involve standardizing its processes and developing a system that can appropriately respond to the basic attacks on such vastly inter-connected infrastructures related to the ODL institutions.

Share best practices

Encourage to build strong trusted network of people in ODL institutions that could enable the sharing of best practices related to CGI operational activities and management. Timely and speedy sharing of such practices would facilitate to mitigate many of the infrastructural security related challenges.

Policies and Regulations

ODL institutions should frame regulatory guidelines so as to facilitate the correct flow of information and data within its jurisdiction and also across the institutional borders. Such institutions may also ensure that such regulations are sufficient to effectively protect the CGI. The already built-in regulations accommodate flexibility and incentives to drive innovation. With added good governance, accountability and transparency these institutions will induce more competitive capabilities, market efficiency and better student support services (Simon, 2017).

Operational safety and default practices

These practices are required to be documented all over the CGI premises. The various risks / threats and security gaps are also required to be identified, documented and dealt with accordingly, while developing new operational safety standards as related to cyber security strategies (O'Halloran, D., & Kvochko, E., 2015). Developing such standards would provide default security to the governance system and also help to establish a resilient CGI (Brandis, 2014).

Raise awareness among policy makers

Many a times it may happen that the institutional policy makers are unaware about the risks and threats on the CGI that might be going to impact the overall educational system in the ODL institution. In today's scenario, it is imperative for them to be skilled and well adapted in the technological and educational policy implications with regard to data security aspects of infrastructural systems and software.

ICT based digital infrastructure

The success of the educational system in ODL institutions depends on the presence of efficient and strong governance infrastructure, realizing ubiquitous network connectivity through the use of modern ICT based systems and devices. Also ensure to make Internet service accessible, affordable, interoperable, secure and resilient so that it may have a fruitful and positive impact.

Establish Computer Emergency Response Teams (CERTs)

The CGI management should ensure to establish emergency warning systems regarding risks and threats emerging from cyber-attacks. It should create and maintain standard crisis management system that will ensure its satisfactory operation even during emergency situations.

Practicing and building cyber aware culture

ODL institutions should be aware of cyber threats and challenges being faced by CGI in recent times. It is imperative for such institution to build awareness among its personnel, students and faculty members about importance of security against threats, risks and challenges. The institutions should encourage cyber security awareness training, inculcate cyber aware culture, practice and prepare every individual who is associated with the institutional governance system to perform effectively while working to protect the CGI.

Establish cyber attribution teams

Cyber-attacks can cause serious damage to CGI. Presently, attribution of such attacks is being mostly overseen and managed by private IT companies, who utilize their expertise to build their own brands and as such can't reveal the resources or its exact techniques. For ODL institutions aspiring to prevent the outbreak of cyber-attacks in CGI, they must form a network of specialists devoted to attributing such attacks.

Adopting and frequently rehearsing security related practices

A good system of Risk / threat intelligence could facilitate to identify and monitor effectively both the external and internal sources of risk. Regular rehearsing CGI related security practices would tend to improve the organization's capabilities and provides better crises management.

Lastly but not least, the Covid-19 precautions and practices that include social distancing, mask-wearing, vaccination, avoiding public-gatherings and washing hands be put into practice at all times. Thus, in addition to the suggested best practices, the Covid-19 precautions or practices be followed and adopted by all for the well-being of the institution as well as its stakeholders that include the students, teachers and other staff during and beyond "new normal".

Conclusions

The CGI presented in this study provides a safe, resilient and robust infrastructure which facilitates to manage institutional governance activities quite efficiently and effectively. It is emphasized that incorporation of such a CGI into the institutional education system would facilitate to establish an excellent governance system that would provide good quality and uninterrupted services considered essential for its efficient operation and effective management during and beyond "new normal". Such a system would overcome the post pandemic challenges for ODL governance while improving the overall efficiency of the ODL institution concerned. In addition, it provides sustainable growth, enhances the overall institutional performance while improving the quality of distance education being provided to its learners.

Acknowledgements

The author would like to thank the following organizations and the associated persons whose work has helped him to undertake and prepare this article:

Atlantic Council and Zurich Insurance Company. (https://www.zurich.com)

Deloitte Touché Tohmatsu Limited (https://www2.deloitte.com/)

Global Conference on Cyberspace 2017. India. (http://pib.nic.in/newsite/PrintRelease.aspx?relid=173571

Indira Gandhi National Open University (www.ignou.ac.in).

The Commonwealth of Learning (www.col.org).

The Ministry of Electronics and Information Technology (MeitY), Government of India.

The Organisation for Economic Co-operation and Development (http://www.oecd.org).

The U.S. Department of Justice. (https://www.justice.gov/).

UNESCO (www.unesco.org/new/en/unesco/).

US-CERT | United States Computer Emergency Readiness Team. (https://www.uscert.gov/).

World Bank (www.worldbank.org/).

References

1. Abhishta, A., Junger, M., Joosten, R., & Nieuwenhuis, L. J. (2019). Victim routine influences the number of DDoS attacks: Evidence from Dutch educational network. In 2019 IEEE Security and Privacy Workshops (SPW) (pp. 242-247). IEEE.
2. AISHE. (2021). All India Survey on Higher Education report for the year 2019–20. Ministry of Education, Government of India. (June, 2021). Retrieved from https://www.education.gov.in/sites/upload_files/mhrd/files/statistics-new/aishe_eng.pdf
3. Biddle, S. (2017). Three of the Biggest Cybersecurity Challenges Facing the Education Sector. Fortinet - Business & Technology. Retrieved from https://www.fortinet.com/blog/business-and-technology/three-of-the-biggest- cybersecurity-challenges-facing-the-education-sector.html
4. Brandis, G. (2014). Opening Address of the Critical Infrastructure Resilience Conference Melbourne, Victoria. Retrieved from www.attorneygeneral.gov.au/Speeches/Pages/2014/Second%20Quarter%202014/6June2014-Opening AddressOfTheCriticalInfrastructureResilienceConference.aspx.
5. Cybersecurity. In The Merriam-Webster.com Dictionary. Retrieved from https://www.merriam-webster.com/dictionary/cybersecurity
6. Daugherty, P., Banerjee, P., Negm, W., & Alter, A. E. (2015). Driving unconventional growth through the industrial internet of things. Accenture technology. Retrieved from https://www.accenture.com/us-en/_acnmedia/Accenture/next-gen/reassembling- industry/pdf/Accenture-Driving-Unconventional-Growth-through-IIoT.pdf
7. EY. (2013). Security Operations: Centers against cybercrime. Ernst & Young Global Limited. Retrieved from http://www.ey.com/Publication/vwLUAssets/EY_-_Security_Operations_Centers_against_cybercrime/$FILE/EY-SOC-Oct-2013.pdf
8. G8. (2003). G8 Principles for Protecting Critical Information Infrastructures. Retrieved from http://www.cybersecuritycooperation.org/documents/G8_CIIP_Principles.pdf
9. Hayden, E., Assante, M., & Conway, T. (2014). An Abbreviated History of Automation & Industrial Controls

Systems and Cybersecurity. A SANS Analyst Whitepaper. Retrieved from https://ics.sans.org/media/An-Abbreviated-History-of-Automation-and- ICSCybersecurity.pdf

10. Harris, C. E., & Hammargren, L. R. (2016). Higher education's vulnerability to cyber attacks. University Business Magazine. Retrieved from https://www.universitybusiness.com/article/0816-wisp
11. Humayun, M., Niazi, M., Jhanjhi, N. Z., Alshayeb, M., & Mahmood, S. (2020). Cyber Security Threats and Vulnerabilities: A Systematic Mapping Study. Arabian Journal for Science and Engineering, 1-19.
12. Johnson, B. (2008). How one clumsy ship cut off the web for 75 million people. The Guardian. Retrieved from www.theguardian.com/business/2008/feb/01/internationalpersonalfinancebusiness.internet
13. Johnston, E. (2010). Governance infrastructures in 2020. Public Administration Review, 70(s122-128). DOI: https://doi.org/10.1111/j.1540-6210.2010.02254.x
14. Johnston, E. W., & Hansen, D. L. (2011). Design lessons for smart governance infrastructures. Transforming American governance: Rebooting the public square, 197-212. Retrieved from https://s3.amazonaws.com/academia.edu.documents/30941690/Johnston_Hansen_Gov_3_0_chapter_final.pdf?AWSAccessKeyId=AKIAIWOWYYGZ2Y53UL3A&Expires=1525684778&Signature=avQUSM0KQtTRhAQbhqBqoQaqo9c%3D&response-content-
15. disposition=inline%3B%20filename%3DDesign_Lessons_for_Smart_Governance_Infr.pdf
16. Khanna, P. (2017). A conceptual framework for achieving good governance at open and distance learning institutions. Open Learning: The Journal of Open, Distance and E- Learning, 32(1), 21-35. DOI: 10.1080/02680513.2016.1246246
17. Khanna, P. (2019). A governance operating model for open and distance learning institutions. Education and Information Technologies, 24(1), 531-547. DOI: 10.1007/s10639- 018-9790-7
18. Kulkarni, P., & Akhilesh, K. B. (2020). Role of Cyber Security in Public Services. In
19. Smart Technologies (pp. 67-77). Springer, Singapore.
20. Kwikkers, P. (2005). Governing governance: organisation law and network – process – design, International Journal for Education Law and Policy. 1, 73. Retrieved from http://heinonline.org/HOL/LandingPage?handle=hein.journals/ijelp1&div=11&id=&page=
21. Luiijf, H. A. M., van Schie, T. C. C., van Ruijven, T. W. J., & Huistra, A. W. W. (2016). The GFCE-MERIDIAN good practice guide on critical information infrastructure protection for governmental policy-makers. Retrieved from https://www.meridianprocess.org/siteassets/meridian/gfce-meridian-gpg-to-ciip.pdf
22. Morag,N. (2014). Cybercrime, Cyberespionage and Cybersabotage: Understanding Emerging Threats. Colorado Technical University. Retrieved from https://www.coloradotech.edu/media/default/CTU/documents/resources/cybercrime-white- paper.pdf
23. O'Halloran, D., & Kvochko, E. (2015). Industrial internet of things: unleashing the potential of connected products and services. In World Economic Forum (Vol. 40). Retrieved from http://www3.weforum.org/docs/WEFUSA_IndustrialInternet_Report2015.pdf
24. OECD. (2007). Working Party on Information Security and Privacy, Development of Policies for Protection of Critical Information Infrastructures: Ministerial Background Report DSTI/ICCP/REG (2007)20/FINAL. OECD. Retrieved from http://www.oecd.org/sti/40761118.pdf
25. OECD. (2008). ICCP Committee: OECD Recommendation of the Council on the Protection of Critical Information Infrastructures. OECD Council. Retrieved from http://www.oecd.org/sti/40825404.pdf
26. Rouse, M. (2018). Posted - infrastructure (IT infrastructure). Tech Targets Information Technology encyclopedia and learning. Contributor(s): Clive Longbottom and Stephen J. Bigelow. WhatIs.com. Retrieved from https://searchdatacenter.techtarget.com/definition/infrastructure
27. Simon, T. (2017). Critical Infrastructure and the Internet of Things. Retrieved from https://www.cigionline.org/publications/critical-infrastructure-and-internet-things-0 and https://www.cigionline.org/sites/default/files/documents/GCIG%20no.46_0.pdf

28. Solomon, H. (2018). RightsCon report: Universities should form cyber attribution network. IT WORLD CANADA. Retrieved from https://www.itworldcanada.com/article/rightscon-report-universities-should-form-cyber- attribution-network/405399

29. UK Parliament (2011). Cyber Security in the UK, Postnote Number 389, Retrieved from http://www.parliament.uk/documents/post/postpn389_cyber-security-in-the-UK.pdf

30. Union, A. (2014). African Union Convention on Cyber Security and Personal Data Protection. African Union: Addis Ababa, Ethiopia. Doc. EX. CL/846 (XXV). Malabo, 27. Retrieved from https://ccdcoe.org/sites/default/files/documents/AU-270614- CSConvention.pdf

31. Wenger, A., Metzger, J., & Dunn, M. (2002). International CIIP Handbook 2002: An Inventory of Protection Policies in Eight Countries. Critical Information Infrastructure Protection. International CIIP Handbook. Retrieved from http://www.css.ethz.ch/content/dam/ethz/special-interest/gess/cis/center-forsecurities-studies/pdfs/CIIP_Handbook_2002.pdf

Shaping the Digital Transformation of the Education Ecosystem in Europe
EDEN Digital Learning Europe Proceedings
2022 Annual Conference | Tallinn, 20-22 June, 2022
ISSN: 2707-2819

HOW DID WE SUPPORT EDUCATION IN PANDEMIC- ROLE OF THE E- LEARNING CENTRE

Sandra Kučina Softić, Tona Radobolja, Zvonko Martinović,

University of Zagreb University Computing Centre SRCE

Abstract

The world is still facing a pandemic that has changed the lives of all of us, it has changed the way we live, work, learn. This period is difficult and challenging, but at the same time we have encountered many opportunities and situations that have opened new vistas and spawned new experiences. We need to recognize what we have learned, what should be done better, what we want education to look like and what actions should be taken from now on. In addition to the disorder, the pandemic also highlighted a number of interesting and provocative topics, such as how online teaching can work and be of the same quality as classroom teaching; why teachers really need digital skills to be able to teach in a new way and why is support to teachers, students and higher education institutions in the implementation of digital technologies very important part in the shaping education for digital age. In this paper we present importance of organized support to online teaching and learning and implementation of digital technologies in educational process. The E-learning Centre at SRCE has provided support to teachers, students and higher education institutions successfully during pandemic and nowadays. In this paper we bring their case study.

Keywords: e-learning centre, organized support, online education, digital technologies

E-learning Centre at SRCE

University of Zagreb University Computing Centre (SRCE) [1] is the oldest infrastructural institution of the academic and research community in the area of application of information and communication technologies (ICT) in Croatia. SRCE is the key institution in planning, designing, construction, and maintenance of the computing, data and information infrastructure, the e-infrastructure for Croatian academic and research community. Furthermore, SRCE is the competence centre for information and communication technologies as well as the centre for education and support in the area of ICT application.

The E-learning Centre [2] was established at SRCE in 2007 and started its work as the central unit at the University of Zagreb for support in systematic implementation of e-learning. Through the years the E-learning Centre expanded its work to other higher education institution in Croatia and today is national centre for support in -e-learning implementation in higher education. The main focus of the E-learning Centre at SRCE (ELC) is to provide accessible and sustainable support to higher education institutions, teachers and students in use and application of new technologies into teaching and learning, ensuring and providing generally accessible e-learning platform and ensuring joint/centralized resources required for application of e-learning and finally, but not less important, promotion and dissemination of information about e-learning.

The ELC supports users in the process of the implementation of e-learning technologies in the educational process. The team provides help to teachers in the preparation and maintenance of e-courses (blended mode or fully online), organizes training for teaching staff in e-learning technologies and course design and supports students in the virtual environment.

The Centre is providing everyday support via helpdesk (phone, e-mail) and consultations to teachers. Also there are number of learning materials like manuals, animations, quick helps, guidelines and frequently asked questions that enable users to find information in the way that best suits them. The ELC has also prepared a number of training courses and workshops for teachers. One of the first activities of the Centre was the establishment and maintenance of a university platform for e-learning. The platform is based on the Moodle open-source software and is continuously upgraded according to user needs. Today, it is a virtual learning environment called Merlin, which consists of an e-learning platform, a videoconferencing system, an e-portfolio system and is connected to the Information System of Higher Education Institutions in Croatia (ISVU). Today the e-learning platform Merlin includes e-courses from the Universities of Zagreb, Dubrovnik, Rijeka, Zadar, Osijek, University North, the Catholic University of Croatia, and other universities in Croatia as well as from polytechnics and colleges. In 2022, the E-learning Centre is celebrating 15 years of continuous work. The Centre today has 12 full time employees who ensure continuous, innovative and efficient work of the Centre.

A significant part of the work with teachers is done through helpdesk via e-mail, online form or telephone. The centre responds very quickly, whether it is simple questions such as why teacher or student does not see his e-course or how to enroll students, to very complex when the teacher presents an idea of what he would like to improve in his/her e-course or trying to find out what went wrong in the online quiz prepared in the e-course. In addition, the ELC team holds daily consultations with teachers, devoting themselves to each individual teacher and his/her e-course. Creating a positive and creative environment, informing about e-learning and its possibilities in the academic community and providing quality and systematic support to users are long-term goals of the E-learning Centre at SRCE.

The E-learning Centre is also very active in collaboration with local teams for e- learning at the higher education institutions and provide them support as well. The Centre has established and maintains a university (and wider) network of people (experts, teachers and students) to share knowledge and experiences in e-learning and works to promote e-learning and encourage the application of new technologies in education.

Pandemic and support to educational process

The pandemic closed universities but did not stop teaching and learning at higher education institutions. Disruption caused huge stress to entire education system. It was necessary to ensure the continuity of education literally overnight. Teaching and learning moved fully to an online environment, using available tools, primarily videoconferencing systems.

Although a number of teachers had already experience in use of digital technologies using them, mostly, as an addition to classroom teaching, still many of them encountered teaching in an online environment for the first time. Another challenge raised soon after the global closure – Zagreb was hit hard by the very strong earthquake in the second half of the March 2020. Number of buildings were severely damaged and among them educational institutions as well. So, teachers and students faced number of challenges – from technical ones like stable and strong internet connection, computer / laptop, to finding premises where they can work and study, then lack of digital skills, incompetence and not knowing which tools and technologies to use; for teachers lack of pedagogical skills to work in a virtual environment and for students lack in learning in virtual environment.

A that moment numerous teachers and higher education institutions turned to the SRCE and the ELC for support and help to move courses into online environment. First task, for those teachers who did not have e-course until then, was to open e- course on the e-learning platform Merlin and to start using videoconferencing system for online lectures. Number of opened e-courses for academic year 2019/2020 on March 1, 2020, was 14.143, and already in the week of March 16, 6.000 new e-courses were opened on the e-learning platform Merlin. At the same time, there was a significant increase in demand for the SRCE videoconferencing system Adobe Connect which was used only vaguely until pandemic. Number of videoconferencing systems became very popular in short time and that was one of the first investment number of higher education institutions did in the pandemic. The vast majority of higher education institutions and teachers managed to ensure the continuity of the academic year. Teachers organized classes as best they knew and at that moment, in the summer semester of the academic year 2019/2020, that was sufficient as it ensured the end of the academic year. The issue of quality was not high on the agenda at that moment.

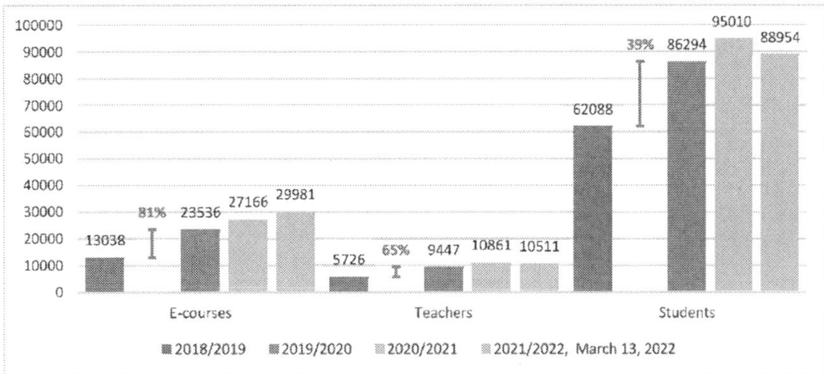

Fig1: E-learning platform Merlin, number of e-courses, teachers and students.

Numbers in Fig 1 show the number of e-courses, students and teachers on the e- learning platform Merlin through academic years 2018/2019 to present academic year. It could be seen that when pandemic hit there were huge sudden increase in the number of e-courses – 81%, following the number of students and teachers. And in the next academic year the numbers continue to increase. At the moment, there are 94 higher education institutions in Croatia who are using e-learning platform Merlin. The pressure on the E-learning Centre team in the March, April, May 2020 was huge. At one moment, it was decided to leave procedures for the e-course opening aside and just open all e-courses upon request. Teachers needed their courses immediately and could not wait longer than day or two... The ELC team worked on Saturdays as well in order to deal with all e-courses requests. One part of the team was opening space on the e-learning platform Merlin for e-courses, another team was on helpdesk and providing consultations how to work with Merlin and develop e-courses.

Due to the pandemic and earthquake, the staff of the E-learning Centre also worked from home at that time answering all day to the user inquiries. It was especially challenging to explain to the teachers over the phone what is the e-learning platform Merlin and how an e-course should look like, especially if the teacher has not encountered these concepts before. Often neither teachers nor students know how to formulate a question or problem, so the expertise and knowledge of the people who provide support is very important. Consultation via phone calls lasted 30 to 45 minutes and were extremely complex as it required knowledge, skills and patience to explain to someone what is an e-course and how to develop one. The E-earning Centre is unique as such as it is supporting users from higher education institutions all over Croatia. Employees are practically constantly on the "quiz" having their knowledge and skills tested as they do not know what question/problem will be next and who will ask the question. This is not easy and it is quite stressful, especially in cases where the inquiry is such that it requires reflection and engagement of more team members and take sometimes even few days. Next challenge were the first online exams in the April 2020, especially when it came to large groups of students (400 to 700). ELC received number of questions on how to prepare exams, how to make sure students do not cheat and how to set up exam so students can see their score after exam. Most of exams were summative tests to assess student's knowledge, and to a lesser extent self-assessment tests. In April 2020 alone, 1758 test activities were held in the Merlin system. Evaluation of student skills was not considered at the time.

From the beginning of the lockdown in Croatia (mid-March) until the end of 2020, the Centre received about 15,000 user inquiries, and the average number of monthly inquiries increased to 2.000, compared to the time before the pandemic when there were about 700 user inquiries per month. Pandemic and earthquake brought significant stress and fear to everyone, and having also challenge to work (teach and learn) in online environment made teachers and students even more vulnerable, so knowing that there is some support where they could ask everything was a tremendous relief for them. Sometimes these calls were made just to hear someone else on the other side and to be able to say how do they feel. Sometimes users were angry and shouting, sometimes crying, sometimes not willing to listen that they are not doing things right; sometimes these were calls from husbands, parents, grandparents for someone... but all of them needed voice on the other side of the phone who will listen. For that, well trained, skilled and experience people are needed who will know how to react in each situation.

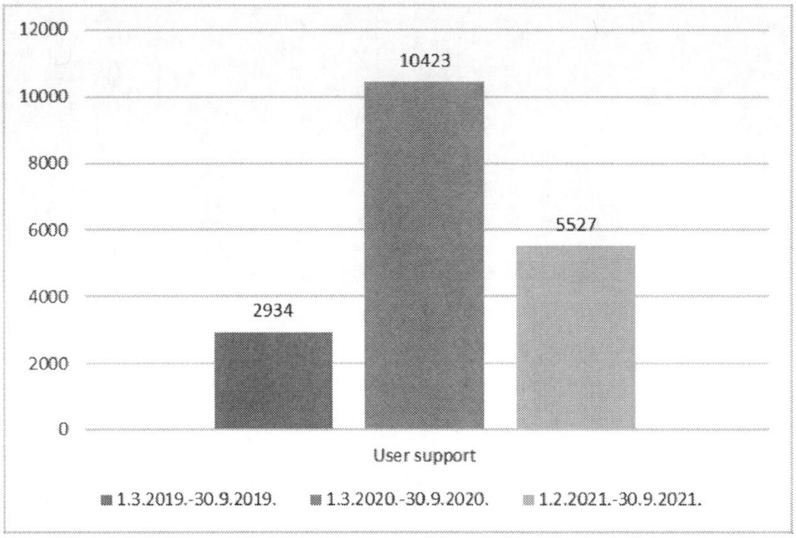

Fig2: Number of inquiries by users answered by the E-learning Centre SRCE team

Fig2 shows the number of inquiries from users to the E-learning Centre team. Significant increase of 255% can be seen between same time in 2019 and 2020. In the 2021 number of inquiries in no longer as big as teachers already have some experience in online teaching and learning and some part of classes are back into classroom. But the number is still almost double to the period in 2019.

In addition to daily live online contacts with teachers, the Centre has prepared and published a number of learning materials for online teaching and learning and additionally highlighted instructions for working in the Merlin e-learning platform so that teachers can immediately find all the information in one place (https://www.srce.unizg.hr/en/elc). Among the materials available are recommendations for online classes, manuals, guidelines, recommendations, animations, and frequently asked questions. New training courses has been prepared for teachers covering various topics, from introductory to the principles of online education and the use of the e-learning platform Merlin based on Moodle, to specifics such as conducting online lectures using videoconferencing systems, how to organize assessment online using for example rubrics or how to set the learning outcomes in Moodle to preparation of the multimedia content in e-course. Although learning materials are widely used, teachers prefer phone contacts as the easiest and the quickest way to solve their problem and advance in their preparation on online teaching.

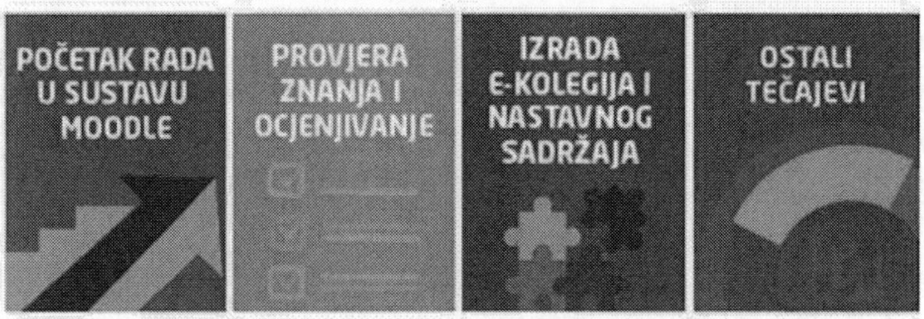

Picture 1: E-course packages for users

Picture 1 represents the four packages of e-courses for users, primarily for teachers, from basics of using Moodle, to courses related to online assessment and grading, e- course development and other courses like those related to e-portfolio development, on importance of digital skills and others. All e-courses are prepared in Moodle, they are self-paced and upon successful completion, participants will get a digital badge. While in March and April 2020 e-courses on basic of using Moodle had the higher number of participants, in April and May 2020 training courses on online assessment had higher number of participants.

In anticipation of the new academic year 2020/2021, some teachers and higher education institutions hoped that the students would soon return to the classrooms and that everything would be the same as before pandemic. However, some higher education institutions saw the crisis caused by COVID-19 as an opportunity to introduce digital technologies in the educational process and to improve its quality.

Unfortunately, the pandemic in the autumn 2020 continued and teaching and learning continues in online environment. This time, teachers had some experience with teaching in an online environment, they know some tools, they have acquired certain digital skills and they prepare and conduct classes online faster and easier. So, the amount of support they need is lesser, first fear and panic is gone, and now they try to stay in line with first experiences. In emergency, teachers and educators will use the most convenient and easy to use tools that do not require major shift in teaching methods.

Why support to users is important?

User support is one of the important factors in process of the implementation of ICT and e-learning technologies into educational process. Knowledge of working with ICT and e-learning technologies is not enough. Lack of support and training in new pedagogical methods and technologies can particularly affect teachers who do not feel comfortable with it [3] [4]. It is therefore necessary to provide teachers with training to gain knowledge on how to improve their pedagogical practice, how to replace traditional teaching and incorporate new educational models that place students at the centre of the educational process [5]. An important factor is the available infrastructure in terms of availability of e-learning tools and technologies, IT support and stable internet connection [6]. According to this, it can be concluded that the skills and competencies of teachers, especially competencies related to ICT and pedagogical competencies, are necessary for the adoption of e-learning.

Survey results from the research with higher education teachers at the University of Zagreb done in 2017 [7] showed that teachers need support in the use of ICT (84,8%), in the use of e-learning technologies (82,1%) and in the preparation and development of e-courses (73,6%). The work and support of the E-learning Centre at SRCE was recognized not only by teachers at the University of Zagreb but also at other higher education institutions in Croatia. 65.7% of teachers believe that the support of the Centre is important in the application of e-learning. During pandemic number of research in education has been done with aim to collect information for further steps and actions in use of digital technologies in educational process. Results from research titled Higher education teachers and pandemic: academic and psychological challenges done in 2021 by Agency for Higher Education and Science [8] on sample of 1204 teachers show that support is very important in preparation and conducting online teaching and learning. Namely, 87% of teachers consider support extremely important and mostly important in the use of e-learning technologies, and 86% of teachers find important support in use of ICT. Support in the preparation and development of e-courses is considered extremely important and important to 78% teachers, and 76% of teachers need support related to pedagogy and teaching methods. If we compare research results before and after pandemic, it can be seen that they there is slight increase in percentage which could be explained that teachers are more aware of the support they need in use of digital technologies in education. Similar results to the ones of the research in 2021 by the Agency for Higher Education and Science were gained in the research done at the University North (Sveučilište Sjever) in 2021 [9] where teachers find support in use of e-learning technologies and preparation of online classes very important. The majority of teachers who participated in the survey find support in the use of ICT (88.9%) extremely important, and another 6.2% believe that it is important. 84.8% of teachers consider support in the use of e-learning technologies to be extremely important and very important, and another 11.7% of teachers consider it important. Support in the preparation and development of e-courses is extremely and very important for 73.1% of teachers, and another 17.2% of teachers consider it important. Regarding the support for pedagogical teaching methods, 59.9% of teachers consider it extremely important and very important, and 27.6% of teachers consider it important. Another research on challenges in online teaching during COVID-19 pandemic done in the Montenegro [10], show that although teachers find their digital competences as being 'good', 26.7% of respondents felt that they did not have the necessary technological and pedagogical skills to support synchronous online teaching, and that they needed additional support and assistance in adapting to the new teaching method. These were the teachers who, despite having basic knowledge of the Internet, were often unfamiliar with the technology needed to conduct synchronous online teaching.

Conclusions

In this paper, aim was to present experience of an e-learning centre and importance of such centre in support to teachers, students and institution in the implementation of digital technologies into educational process, especially during pandemic. Pandemic highlighted the need for a more "professional" approach to teaching and learning in higher education. Setting the education for digital age and digital transformation of education requires significant investment into number of issues and one of them is reliable and accessible support and available and easy to use tools and technologies.

References

1. University Computing Centre SRCE Homepage, https://www.srce.unizg.hr/en/
2. E-learning Centre at SRCE Homepage, https:// www.srce.unizg.hr/elc
3. Buabeng-Andoh, C.: Factors influencing teacher's adoption and integration of information and communication technology into teaching: a review of the literature. IJEDICT, 8(1), pp. 136-155 (2012)
4. Mahdizadeh, M., Biemans, H. & Mulder, M. Determining factors of the use of e-learning environments by university teachers. Computers& Education, 51(1), pp. 142-154(2008).
5. Oldfield, A.: A summary of teacher attitudes to ICT use in schools. iTECfuturelab (2010)
6. Jokiaho, A., May, B. & Specht, M. S. S.: Barriers to using E-learning in an Advanced Way. International Journal of Advanced Corporate Learning, 11(1), pp. 17-22 (2018)
7. Kučina Softić, S.: Digitalne kompetencije nastavnika za primjenu e-učenja u visokom
8. obrazovanju [Disertacija]. Zagreb. (2020).
9. Agencija za znanost i visoko obrazovanje, Sveučilišni računski centar Sveučilišta u Zagrebu, Sveučilište u Rijeci.: Visokoškolski nastavnici i pandemija: akademski i pshiološki izazovi. Zagreb. (2021).
10. Kučina Softić, S., Lasić Lazić, J., Tropša, V.: Analiza ankete o stavu nastavnika prema tehnologijama e-učenja u visokom obrazovanju te koje digitalne kompetencije su im potrebne kako bi na kvalitetan način primijenili e-učenje u obrazovnom procesu. Sveučilište Sjever (2022)
11. Kavarić M, Kavarić A, Djokovic R.: Challenges in online teaching during the COVID-19 pandemic: Higher education survey in Montenegro, Innovations in Education and Teaching International, DOI: 10.1080/14703297.2021.2013287 (2021)

ISSN: 2707-2819

GETTING READY FOR EFFECTIVE ONLINE LEARNING THROUGH PANDEMIC TERM EXPERIENCES

Hale Ilgaz, Ankara University

ABSTRACT

Online learning has been an essential part of education and people's lives. Especially due to the COVID-19 pandemic, people have experienced online environments for both educational activities and professional activities. But at the same time, as a result of the rapid shift, most of the implementations couldn't reflect the correct online learning method. To create effective and successful online learning environments two institutional reports (EDUCAUSE Horizon Reports and European Union Digital Education Action Plan) have been reviewed by focusing on converging dimensions. Both of these reports have emphasized 4 main dimensions. These have been categorized as learning models, digital skills, new technologies and applications, and administrative issues. With the pandemic, the online learning method has gained great importance, and this can be considered an opportunity to develop and sustain effective learning environments by taking these reports' suggestions.

Keywords: Online Learning, Digital Transformation, New technologies.

Introduction

Even if online learning has an old history, it has always been compared with face-to-face education in studies that have been going on for years. Although the focus of these comparisons is different in each study such as effectiveness, learner success, motivation, interaction, perception, and attitude dimensions are seen in the foreground [1-3]. Especially during the past two years, it's easy to observe that there are differences in the perspectives on online education experienced by all segments. Nothing is the same anymore, in every sense.

In these past two years, digital transformation has gained importance in every sector and field, and it has been seen that it is impossible to exclude the online learning option while integrating technology into educational environments in the digital transformation process. Content, stakeholders, pedagogy, and digital technologies are the most important components of online learning. The acceleration of integration of artificial intelligence and internet of things applications is expected to be one of the driving forces of this digital transformation. In this study, the online learning process was examined within the framework of the existing literature and global reports. Also, suggestions regarding the steps that can be taken after the experience of the COVID-19 period are presented.

Methodology

In this study, the traditional literature review method has been used to put an overview of the current situation [4]. Traditional literature reviews provide a comprehensive, critical, and objective analysis of the current knowledge or facts on a specific topic.

Literature Review

Nowadays, we often hear the concepts of online learning, e-learning, and distance education, and in fact, we use each of them interchangeably for the same purpose. However, when we look at the development of this field, it is seen that these concepts differ from each other. Looking at the historical flow, it is seen that the concepts used generally change as a result of technological developments. This change and development are seen in a study that was conducted 17 years ago in which the relations between the concepts were revealed [5]. The distance learning process, which started with letters (postal services), has been moved to the technology dimension with the use of radio and television and has taken its current form with the inclusion of computers and the internet in the process. Essentially each of these conceptual changes can be considered one of the keystones of the distance education journey.

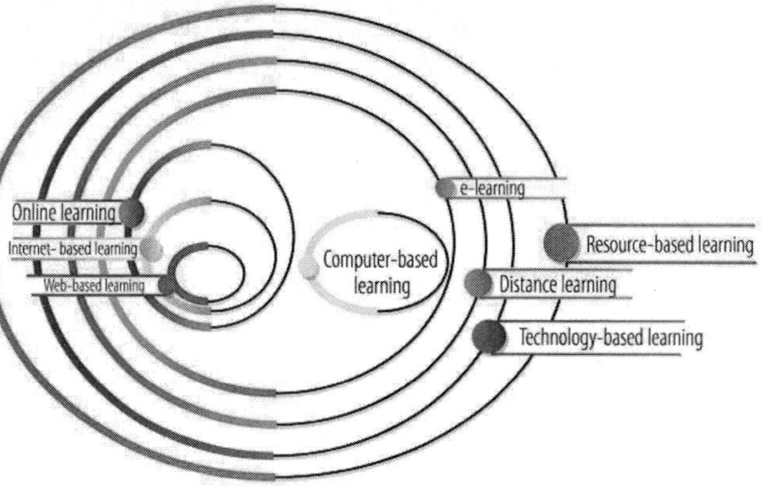

Fig 1. The subset relationships between the groups of the terms [5]

Although conceptual changes have an important place in the distance education process, it can be said that sociological phenomena also have an important effect on this process. The reflection of these sociological phenomena in the conceptual process was with the declaration of the pandemic in 2020. It is known that before the COVID-19 pandemic, a similar situation occurred in history. The polio epidemic had been in 1937 in Chicago, USA. In this incident, which is similar to the COVID 19 pandemic, but with a more localized one, the radio stations in the city broadcast specific courses on certain days of the week for children who could not go to school due to the polio outbreak, ensuring the continuation of educational activities [6].

This epidemic case and the current pandemic reveal that such situations can always happen. For educational processes, how ready we are for such situations in terms of institutions, learners, teachers, families, and the learning environment is a critical point. The necessity of creating a new concept has arisen because the sudden shift and online learning process experienced with the declaration of the pandemic are different from each other. And this is called "Emergency Remote Teaching (ERT)" [7]

Comparing the ERT, with online learning or calling it online learning reinforces the "weak" situation, which is a general perception of the online learning method. Whereas online learning as a whole includes instructional design, planning, development, implementation, and assessment and evaluation activities. However, the experience in ERT enabled the teacher, who is the narrator, and the learner, who is the listener, to meet in a virtual video conference tool instead of the classroom. Therefore, accepting that the ERT is different from online learning is important for a successful online learning process and eliminating negative perceptions [7].

It is not that easy to say that online learning is equal to face-to-face learning, but researchers have shown that if the requirements of online learning are met, it can be as effective as face-to-face education [1, 8, 9]. Even if many studies show online learning can be as effective as face-to-face education, there is a tendency for a negative opinion and this is one of the barriers to online learning [10, 11]. But the pandemic played a pushing role for the online education area.

Somehow, most people have experienced online learning during the pandemic. And due to the sudden shift transition process was not successfully ended for most of the cases. For creating an effective and successful online learning environment to be as much as equal to face-to-face learning, there are some key dimensions. These dimensions have been studied in several review types of research [8, 12, 13].

Based on regional initiatives EDUCAUSE Horizon Reports and European Union Digital Education Action Plan are providing a detailed and comprehensive framework for online learning integration. Both of these studies aimed to reshape education for digital environments after COVID 19. Before discussing converging points, the general overview has been stated below:

European Union (EU) Digital Education Action Plan 2021-2027 & 2022 EDUCAUSE Horizon Report

Right after the first year of the pandemic, the EU has stated a digital action plan for education and training systems to support their adaptation to the digital age. This action plan has two main focuses that are fostering the development of a high-performing digital education ecosystem and enhancing digital skills and competencies for the digital transformation [14].

Effective digital capacity planning and development, including up-to-date organizational capabilities, digitally competent and confident teachers and education and training staff, high-quality learning content, user-friendly tools, and secure platforms which respect e-privacy rules and ethical standards have been stated in fostering the development of a high-performing digital education ecosystem. On the other hand, basic digital skills and competencies from an early age, digital literacy, including tackling disinformation, computing education, good knowledge and understanding of data-intensive technologies, such as artificial intelligence (AI), and advanced digital skills, which produce more digital specialists, ensuring that girls and young women are equally represented in digital studies and careers have been emphasized under enhancing digital skills and competences for the digital transformation dimension [14].

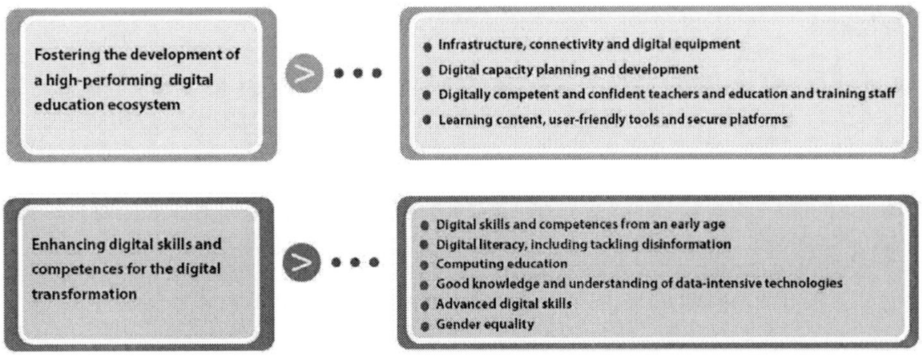

Fig. 2. EU Digital Action Plan (2021-2027) Priority Areas

On the other side, EDUCAUSE Horizon Report consists of five main trends that are social, technological, economic, environmental, and political [15].

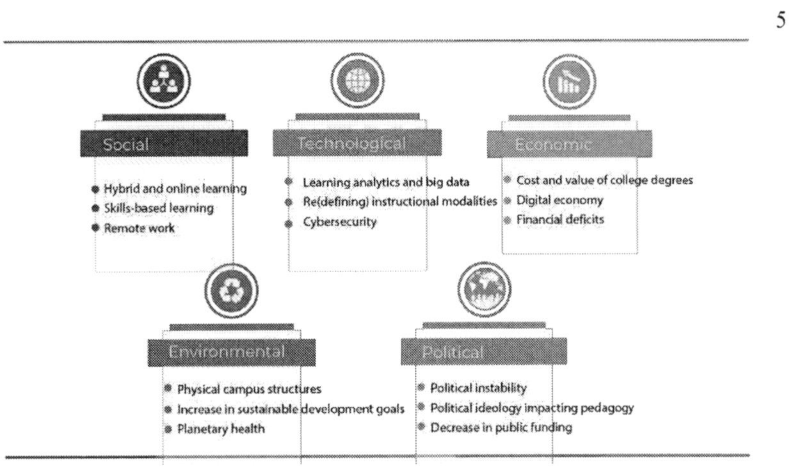

Fig. 3. EDUCAUSE 2022 Horizon Report Trends

Although these reports were created through two different institutions, it is seen that the basis of both is to realize digital transformation and to provide this by increasing digital skills and competencies. The convergent points of these two frameworks can be grouped as learning models, digital skills, new technologies and applications, and administrative issues.

Learning Models

In today's world, there is no single best solution for educational activities and COVID 19 pandemic has shown this clearly. After the first shock of the pandemic, most of the institutions revised their information and communication technologies (ICT) infrastructure and learning models. Fully online learning [16-18], flipped learning [19, 20] or blended learning [21] models have been also using by the institutions before the pandemic. During the pandemic, due to the physical isolation, the face-to-face (F2F) option couldn't be used. But according to the studies revealed during and after the pandemic's pick time showed that there were no significant differences between online and F2F in terms of learning levels [22]. One of the most important problems experienced in this process has emerged as the lack of an effective interaction [22, 23]. Therefore, diversifying the interaction designs in the dimension of learners, teachers, and content in online learning environments will provide more effective learning experiences. Another challenge emerges as assessment design [24, 25]. Especially academic dishonesty and efficiency are the major problems due to the unsupervised and electronic assessment processes [26]. To overcome this obstacle, combining formative assessment and summative assessment strategies reasonably will be a better and fair solution. These difficulties revealed by the researches how the importance of the design process in online learning environments.

Digital Skills

Another common component is digital skills. In the digital information age, the characteristics of individuals are also changing, and it is important to raise individuals who keep up with it, to catch up with the society and the age [27]. The lack of digital skills is one of the most important barriers to online learning [10, 28, 29]. This is valid not only for learners but also for the teachers too [30]. Such that one of the most preferred MOOC platforms, Coursera has created SkillSets for preparing learners for professional life. According to the World Economic Forum statistics 85 million jobs will be displaced globally by 2025, and 149 million new digital jobs are expected by 2025 [31]. From this point of view, skills-based learning has gained more importance for both the individual development of learners and educational curriculums.

New Technologies and Applications

During the pandemic process, the massive open online course (MOOC) concept has gained great popularity. Especially Coursera and edX have provided access to their content free of charge to all educational institutions, enabling them to reach and benefit from those who have not experienced these platforms before. In this way, the concept of MOOC, which has reached a much wider audience, has drawn attention to alternative ways of education [32]. Another salient point is the need for and integration of artificial intelligence, augmented reality, and virtual reality applications into online learning environments [33]. The argument that every innovation emerges out of a need has been experienced especially during the pandemic period. The need for learning analytics and decision support systems has increased in order to individualize learning environments and establish learner tracking and effective feedback mechanisms [34, 35]. During the presentation of applied content, which is one of the biggest handicaps of online learning environments, the effectiveness of learning environments can be increased with the integration of augmented reality [36- 38], and virtual reality [39, 40] applications.

Administrative Issues

In both reports, it is seen that administrative processes, policies, and regulations are emphasized. In this context, the Digital Competence Framework put forward by the EU can be a baseline for institutional decisions for all levels of education. The framework consists of five main dimensions that are information and data literacy, communication and collaboration, digital content creation, safety, and problem-solving [41].

Another value is micro-credentials. Although it is still a new method in -practice, it is one of the applications that best reflects the flexibility of learning environments in the digitalized world. Micro-credentials, which can be used for both diploma programs, personal development, and professional development purposes, are becoming more and more common [42-44]. Policy and regulation adjustments are needed to overcome barriers to the acceptance of micro-credentials [45].

Another administrative issue is seen as privacy and security. Although the terms of use have been determined by many laws and regulations, especially in digital environments, such as data privacy, copyrights, and personal data, the use of these data in educational activities, the scope of the permissions and the sanctions are still controversial [46, 47]. Therefore, it is considered important for institutions to open their corporate decisions to their stakeholders in a transparent manner, based on legal regulations as the upper roof.

Discussion & Conclusions

In the light of these reports; institutions, instructors, administrators, and policymakers need to reshape, revise, and also integrate new learning models, and new technologies into the current programs and curriculums. Although researches suggest otherwise, online learning bears the stigma of being of lower quality than F2F learning. However, this situation has begun to reverse with the pandemic experienced in the past two years. It is seen that online learning is used in educational institutions at all levels, albeit in different models, with the detection of implementation errors and the spread of good practice examples. This global experience has shown that this will not be the last issue as a disruption. Wars, outbreaks, scarcities, or economical restrictions can cause such disruptions anytime. So it is important to be ready for these kinds of situations. Because educational activities are vital and cannot be discarded. At the same time, it has been seen that rapid digital transformation is inevitable for online learning processes to be effective and successful Aside from the devastating effects of the pandemic, when looked at from an optimistic point of view, many institutions have had the chance to progress with the momentum gained from this transformation, as it initiated or accelerated this transformation.

Of course, it is not that easy to create a qualified online learning environment for all the institutions due to economic, technical, or infrastructural issues. For this kind of case, it can be better to choose a more centralized system in which a few institutions come together and use or customize a platform and use it.

References

1. Herman, T. and S. Banister, Face-to-Face versus Online Coursework: A Comparison of Learning Outcomes and Costs. Contemporary Issues in Technology and Teacher Education, 2007. 7(4): p. 318-326.
2. Bagrıacık Yılmaz, A., Distance and Face-To-Face Students' Perceptions Towards Distance Education: A Comparative Metaphorical Study. Turkish Online Journal of Distance Education, 2019. 20(1): p. 191-207.
3. Price, L., J.T.E. Richardson, and A. Jelfs, Face-to-face versus online tutoring support in distance education. Studies in Higher Education, 2007. 32(1): p. 1-20.
4. Baumeister, R. and M. Leary, Writing Narrative Literature Reviews. Review of General Psychology, 1997. 1: p. 311-320.
5. Anohina, A., Analysis of the terminology used in the field of virtual learning.
6. Educational Technology & Society, 2005. 8(3): p. 91-102.
7. Foss, K. Remote learning isn't new: Radio instruction in the 1937 polio epidemic. The Conversation 2020 2021/09/23]; Available from: https://theconversation.com/remote-learning-isnt-new-radio-instruction-in- the-1937-polio-epidemic-143797.
8. Hodges, C., et al. The Difference Between Emergency Remote Teaching and Online Learning.EDUCAUSE Review 2020; Availablefrom: https://er.educause.edu/articles/2020/3/the-difference-between-emergency- remote-teaching-and-online-learning.
9. Nortvig, A.M., A.K. Petersen, and S.H. Balle, A Literature Review of the Factors Influencing E-Learning and

Blended Learning in Relation to Learning Outcome, Student Satisfaction and Engagement The Electronic Journal of e-Learning, 2018. 16(1): p. 44-65.

10. Paul, J. and F. Jefferson, A Comparative Analysis of Student Performance in an Online vs. Face-to-Face Environmental Science Course From 2009 to 2016. Frontiers in Computer Science, 2019. 1.
11. Muilenburg, L.Y. and Z.L. Berge, Student barriers to online learning: A factor analytic study. Distance Education, 2005. 26(1): p. 29-48.
12. Keengwe, J. and T.T. Kidd, Towards Best Practices in Online Learning and Teaching in Higher Education. Journal of Online Learning and Teaching, 2010. 6(2): p. 533-541.
13. Bozkurt, A. and O. Zawacki-Richter, Trends and Patterns in Distance Education (2014–2019): A Synthesis of Scholarly Publications and a Visualization of the Intellectual Landscape. The International Review of Research in Open and Distributed Learning, 2021. 22(2): p. 19-45.
14. Martin, F., T. Sun, and C.D. Westine, A systematic review of research on online teaching and learning from 2009 to 2018. Computers & education, 2020. 159: p. 104009-104009.
15. Commission, E. Digital Education Action Plan (2021-2027). European Education Area 2021; Available from: https://education.ec.europa.eu/focus- topics/digital-education/about/digital-education-action-plan.
16. EDUCAUSE, 2022 EDUCAUSE Horizon Report | Teaching and Learning Edition. 2022.
17. van Oostveen, R., et al., New conceptions for digital technology sandboxes: Developing a Fully Online Learning Communities (FOLC) model, in EdMedia + Innovate Learning 2016. 2016, Association for the Advancement of Computing in Education (AACE): Vancouver, BC, Canada. p. 665-673.
18. Tibingana-Ahimbisibwe, B., et al., A systematic review of peer-assisted learning in fully online higher education distance learning programmes. Open Learning: The Journal of Open, Distance and e-Learning, 2020: p. 1- 22.
19. Trenholm, S. and J. Peschke, Teaching undergraduate mathematics fully online: a review from the perspective of communities of practice. International Journal of Educational Technology in Higher Education, 2020. 17(1): p. 37.
20. Karabulut-Ilgu, A., N. Jaramillo Cherrez, and C.T. Jahren, A systematic review of research on the flipped learning method in engineering education. British Journal of Educational Technology, 2018. 49(3): p. 398-411.
21. Bond, M., Facilitating student engagement through the flipped learning approach in K-12: A systematic review. Computers & Education, 2020. 151: p. 103819.
22. Müller, C. and T. Mildenberger, Facilitating flexible learning by replacing classroom time with an online learning environment: A systematic review of blended learning in higher education. Educational Research Review, 2021. 34: p. 100394.
23. Baczek, M., et al., Students' perception of online learning during the COVID-19 pandemic: A survey study of Polish medical students. Medicine, 2021. 100(7): p. e24821.
24. Shambour, M.K.Y. and M.A. Abu-Hashem, Analysing lecturers' perceptions on traditional vs. distance learning: A conceptual study of emergency transferring to distance learning during COVID-19 pandemic. Education and Information Technologies, 2022. 27(3): p. 3225-3245.
25. Adedoyin, O.B. and E. Soykan, Covid-19 pandemic and online learning: the challenges and opportunities. Interactive Learning Environments, 2020: p. 1- 13.
26. Su, H., Educational Assessment of the Post-Pandemic Age: Chinese Experiences and Trends Based on Large-Scale Online Learning. Educational Measurement: Issues and Practice, 2020. 39(3): p. 37-40.
27. Guangul, F.M., et al., Challenges of remote assessment in higher education in the context of COVID-19: a case study of Middle East College. Educational Assessment, Evaluation and Accountability, 2020. 32(4): p. 519-535.
28. Bozkurt, A., et al., Dijital bilgi çağı: Dijital toplum, dijital dönüşüm, dijital eğitim ve dijital yeterlilikler. Açıköğretim Uygulamaları ve Araştırmaları Dergisi, 2021. 7(2): p. 35-63.
29. Garcia, K.R., et al., Improving the digital skills of older adults in a COVID- 19 pandemic environment.

Educational Gerontology, 2021. 47(5): p. 196- 206.

30. Sciacca, B., et al., Parental mediation in pandemic: Predictors and relationship with children's digital skills and time spent online in Ireland. Computers in Human Behavior, 2022. 127: p. 107081.

31. Chakraborty, P., et al., Opinion of students on online education during the COVID-19 pandemic. Human Behavior and Emerging Technologies, 2021. 3(3): p. 357-365.

32. Mittal, S. Launching SkillSets for Coursera for Campus: Preparing Students for High-Growth Entry-level Jobs. Coursera Blog 2021; Available from: https://blog.coursera.org/launching-skillsets-for-coursera-for-campus/.

33. News, I. Coursera and edX Launch Initiatives to Support Universities Impacted by the Outbreak. 2020 2022/04/03]; Available from: https://iblnews.org/coursera-and-edx-launch-initiatives-to-support- universities-impacted-by-the-coronavirus/.

34. Ara Shaikh, A., et al., The Role of Machine Learning and Artificial Intelligence for making a Digital Classroom and its sustainable Impact on Education during Covid-19. Materials Today: Proceedings, 2022. 56: p. 3211-3215.

35. Petrescu, D., D. Enache, and L. Duta, Collaborative decision-making in online education. Procedia Computer Science, 2022. 199: p. 1090-1094.

36. Kaloudelis, D., et al., Design of a University Pandemic Response Decision Support System. Industrial and Systems Engineering Review, 2022. 9(2): p. 117-133.

37. Eldokhny, A.A. and A.M. Drwish, Effectiveness of Augmented Reality in Online Distance Learning at the Time of the COVID-19 Pandemic. International Journal of Emerging Technologies in Learning (iJET), 2021. 16(09): p. pp. 198-218.

38. Saleem, M., et al., Influence of augmented reality app on intention towards e-learning amidst COVID-19 pandemic. Interactive Learning Environments, 2021: p. 1-15.

39. Maiti, M., M. Priyaadharshini, and B. Vinayaga Sundaram. Augmented Reality in Virtual Classroom for Higher Education During COVID-19 Pandemic. 2021. Cham: Springer International Publishing.

40. Raja, M. and G.G. Lakshmi Priya, Using Virtual Reality and Augmented Reality with ICT Tools for Enhancing Quality in the Changing Academic Environment in COVID-19 Pandemic: An Empirical Study, in Technologies, Artificial Intelligence and the Future of Learning Post-COVID-19: The Crucial Role of International Accreditation, A. Hamdan, et al., Editors. 2022, Springer International Publishing: Cham. p. 467-482.

41. Tsekhmister, Y., et al., Evaluation of Virtual Reality Technology and Online Teaching System for Medical Students in Ukraine During COVID-19 Pandemic. International Journal of Emerging Technologies in Learning (iJET), 2021. 16(23): p. 127-139.

42. Hub, E.S. The Digital Competence Framework 2.0. 2022; Available from: https://joint-research-centre.ec.europa.eu/digcomp/digital-competence- framework-20_en.

43. White, S., Developing credit based micro-credentials for the teaching profession: An Australian descriptive case study. Teachers and Teaching, 2021. 27(7): p. 696-711.

44. Woods, K. and J.A. Woods, Less Is More: Exploring the Value of Micro- Credentials Within a Graduate Program. The Journal of Continuing Higher Education, 2021: p. 1-9.

45. Fitzgerald, R. and H. Huijser. Exploring industry-university partnerships in the creation of short courses and micro-credentials. in Back to the Future – ASCILITE '21. 2021. Armidale: Proceedings ASCILITE 2021.

46. McGreal, R. and D. Olcott, A strategic reset: micro-credentials for higher education leaders. Smart Learning Environments, 2022. 9(1): p. 9.

47. Turnbull, D., R. Chugh, and J. Luck, Transitioning to E-Learning during the COVID-19 pandemic: How have Higher Education Institutions responded to the challenge? Education and Information Technologies, 2021. 26(5): p. 6401-6419.

48. Dwivedi, Y.K., et al., Impact of COVID-19 pandemic on information management research and practice: Transforming education, work and life. International Journal of Information Management, 2020. 55: p. 102211.

Shaping the Digital Transformation of the Education Ecosystem in Europe
EDEN Digital Learning Europe Proceedings
2022 Annual Conference | Tallinn, 20-22 June, 2022
ISSN: 2707-2819

INSTITUTIONAL READINESS TO OFFER DIGITAL AND MICRO-CREDENTIALS

Elena Trepulė, Airina Volungevičienė, Estela Daukšienė and Giedrė Tamoliūnė,

Vytautas Magnus University

Abstract

The paper provides a concise overview of 6 stage institutional preparation to get ready offering and recognizing digital and micro-credentials in universities or other educational institutions. Organization needs to implement changes in all 6 stages to prepare for the implementation and recognition of digital and micro-credentials in the institution: (1) strategic decisions to make links to the European digital learning infrastructure, (2) transparent internal procedures, (3) academic and administrative staff competence development, (4) a standardized digital metadata template needs to be developed and approved in the organization, (5) the virtual learning environment needs to be adjusted accordingly to allow issue of digital credentials; (6) and finally the learning opportunity descriptions need to be updated to correspond to the standardized digital metadata template and virtual learning environment.

Keywords: micro-credentials, institutional readiness, digital credentials.

Institutions and countries are experimenting with issuing digital and micro-credentials, however, there are those who are interested in possibilities to start issuing micro-credentials but need to prepare interacting with the European digital infrastructures in issuing digital credentials. The goal of this paper is to offer a system of 6 steps for the organizational transformation to become ready to offer and recognize digital and micro-credentials.

Organization needs to implement changes in all 6 stages to prepare for the implementation and recognition of digital and micro-credentials in the institution (Figure 1): it all starts with making strategic decisions (1) regarding the fact of adopting digital micro- credentials, making it legalized in the institutional documentation and choosing to make links to the European digital learning infrastructure; (2) these decisions are being implemented through transparent internal procedures; (3) accordingly academic and administrative staff needs to gain professional development to know how to implement and recognize micro- credentials; (4) a standardized digital metadata template needs to be developed and approved in the organization; (5) then the virtual learning environment needs to be adjusted accordingly to allow issue of digital credentials; (6) and finally the learning opportunity descriptions need to be updated to correspond to the standardized digital metadata template and virtual learning environment. We will now accordingly discuss all 6 stages.

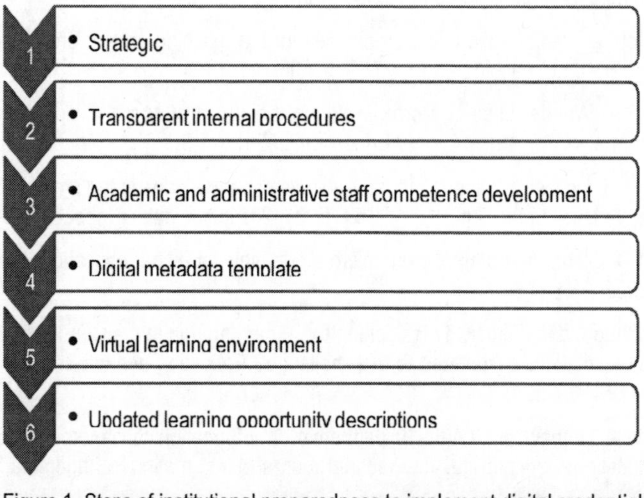

Figure 1. Steps of institutional preparedness to implement digital credentials

Strategic decisions

European education and research projects have been experimenting with different technical solutions to implement digital credentials in education institutions. Meanwhile, in 2020 European Commission Europass platform has launched a whole a new Europass platform with Digital Credential Infrastructure. The Europass platform is currently still being piloted but it already has tools for institutions to issue credentials, certificates at different levels, in digital format with automatic verification of authenticity.

Institutions ready to implement Europass infrastructure in their organizations would be able to issue qualifications and certificates in an efficient, secure, and fraud-resistant digital infrastructure. This technical infrastructure could be used by the Member States and various stakeholders when issuing Europass digital credentials to learners. For example, IT systems of awarding bodies could implement this infrastructure to create diplomas and certificates for students. Any school, college, university, or training provider in Europe may use this tool to issue credentials for free and secure them with their e-seal. Credentials can be e-mailed to learners or directly deposited to their Europass profiles. Organizations willing to start issuing digital credentials using Europass digital infrastructure need to undergo a 3-step approach:

1. Prepare data to obtain a qualified electronic seal for issuing digital credentials;
2. Use the online credential builder or existing XLS template to describe digital credentials and add necessary information;
3. Upload prepared credential information to the system.

Further detailed instructions how institutions need to prepare their data for Europass Digital Credentials can be accessed in the Europass website1. While Europass is evolving and further development will be oriented for creating open metadata formats for sharing and storing of micro-credentials and interoperability between various infrastructures institutions should be following this path, preparing institutional roadmaps for digital credentials' storage and recognition and integrate already-existing Europass Digital Credentials Infrastructure in organization's IT systems.

Setting transparent internal procedures

Higher education institutions getting ready to issue digital credentials need to get ready likewise to recognize the incoming digital credentials from other institutions as well. First, external challenging factors in the process of open online learning recognition closely relate to political decisions, such as standards and guidelines that lead recognition procedures within Europe, that those should be the same, when it comes to open online learning.

The different attitudes and trust in open learning, labour market flexibility needs to be emphasized both by society and universities. The internal requirements for universities mostly deal with 1) internal readiness of university; and 2) learner-provided evidence on open online learning. Requirements for university readiness to recognize open online learning lead to changes in institutional values and culture. The university needs strategic decisions and setting internal transparent procedures, in order that the staff and learners are confident on how and when, and through which type of learning digital credentials are issued or could be recognized. This also means that professionals in recognition, human resource managers, as well as academic staff should be instructed on procedures of recognition and possible activities around it.

Academic and administrative staff competence development

Moreover, academic, and non-academic staff should not only be informed about strategic decisions and processes required to prepare for micro-credentialization, but also targeted programs for continuous professional development should be prepared and staff competences need to be developed and constantly updated. Even though digital competences of staff are already under discussion, there are no yet clear concepts and guidelines for training programs established now for micro-credentialization. In such a way clearly defined quality assurance procedures and standards could increase trust among all stakeholders. The role of stakeholders, when open online learning recognition is in focus, is of high importance, as strong networks with a variety of stakeholders contribute to easier solutions when it comes to questions of openness, transparency, trust, and digital credentialization. University openness also means a change in teacher's attitude towards openness, sharing and use of online learning content

[1] https://europa.eu/europass/en/preparing-credentials-european-digital-credentials-learning

created by others, and the new modes of teaching and learning.

The process of recognition inside the university, as based on evidence provided by open online learning providers, offers a variety of quality assurance scenarios already available from the good practices of most advanced universities in this area. The collected evidence on how learning and assessment was done and what results were reached in many situations allows us to get more objective data. Information, data, and qualitative evidence are the main requirements for open online learning providers to ensure a successful process of digital credential recognition in the university.

Digital metadata template

According to MicroHE definition "credential is a documented statement that acknowledges a person's learning outcomes or achievements". In other words, the term "credential" is used to refer to any type of formal certification usually awarded to acknowledge a completion of an academic degree or professional/vocational training (LaMagna, 2017). Examples of credentials include the following: diplomas, certificates, degrees, etc. Higher educational institutions face challenges in attempting to recognize students' achievements, skills, competences, and knowledge. Thus, there is growing interest in making credentials more valuable and informative. Recently, there has been an attempt to improve the design of the credentials, so they become more informative and comprehensive. For instance, the ECCOE (European Credit Clearinghouse for Opening up Education) project aims at simplifying certification within the higher education sector, as well as raising approval rates and appreciation of technology-enabled credentials with different stakeholders, such as students, higher education institutions, and employers.

Virtual learning environment

European higher education institutions have already for a long-time organized distance or blended learning and have their digital learning environments in operation. Some institutions rely on commercial decisions; however, the most popular institutional, non-commercial digital learning environment which is used by European universities is Moodle. It is an open-source platform which requires the institutional staff for administration. However, the requirement to have it administered by institutional staff provides opportunities for its adaptation to institutional needs, and thus opens possibilities for flexible use of micro-credentials. EHEA institutions organise different types of educational initiatives and issue different types of credentials (see Camilieri and Rampelt, 2018, for classification types of credentials).

Generating learning outcomes to the digital certificate allows a micro-credential to collect metadata from a digital learning environment and transfer the data to a digital certificate; the more of the elements are generated by the platform and automatically is transferred to the certificate, the more the metadata digital certificate has. For the digital learning platform to generate metadata it needs to collect it during the learning process. Thus, the teacher (or institution providing the digital learning experience, such as a course(s) or module) not only needs to design and prepare educational activities, but also need to use the digital learning environment functionality properly for learning process organization.

First, it is learner authentication and administration. For the learner to be provided with the digital learning opportunity it needs to be enrolled in the platform. Second, when the selected learning activity (for example a course or module) is designed and prepared in the digital learning environment it needs to be associated with the learning outcomes. The learning activity outcomes need to be added to the course, linked with the learning activities, and later, when the teacher assesses the learner activities, learning outcomes linked to the activity also need to be evaluated and marked if they have been reached. Third, there are certain digital learning environment plugins (such as Simple certificate, Custom certificate or similar) that need to be installed in the Moodle and based on their possible templates the digital certificate is formed and may be issued. It is possible to add different data that goes along with the digital certificate, such as issuing body and its details, the learner details, title of the course, module, learning outcomes, learning volume and date range, assessment methods and grades, teacher(s) name(s) and other necessary information. When the learning process is over and the learning activity – a course or several courses or modules – is finished, either the teacher or the Moodle platform itself allows the learner to generate the certificate if the learning activity conditions are fulfilled.

Updating learning opportunity descriptions

Open learning requires us to rethink curriculum, course design, teaching and learning approaches and how to support learners. An open online course should meet national competence standards that have been endorsed by a national authority. In the absence of national standards, course outcomes should be based on the authority's definition of competence and endorsed by industry training boards or by relevant industry parties. Where non-formal learning is guided by a formal curriculum, it should meet formal education standards e.g., learning outcomes defined by educational institutions. Structural elements of open online course descriptions include general information, learning outcomes, pedagogical approach, assessment strategy and certification.

To make a course description more attractive, some key question(s) addressed in the course could be identified, relating the questions and topics to the latest news and viral social media discussions. Furthermore, it is necessary to indicate the main target group, tuition language, course level (if applicable), providing course delivery specifications and letting a learner know about the planned type of learning - mentored or self-learning and finally course duration in weeks. The key point is that learning opportunity description templates need to be in close coherence with the digital credential metadata template and virtual learning environment course descriptions to allow cohesion and interoperability of course and credential data.

To conclude

The following 6 steps need to be taken by the organization centrally and in a unified way. The implementation of the discussed steps need to be adjusted internally to achieve compatibility among organization's strategic decisions, clarity of internal procedures, staff development, metadata template preparation and adjustment of virtual learning environment and learning opportunity descriptions.

A more in-depth analysis of the institution's readiness to issue and recognize digital and micro- credentials may be found in publication *„Guidelines for Open and Online Learning Assessment and Recognition with Reference to the National and European Qualification Framework Micro-Credentials as a Proposal for Tuning and Transparency"* (2021) prepared by the Vytautas Magnus university research team working in a research project *"Open Online Learning for Digital and Networked Society"*, supported by Lithuanian Research Council.

References

LaMagna, M. (2017). "Placing digital badges and microcredentials in context". In: Journal of Electronic Resources Librarianship. 29(4), 206-210. DOI:10.1080/1941126X.2017.1378538.

Camilleri, A. F. and Rampelt, F., 2018, Concept paper on quality assurance on credentials. Retrieved from https://oepass.eu/wp-content/uploads/sites/22/2019/03/OEPass_O1A1- report_v5.pdf

Shaping the Digital Transformation of the Education Ecosystem in Europe
EDEN Digital Learning Europe Proceedings
2022 Annual Conference | Tallinn, 20-22 June, 2022
ISSN: 2707-2819

DIGITAL INCLUSION FOR ALL (DI4ALL)

Ebba Ossiannilsson, Swedish Association for Open, Flexible and Distance Education; International Council for Flexible and Distance Education, Sweden

Egle Celiešienė, Lithuanian College of Democracy

Abstract

The object of this article is to present an on-going two-year project 2022-2024 Digital Inclusion for all learners (DI4all), financed by ERASMUS + program (2021-2-SE01-KA210- SCH -000050728 project) as a best practice example. DI4all aims to improve the key competencies, skills, and learning outcomes of young people in schools by promoting quality improvement, innovation excellence at the educational level and mainstreaming digital inclusion, as well as improving the competencies of teachers and educators to promote digital inclusion and combat disinformation through education and training. The expected outcomes are: training of educators for the implementation of digital inclusion developed based on analyzed results and best practices of teachers and educators in the field of digital inclusion, development of a guide for educators that includes materials from the intellectual results of the project, studies of best practices, and case studies, and the implementation of an online contest for schools that present their best practices for digital inclusion of all learners. This project is based on main strategies and influenced by the UNESCO SDG4, and EU programs such as the European Commission EU Digital Agenda, the DigComp2.2, DigCompEdu, the Selfie, My Digiskills. The four priority areas for ERASMUS+ also serve as a basis, such as digital transformation, inclusion and diversity, green sustainability as well as the overall aim on active citizens for all.

Keywords: Active citizenship, Digital Inclusion, Education, DigComp2.2, Green Sustainability, Transformation.

Introduction

The purpose of this paper is to present the structure of the on-going two-year project 2022-2024 Digital Inclusion for all learners (DI4all) [1] that aims to improve the key competencies, skills, and learning outcomes of young people in schools by promoting quality improvement, innovation excellence at the educational level, and mainstreaming digital inclusion, as well as improving the competencies of teachers and educators to promote digital inclusion and combat disinformation through education and training. The expected outcomes are: Training of educators for the implementation of digital inclusion developed based on analyzed results and best practices of teachers and educators in the field of digital inclusion, development of a guide for educators that includes materials from the intellectual results of the project, studies of best practices and case studies, and the implementation of an online contest for schools that present their best practices for digital inclusion of all learners. A final conference will also be held. The foundations for the project are UNESCO SDG4 [2], the four priority areas for ERASMUS + such as active citizenship, digital transformation, inclusion and sustainability [3], the European Commission Action Plan 2021-2027 [4], the DigComp2.2 [5], the EU DigCompEdu [6], European Commission MyDigS kills [7] and the Selfie [8]. They will all shortly be summarized as below in section 2.

Foundation guidelines for Digital Inclusion for all learners (DI4all)

The United Nation Agenda 2030 is "an action plan for people, planet and prosperity." It includes 17 Sustainable Development Goals (SDGs). These goals are indivisible and include economic, social and environmental dimensions. The UNESCO Sustainable Development Goal 4 (SDG 4) is the education goal, which aims to "ensure inclusive and equitable quality education and promote lifelong learning opportunities for all." [2]. Figure 1.

Fig. 1 UN UNESCO SDG4

The EU Action Plan on Integration and Inclusion 2021-2027 by the European Commission outlines concrete steps, provides guidance, and identifies funding for initiatives that promote inclusion for all [3]. It focuses on multi stakeholder partnerships, including close collaboration with immigrant-led organizations.

Its key actions include:

- Inclusive education and training from early childhood through higher education, with a focus on facilitating recognition of qualifications and continued language acquisition;
- Improving employment opportunities and recognition of qualifications to fully recognize the contribution of migrant communities, particularly women, and ensure that they are supported to reach their full potential;
- Promote access to health services, including mental health care, for
- people with migrant backgrounds;
- Access to adequate and affordable housing, funded by the European Regional Development Fund (ERDF), the European Social Fund Plus (ESF+), the Asylum and Migration Fund (AMF) and Invest EU.

The four prioritized Areas ERASMUS+

The new ERASMUS + program aims to promote participation in democratic life, shared values and civic engagement [3]. The program supports active citizenship and the ethic of lifelong learning; it promotes the development of social and intercultural skills, critical thinking and media literacy. Priority is given to ERASMUS+ projects that provide opportunities for people to participate in democratic life and social and civic engagement through formal or non-formal learning activities. Emphasis is placed on raising awareness and understanding of the context of the European Union, particularly with regard to the EU's common values, principles of unity and diversity, and social, cultural, and historical heritage. In the area of youth, a strategy for youth participation has been developed to provide a common framework and support the use of the program to promote youth participation in democratic life. The program has four focus areas:

- Active Citizenship
- Digital Transformation
- Inclusion and Diversity, and
- Green Sustainability.

Active citizenship

Active citizenship can be considered as an overall goal for the program and the three others are facilitating this aim.

Digital transformation

One of the main objectives of Erasmus+ is to make greater use of the possibilities of digitalization in international cooperation. In addition to physical mobility, virtual learning will be introduced to complement stays abroad. One of the horizontal priorities of Erasmus+ is digital transformation and digital skills development. The European Commission has developed an action plan for digital education that covers the same period as the new Erasmus+ program, from 2021 to 2027, with the two main priorities being capacity building for the use of available digital teaching methods across the education sector and the dissemination of digital skills throughout society.

Digital literacy is about being familiar with digital services and being able to use different tools depending on one's skills. It's about using cell phones and computers to do things we normally do, but also to do completely new things in a digital way. It's also about being able to cope with the change that digitization is bringing to all areas of life without too much difficulty.

The COVID -19 pandemic further highlighted the importance of digital literacy for the digital transformation that Europe needs. In particular, it underlined the need to harness the potential of digital technologies for teaching and learning and to develop digital literacy for all. In line with the strategic priorities of the Digital Education Action Plan (2021-2027) [4], the program aims to support these efforts to help learners, educators, youth workers, young people, and organizations on the path to digital transformation.

The program will support the first strategic priority of the action plan, the development of a powerful digital education ecosystem The program will also support the second strategic priority of the Action Plan by supporting actions aimed at improving digital skills and skills development at all levels of society and for all (including disadvantaged young people, students, job seekers, and workers). In line with these two strategic priorities of the Action Plan, a European Digital Education Hub will be launched

Inclusion and diversity

In multicultural society the social equity and inclusion is one of the major challenges of today. The 2020 Global Education Monitoring Report by

UN underline that about 258 million children, adolescents and youth (17% of the global total) are not in school, children with disabilities were 19% less likely to achieve minimum proficiency in reading than those without disabilities, unequal distribution of resources and opportunities and in the same time argue the need of ensuring opportunities to take part in the society to all individuals. Moreover, taking into account the global pandemics the social equity and inclusion has become more important than ever. Most governments around the world have temporarily closed educational institutions impacting almost 70% of the world's student population or some 1.6 billion students.

The importance to social equity and inclusion thought digital interaction is revealed in the Digital Education Action Plan (EC, 2018), where it is described as the opportunity, which must be accessible to all. Over the past few decades, the usage of the internet has grown substantially accounting for nearly 2 billion users globally and the majority of Internet users are adolescents and young adults (Bremer J, 2005; Aslanidou S, Menexes G, 2008; Giles G, Price IR, 2008). In Europe more than 80 % of young people use the internet for social activities. Digital interaction is also highlighted by the international organization: OECD report “Education 2030” has identified three pillars of “transformative competencies”: creating new value; reconciling tensions and divisions and taking responsibility (OECD Future of Education and Skills 2030) and World Economic Forum presented new competences development in order to succeed in nowadays society and participate in all facets of society from civic duties to the workplace (World Economic Forum (2018), and (2020).

All people - regardless of their circumstances - must have the opportunity to participate and develop in Erasmus+. One of the goals of Erasmus+ is to enable more people with limited opportunities or underrepresented groups to participate in international exchange programs. Encounters between people of different origins and backgrounds are an important component. An international exchange not only contributes to a higher quality of education, but also offers new perspectives and new knowledge that can contribute to a stronger cohesion in society. In a partnership project, you can also work with organizations in other countries to contribute to inclusion and diversity in different ways. Environmentally sustainable projects are one of the four priorities of Erasmus+ for the program period starting in 2021. At a detailed level, they include

- Disabilities
- Health problems
- Barriers related to education and training systems
- Cultural differences
- Social barriers
- Economic barriers
- Barriers related to discrimination
- Geographical barriers

Green sustainability

Combating climate change and contributing to long-term sustainable development is the goal of the Paris Agreement and Agenda 2030, which form the basis for the European Commission's sustainability work. For the Erasmus+ program period 2021-2027, one of the news is that all projects must be environmentally sustainable. This means that as a project promoter, one has to think green consistently when planning and implementing the project. Alternative to physical visits, conferences, exchange programs or other activities abroad is virtual mobility. The advantages are not only lower environmental impact, but also factors such as higher availability and lower costs.

The Digital Competence Framework for Citizen (DigComp) provides a common understanding of what digital competence is [5]. The DigComp framework identifies the key components of digital competences in five areas., which are; (i) Information and data literacy, (ii) Communication and collaboration, (iii) Digital content creation, (iv) safety, and (v) Problem solving.

The framework is also provided in alignment with the Digital Accessibility Guidelines, as creating accessible digital resources is an important priority today. Fig 2.

Fig. 2. The Digital Competence Framework for Citizen (DigComp) 2.2.

The European Framework for Educators' Digital Literacy (DigCompEdu) is a science-based framework that describes what it means for educators to be digitally literate [6]. It provides a general reference framework to support the development of education-specific digital literacy in Europe. DigCompEdu is aimed at educators at all levels of education, from early childhood to higher and adult education, including general and vocational education, special education, and non-formal learning, Fig 3.

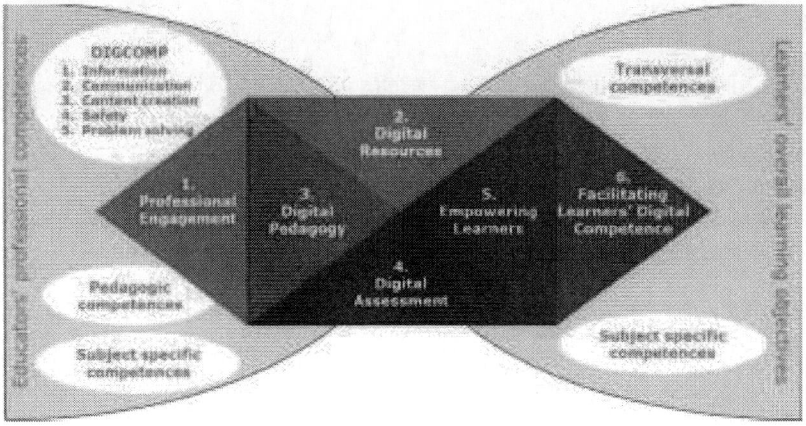

Fig. 3. DigCompEdu framework

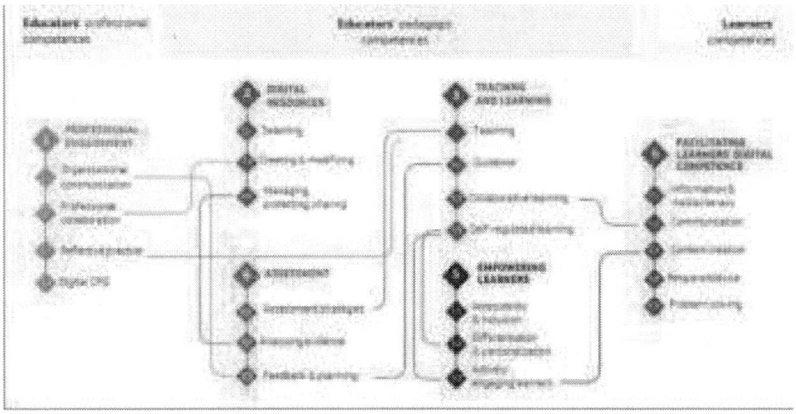

Fig. 4. Details of DigCompEdu Framework

MyDigiSkills [7] helps to better understand ones level of digital skills based on knowledge, skills and attitudes in each of the five areas of the European Framework of Digital Competences for Citizens, known as DigComp, Figure 5. Educators' competencies play an important role in nowadays society, and in one hand it could be described as a formal requirement fulfillment, involving knowledge, skills and values. In another hand, it became a life-long learning process and the synergy between the educators' professional and pedagogical competencies and learners' competencies is highlighted. At the same time, it is important to highlight educators' social-emotional competencies (Kvieskienė et al., 2022), especially targeting vulnerable youth. This holistic view of educators' competencies ensures a favorable action policy (optimistic socialization scenario) by determining the components of positive socialization and preventing socially unacceptable cultural consequences (Kvieskienė et al., 2022).

Fig. 5.My Digiskills

SELFIE is a free, easy-to-use, customizable tool to help schools assess where they stand with learning in the digital age [8]. Figure 6.

Fig 6. Selfie tool for schools

About the ERASMUS+ project Digital Inclusion for all learners (DI4all)

Many of the digital inequalities that exist in the world today were highlighted by COVID -19 and the impact it has had on learning around the world. Learners around the world have moved from traditional to digital learning. The pandemic highlighted the importance of creating an education and training system that is compatible with the digital world. While the COVID - 19 pandemic has demonstrated the need to build digital capacity in education and training, it has also exacerbated a number of existing difficulties and inequalities between those who have access to digital technology and those who do not, particularly among those from poor backgrounds. The pandemic has also exposed a number of issues for education and training systems, including institutional digital capacity, teacher training, and overall levels of digital skills and competencies.

The objectives of the project are as follows.

- improve key competences, skills and learning achievements of young people in schools by promoting quality improvement, innovation excellence at the educational level and mainstreaming digital inclusion, in particular through increased transnational collaboration between education and training providers and other stakeholders in the field of digital inclusion in schools.
- improve the skills of teachers and educators to promote digital inclusion and combat disinformation through education and training.

The project builds on long-term collaboration between schools and other research and training institutions targeting digital inclusion by promoting the exchange of best practices and enabling the creation of a network for sharing best practices.

The expected outcomes are as follows:

- Training of educators for the implementation of digital inclusion, developed based on the analysed results and best practices of teachers and educators in the field of digital inclusion.
- Guide for educators with materials from the intellectual results of the
- project.
- Best Practices Study and Case Studies: participants select best practices to explore and deepen. In addition, the project's case studies provide some scenarios of how different types of schools are approaching digital inclusion, with practical ideas for how they might approach implementing inclusion in their own schools.
- Competition: creating an online competition for schools (website and Facebook) to showcase their digital inclusion activities for all learners. Participants and participating organizations will

select the best practice implementation project for each of the three key practices described in the program.

- Final seminar to present the project results and the winners' experiences in the field of digital inclusion.

The target group are all stakeholders within a schools and organizations, such as students, school staff, schools, other educational providers, public bodies, and national agencies

The Di4all project has sustainability and maintenance activities built in. The project has embedded all four priority areas, such as active citizens, inclusion and diversity, digitalization, and green sustainability, both in its application, but will integrate them even more in its activities, dissemination, and sustainability.

Conclusion and recommendation

It is important to underline that mentioned various strategies and methodologies of digital inclusiveness identify multi-aspects and ambiguity of its content expanse presupposed by the methodological attitude. Digital inclusiveness highlight new requirements for the entire sector and the collaborating educational bodies will have to professionalize to cope with these challenges.

DI4all project is based on main international strategies and methods such as the UNESCO SDG4, the EU Digital Agenda, the DIgComp2.2, the EU DigCompEdu, the Selfie, My Digiskills. The three priority areas for ERASMUS + also serve as a basis, such as digital transformation, inclusion, and sustainability.

DI4all project could be described by the main key elements: digital transformation, inclusion, and sustainability. The essence of DI4all project can be disclosed through the constituent parts of those parameters: a) digital transformation, empowering people with limited opportunities or underrepresented groups to participate in the project; b) inclusion, involving knowledge about psycho-cultural, socio-cultural and cultural environment; motivation for communication and cooperation; competence for communication and cooperation in inner and outer networks; c) sustainability - ensuring DI4all project live after the official end of the project.

The results of DI4all project are interested not just schools as the main beneficiaries and target group of the project, but different stakeholders, implementing digital inclusiveness practices or policy.

The success of DI4all project depends on the active engagement and exchange of the best practice of the mentioned above-interested parties and created spread at local, regional, national, and international levels.

References

1. ERASMUS+ Application Di4all learners, http://www.lduk.lt/en/digital inclusion-for-all-learners-di4all/, last accessed 2022/06/19.
2. European Commission Action Plan 2021-2027 https:/ec.europa.eu/migrant-integration /news/one-year-eu-action plan-integration-and-inclusion-2021-2027_en, last accessed 2022/06/19.
3. [Vuorikari, R., Kluzer, S. and Punie, Y., DigComp 2.2: The Digital Competence Framework for Citizens - With new examples of knowledge, skills and attitudes, EUR 31006 EN, Publications Office of the European Union, Luxembourg, 2022, ISBN 978-92-76-48883-5, doi:10.2760/490274, JRC128415
4. European Commission DigCompEdu. Digital Competence Framework for Educators (DigCompEdu). https://joint-researchcentre.ec.europa.eu/digcompedu_en
5. European Commission mydigskills. https://mydigiskills.eu, last accessed 2022/06/19.
6. European Commission SELFIE https://education.ec.europa.eu/selfie, last accessed 2022/06/19.
7. Eurostat (2015): Being young in Europe today - digital world: http://ec.europa.eu/eurostat/statistics-explained/index.php/Being_young_in_Europe_today_-_digital_world,last accessed 2022/06/17
8. Global education monitoring report, Inclusin and education: all means all: https://unesdoc.unesco.org/ark:/48223/pf0000373718/PDF/373718eng.pdf.multi, last accessed

2022/06/20

9. InternetWorldStats: Usage and Population Statistics. Bogota, Miniwatts Marketing Group, 2010
10. Kvieskienė, G., (Volume editor) Gerd-Bodo von Carlsburg (Volume editor), (2022). Prototype: Modelling in Social-Emotional Education. Edited Collection. 270 Pages.
11. Kvieskienė, G., Ivanova, I, Trasberg, K., Stasytytė, V., Celiešienė, E., (2021). Modeling of Social Policy and Initiatives under COVID-19: Rural NEET Youth Case Study.: https://www.mdpi.com/2076-0760/10/10/393, last accessed 2022/06/19.
12. Kvieskienė, G., Kvieska, V., Gerd-Bodo von Carlsburg. Social Clustering: Paradigm of Trust. (2021). https://www.peterlang.com/document/1111457, last accessed 2022/06/19.
13. OECD: Learning for 2030: http://www.oecd.org/education/2030- project/, retrieved March 2020
14. Prioritiese of the ERASMUS+ Program https://erasmus plus.ec.europa.eu/programme-guide/part-a/priorities-of-the-erasmus programme, last accessed 2022/06/19.
15. The Future of Jobs Report: http://www3.weforum.org/docs/WEF_Future_of_Jobs_2018.pdf, retrieved 6th March 2020
16. UNESCO COVID-19 Education issue notes: https://en.unesco.org/covid19/educationresponse/issuenotes, last accessed 2022/06/21
17. UNESCO SDG https://en.unesco.org/sustainabledevelopmentgoals, last accessed 2022/06/19.
18. World Economic Forum, Jobs of Tomorrow: Mapping Opportunity in the New
19. Economy:http://www3.weforum.org/docs/WEF_Jobs_of_Tomorrow_2020.pdf, retrieved March 2020

Shaping the Digital Transformation of the Education Ecosystem in Europe
EDEN Digital Learning Europe Proceedings
2022 Annual Conference | Tallinn, 20-22 June, 2022
ISSN: 2707-2819

DIGITAL EDUCATION IN THE POST-COVID: PERSPECTIVES FOR REDUCING INEQUALITIES

Eucidio Arruda, Federal University of Minas Gerais

Abstract

The main objective of this manuscript is to build analyzes that allow political decision- making that consider technological training in basic education as a priority so that the country can develop effective actions to expand and universalize technological access for students and teachers. It also seeks to problematize how it is possible to rethink the technological training of teachers and students and how this can be directed towards the construction of a more democratic society, producing, and distributing more wealth. From the moment that digital technology is the main pedagogical resource to reduce distances and thus guarantee the maintenance of the school's functioning, political and pedagogical conditions are created to think about contexts in which technologies are more integrated into the school environment. in person. It is not just a case of defending digital technologies in schools, but planning properly so that the school is prepared for future challenges that prevent physical approaches and contacts again. In addition, it is up to the school to train subjects who are able to position themselves and integrate technological knowledge into their lives. These questions help to build readings and analyzes about possible educational impacts in the country, and open paths for interpretations about the educational structures in Brazil that may imply in curricular discussions that involve, in a transversal way, digital information and communication technologies both in teacher training, as well as in student education.

Introduction

The advent of the Covid-19 pandemic has brought new and old challenges to basic education and higher education, especially with regard to access and technological training for students and teachers to respond to contemporary demands, including those involving teaching and learning in different times and spaces with technological mediation.

In the school aspect, the technological demands coincide with the sudden closing of the physical spaces of the schools. At the same time, financial, software and hardware limitations were observed to guarantee access to education for students, in addition to the difficulties faced by teachers to perform their duties.

As an element of even greater challenge for Brazilian education, according to UNESCO data for 2021, Brazil was one of the rich and emerging countries that extended the total closure of schools the longest, exceeding 40 weeks in 2020.

The so-called emergency remote education (Arruda, 2020) made the school suddenly migrate to the homes of students and teachers. Although Brazil has public policies for the inclusion of digital technologies in basic education for more than 20 years, it was observed that the reality of access and technological training is not a reality in the country.

According to Novoa and Alvim (2020), distance learning made the school suddenly migrate to the homes of students and teachers. Then came the implementation of various pedagogical models, on an exceptional basis, such as the transmission of classes on TVs and the development of teaching materials in an emergency way.

Distance learning and other terminological and technological variations to address education mediated by digital technologies (Schlemmer and Moreira, 2021) was not a reality in Brazilian basic education. From the moment that digital technology is the main pedagogical resource to reduce distances and thus guarantee the maintenance of the school's functioning, political and pedagogical conditions are created to think about contexts in which technologies are more integrated into the school environment. in person. It is not just a case of defending digital technologies in schools, but planning properly so that the school is prepared for future challenges that prevent physical approaches and contacts again. These questions help to build readings and analyzes about possible educational impacts in the country, and open paths for interpretations about the educational structures in Brazil that may imply in curricular discussions that involve, in a transversal way, digital information and communication technologies both in teacher training, as well as in student education.

In other words, it is about thinking of a school that is linked to contemporary challenges and problems, which has digital technologies as elements that become increasingly central in social life, despite its contradictions and paradoxes. School is the right place to understand everything that transforms life in society and digital technologies have become elements of great economic and social impact.

A school that does not have educational technological equipment (computers, internet, etc.) accessible to all students is a school that helps to increase inequalities and the impoverishment of the population.

In addition to the lack of equipment, there are still pedagogical-curricular limitations. Moreira et al (2020) draws attention to an emergency remote education that is based on distance learning, but which uses educational methodologies and practices typical of physical learning territories. In a context like this, curriculum or teaching innovation is not seen, but an anachronistic integration between a teaching methodology from a past time and contemporary technologies that demand other ways of learning and, therefore, of teaching.

For Shalberg (2021), the pandemic has shown that the school is more than a place for acquiring knowledge, it is integrated into the social fabric, in which poverty, lack of health and violence are directly related to learning opportunities. For this author, in a post- covid world, educational financial resources are more likely to be scarce and more "results with less" are demanded – which can result in a school that diminishes the autonomy, innovation and self-reflection of the school community. From the perspective of political choices, this is a plausible reality, in which teaching work can be replaced, in part, by automated or artificial intelligence-based software.

Arruda et al (2021) analyze that in Brazil this arrangement could be seen in remote education initiatives in the 27 Brazilian states. All of them adopted centralized curricular initiatives, with a model built without the participation of the school community, with television productions and handouts in PDF format prepared by unknown pedagogical teams and with little transparent costs. A model was implemented in which the teacher is responsible for the operationalization of the pedagogical proposal conceived by others.

The risk is that the exceptionality regime of the pandemic becomes the "new normal" of curricular models, with the elaboration of closed national "educational packages".

This movement is what Morgado et al (2020) call curriculum isolation. It is a use of digital technologies centered on instruction, on the development of content mediated by technologies whose greater interaction takes place between student and material, undoing the processes of interaction, socialization and curricular reconfiguration that would be typical in a context of physical interactions.

When considering the fluid movement of teachers who leave school activities together with the number of undergraduate students who, according to OECD data, are equivalent to close to 20% of undergraduate students, an important space opens up. curricular education policies integrated with technologies. This movement is important because it allows teacher training to be transformed and empower the next generation of teachers to have a more "technological" training.

It is imagined that such a movement of curricular transformation involves what Barroso (2018) calls regulatory instruments:

Whether they are legislative, economic, informative, communicational, management or other instruments, these devices always configure, in addition to their own effects, a certain conception of public action (its meaning, its cognitive and normative framework) and a specific way of materializing and operationalizing governmental action. (Barroso, 2018)

This set of instruments indicates a complexity of this process that involves not only curricular changes in basic education, but also curricular restructuring in teacher training courses.

Pandemic, technological-educational demands, and Brazilian curriculum structure

The Covid-19 pandemic raises a classic question for historians, which is the inability to predict the future. Knowledge of the past, according to Legoff (1990), can be an instrument of liberation, in the sense that we are not stuck in the past to determine the present and future – a condition that we perceived at the beginning of the pandemic, as I will discuss below.

We live in a context of technological transformations, in which Vieira Pinto (2005) claims that the techniques are more valued than technology today, although technology goes beyond the technique itself, as it is a science and allows epistemological inquiries. The same author also states that, as the perspective of technological development in the Western world is presented to us, it is configured from an evolutionary logic, of control over people and processes from a supposed promise of solving all our problems.

Giddens (1991) understands this movement as a symptom of modernity in which the guiding axis is the belief in the functioning of technological systems in which their full functioning generates a sense of control and defense against adversities. This is what the author calls trust mechanisms and disembedding systems. The organization of social life, therefore, would be supported by the trust that people have on these systems, since it is not possible for everyone to have all the knowledge about everything. Our trust in health is also trust in the system, that, despite the risks, the functioning of things still overlaps with social instabilities.

Covid-19 has deconstructed this conceptual direction, insofar as the future cannot be predicted, but the implications of a pandemic present have deconstructed many of the accumulated knowledge about how society, the economy, culture and, in the specific case of this proposal, scientific research, school education would respond to extreme situations worldwide. There was a tacit understanding that, with the exception of traditional wars between nations, we would be prepared to meet other calamities with relative speed and safety. However, it is possible to infer that some signs of the destabilization of Covid-19 were little observed or were not given adequate importance. The case of the emergence of Covid-19 in China and the way in which the world watched the country's defense strategies are important elements to understand the delay in recognizing the gravity of the situation.

To corroborate this thesis, the world has watched China2 completely close a region since December 2019 – which, despite the lack of more accurate information, would already demonstrate the health severity of the situation. Only in March 2020, global actions (disjointed between countries) to contain transmission were started, after the declaration by the World Health Organization (WHO) that Covid-19 should be considered a pandemic. From a scientific point of view, there were strong signs about the virus's social disruptive capacity, but at the same time, possible political and scientific readings that it was possible to contain it in the short term.

Although we lived with a major pandemic between 1918 and 1920, incorrectly called the Spanish flu, as stated by Kolata (1999), which caused school closures around the world, it is possible to say that Covid-19 impacted even more the systems of education around the world. According to Unesco data (2020), we reached more than 90% of schools completely closed between April and May 2020 and numerous countries, such as Brazil, Mexico and the United States, have extended the total school closures to more than 40 weeks in 2020 (Unesco, 2021).

Digital technologies, despite being discussed as educational possibilities in numerous scientific works (the OECD and UNESCO websites have numerous productions), emerge as the great news in the school context

---

[2] City of Wuhan, China, at the end of December 2019, the Sars-CoV-2 virus was already circulating undetected. https://www.bbc.com/portuguese/geral-51060492

of the pandemic, as pointed out by Irfam et al (2020). It is not possible to question the dimension of novelty, but perhaps the dimension of the inexistence of another possibility to keep school activities active, due to the imposed social distance.

On the one hand, the pandemic demonstrates an urgent need for schools to incorporate technological knowledge already disseminated by students and teachers. On the other hand, it was possible to perceive a misalignment between educational policies, the reorganization of teaching work and curricular reconfigurations based on technological mediation. These curricular reconfigurations bring a centrality of digital technologies that until then were not part of everyday school life, but that with the pandemic are perceived as necessary for the construction of a more inclusive education (Mulumba and Schmidt, 2021).

In line with this perception, a study carried out by Dorn et al (2021) indicates changes that will likely remain post-pandemic. Among them, the increase in e-commerce, which grew more than four times in some countries, the maintenance of homeworking for a significant percentage of workers, greater demand for technological training, increased automation, especially through Artificial Intelligence. These changes directly and indirectly affect school structures, as they bring new training demands and an expansion of educational inequalities given the difficulties in modifying national curricula in the short term.

It is relevant to understand how such changes affect educational policies around the world, especially in relation to teacher training and reconfigurations of curricular structures in compulsory basic education. Technological training no longer involves a search for technological distinction, but as an attribute that can help reduce educational inequalities.

Studies by UNESCO (2021) and the World Bank (World Bank, 2021) already indicate that educational losses will be felt for many years, especially in the poorest countries, which experience a lack of digital literacy in schools and the reality of digital exclusion. At the same time, it is up to us to create a hypothesis in which the pandemic stimulates planning and strategies that have technology as a political and pedagogical axis.

In 2017, I prepared a large-scale study on the OECD (Arruda, 2017)3, at the request of the National Education Council of Brazil, in which I analyzed how member countries of the Organization for Economic Cooperation and Development (OECD) were implementing digital technologies of information and communication (TDIC) in the curriculum of basic education schools (primary and secondary education), considering the methodology, contents and workload. Among the results obtained, Arruda (2018) states that there was a movement of curricular reformulation in most OECD member countries, aimed at the need to train a young person who is critical, who manages to position himself in a world with the primacy of the development of techniques and technologies that transform human life more and more quickly.

We note, however, that there is still an incipience regarding this theme, of implementing more "technological curricula and more universal access to digital technologies, as detected by Tied and Grafe (2019) in the case of Germany.

THE leave of questions posts The respect of policies public promoters of use in TDIC and the discourses that are created around this subject, we point to gaps that are possibly likely to be recognized in the space of teacher training. Our hypothesis is that teacher training courses still keep traditions, in their historical sense, that limit discussions about the role of TDIC in the training of basic education students, which directly reflects on the teacher training strategies used for the higher education, embodied in courses such as the Doctorate in Education, for example.

Cifuentes (2016) states that the political dimension is extremely important to think about technologies in teacher training processes. According to the author, these issues even involve a dimension of university reform that would bring the university closer to contemporary social, economic and cultural issues and problems. Gonzáles and Martín (2019) consider that the digital training of teachers should involve the

---

[3] Available on the Ministry of Education website http://portal.mec.gov.br/docman/dezembro-2017- pdf/77891-produto-estudo-sobre-processo-implementacao-tecnologias-digitas-pdf/fileAccessedon06/ 11/2021.

technological literacy of students, to reduce the digital and unequal gaps in society, whose technological knowledge becomes a premise of contemporary inclusion.

In Brazil, Gatti (2009) and Arruda (2018) already point out that there are few changes in the organization of courses in formation in teachers at Brazil, especially with regard to the implementation of technologies in teacher training. Both authors, in different and temporally separated research, observe that there are few changes in the curricular structures of teacher training courses in Brazil. The results point to generic formations, with a massive presence of critical discourses that present little about the contents and way of functioning of the courses, in addition to the almost non-existence of discussion about technologies in the school environment.

The problem does not lie in offering a specific subject to discuss possibilities for introducing ICT in the teaching and learning process. Even if the percentage of disciplines in the area of technologies and education were higher, what guarantees that their theoretical and empirical assumptions were objects of dialogue with the other disciplines of a course?

The question, therefore, does not start from the insertion of specific disciplines, but from more complex what leave gives relationship in between at technologies old and new and you necessary content The formation teacher in one society whose students (and teachers) live surrounded by digital media that transform their social, cultural and economic relationships.

Data from the OECD (2015) show, for example, that young people with more privileged access to digital technologies have broader experiences of obtaining content or practical information (oriented to solving problems). This same research demonstrates that the most favored students have greater skills to read and interpret digital documents, which favors their positioning in the world in which they live, in addition to other inclusive elements in a society whose mediation has been increasingly operated by these technologies.

We observed that Israel, Poland, New Zealand, United Kingdom, Slovakia and Australia (Arruda, 2018 and Webb et al, 2018) present proposals for more consolidated implementation of technologies in basic education in recent years.

In Israel, from primary education onwards, everyone must learn Computer Science, technological literacy and computational thinking. According to Goldstein et al., 2011, in the late 2000s most teachers in Israel lacked training and practical experience in integrating ICT in teaching. Goldstein and Tesler (2017) state that the national policy for teacher training for the incorporation of ICT in teaching began in 2011 and the authors' data demonstrate that there have been significant changes in teacher profiles, especially with regard to promoting ICT integrations in their practices.

In Australia, from the age of five, people start studying computer science. Poland has had, for at least 20 years, a curriculum that privileges technological training.

In the United Kingdom, according to information from the British government (www.gov.uk), the implementation of the "National Curriculum" began in 2014 and one of the greatest difficulties encountered in incorporating digital technologies into the curriculum in a transversal way, that is, integrated into all curricular components, took place with the training of teachers. Teachers were not able to work under the new curricular perspective and it was necessary to undertake a set of actions to train teachers who were already working and change the training structures of undergraduate courses. It is a process with medium and long-term results, as the time required for teacher training, their insertion in the market and responses/results of this training can take more than a decade to be observed.

OECD data (2020), in the study called " School education during COVID-19: Were teachers and students ready?", demonstrate that at least the United Kingdom, Australia, Israel and New Zealand are in an advantageous situation compared to other countries in terms of: teacher training in the use of technologies, teaching support for students, preparation of young people, access to good quality equipment and internet, cooperative teaching work mediated by technologies and continuing education.

It cannot be concluded that the measures adopted by these countries have had a positive effect on the quality of education, as further studies and deeper analyzes are needed to allow us to compare the curricular structures, the educational policies of each country, the strategies for change, etc. This is necessary so that we can understand that the introduction of ICT is not something that will promote an immediate change in educational quality or the reduction of inequalities in a country, but it indicates the temporal proximity of school policies in these countries with the social transformations that involve digital technologies.

We observe that other countries are in a situation of studies and analyzes for the implementation of the TDIC as problematized knowledge and discussed in the curricular structures (Storte et al, 2019). In general, what was perceived was an understanding of the importance of the school bringing dimensions of contemporary technological knowledge, but still lacking in relation to the modification of curricular structures and the bases of teacher training.

When analyzing the data obtained in different countries, it is clear that difficulties with DICT in education are common (OECD, 2020). The greatest difficulty, highlighted by the pandemic, continues to be economic and social inequality, since even in rich countries, such as the United States, access to remote classes by students and teachers is hampered by financial and/or geographical difficulties (UNESCO, 2021)

On the other hand, the pandemic opened an important analytical perspective, presenting digital technology as the new demand for training and mandatory educational access. Let us also note that if, before, minimum training was a requirement for a country to grow, generate and distribute wealth, what is observed today is that the dissemination of technological knowledge becomes the new demand for the future planning of the distribution of social welfare. between countries.

Reich (2020) states that education is reasonably complex, as there are numerous systems and subjects that have unique social demands, needs and challenges, which directs an educational system in a particular country to strengthen certain school knowledge to the detriment of another. In addition, the author states that technologies will not be so well suited to all curricular components, with some having greater adherence than others.

Despite considering that there is knowledge that requires greater contemporary technological knowledge, based on TDIC, it is relevant to consider that social knowledge of technology is historical knowledge that is related to the ways in which we produce and appropriate knowledge in contemporary times. This means that understanding the implications of technological development in contemporary society becomes an important action for current and future school systems.

It is important to highlight that, therefore, it is not a question of incorporating technologies into a certain area of knowledge, through artificial intelligence systems, big data or individual computerized tutorials, but understanding the impacts of technological development on the different components of social life.

What we intend to problematize is that the TDICs, regardless of how well their algorithmic, programming, hardware or software aspects are known, establish new ways of producing knowledge in different areas. It is relevant for those who determine educational policies to pay attention to these transformations, so that the propositions of thinking of the school as a space for preparing young people for a future active adult life and for socio-economic and cultural protagonist are strengthened.

We observe, therefore, a look that directs technologies to the interior of the school, but on the other hand, an apparent slowness in the appropriation of technological innovations, insofar as they are infrequent in curricular structures, as we observed previously.

We can infer that this movement is what Hobsbawm (2013) announces as cultural resistance, in which technology is not accepted when it promotes significant changes in our cultural and hierarchical structures. According to the author, technological transformations that represent, in the imagination, technical improvements in our actions, such as an increase in the speed of locomotion made by air transport, are better accepted than technologies that reconfigure power relations, such as access to information without teacher intermediation.

We are therefore living in a period of great challenges, in which efforts must be integrated to understand that the technological training of teachers and students is fundamental for the political and economic strengthening of a country of dimensions such as Brazil.

Final considerations

The advent of the Pandemic pointed out numerous gaps in educational policies for the implementation of technologies in basic education, when it was observed that, despite being in a much more connected world through the internet, reports around the world showed educational systems taken by surprise. as they found it difficult to offer other educational options to the face-to-face education that had hitherto been predominant. Brazil experienced a similar situation, perhaps even worse, because in addition to the initial difficulties, data from transparency portals showed that there was investment below the constitutional percentages in Education, showing little attention to fundamental elements, such as network infrastructure, teacher training, equipment technological etc.

From the moment that digital technology is the main pedagogical resource to reduce distances and thus guarantee the maintenance of the school's functioning, political and pedagogical conditions are created to think about contexts in which technologies are more integrated into the school environment. in person. It is not just a case of defending digital technologies in schools but planning properly so that the school is prepared for future challenges that prevent physical approaches and contacts again. In addition, it is up to the school to train subjects who are able to position themselves and integrate technological knowledge into their lives.

These questions help to build readings and analyzes about possible educational impacts in the country, and open paths for interpretations about the educational structures in Brazil that may imply in curricular discussions that involve, in a transversal way, digital information and communication technologies both in teacher training, as well as in student education.

In other words, it is about thinking of a school that is linked to contemporary challenges and problems, which has digital technologies as elements that become increasingly central in social life, despite its contradictions and paradoxes. School is the right place to understand everything that transforms life in society and digital technologies have become elements of great economic and social impact.

We consider, therefore, that the integration of technologies in the entire curricular structure is the condition to allow school subjects to weave choices and define formative paths that lead them to a critical and analytical formation of a society whose technological centrality has guided many political decisions in the world.

The pandemic opened an important analytical perspective, presenting digital technology as the new demand for training and mandatory educational access. Let us also note that if, before, minimum training was a requirement for a country to grow, generate and distribute wealth, what is observed today is that the dissemination of technological knowledge becomes the new demand for the future planning of the distribution of social welfare. in the country.

References

1. Arruda, EP Implementation of digital technologies in the curricula of Basic Education schools in OECD member countries. Subsidies for the preparation of the BNCC, 32. 2018
2. Arruda, EP Emergency remote education: elements for public policies in Brazilian education in times of Covid-19. EmRede - Journal of Distance Education, 7 (1), 257- 275. 2020
3. Arruda, EP, & Mill, DRS Digital technologies, training of professors and researchers in graduate studies: relations between Brazilian and international initiatives. Education (UFSM), 46 (1), 25-1.ko. 2021
4. Arruda, EP. Study on the process of implementing OECD digital technologies. Available at http://portal.mec.gov.br/docman/dezembro-2017-pdf/77891-produto-estudo-sobre-processo-implementacao-tecnologias-digitas-pdf/file. 2017 Accessed on 09/06/2021.
5. Moreira, JA, Henriques, S., & Barros, DMV Transitioning from an emergency remote teaching to a networked digital education, in times of a pandemic. Dialogia, 351-364, 2021. https://doi.org/10.5585/dialogia.n34.17123
6. Morgado, JC, Sousa, J., & Pacheco, JA Educational transformations in times of pandemic: from social

confinement to curricular isolation. praxis Educational (Brazil), 1, 20205. https://doi.org/10.5212/PraxEduc.v.15.16197.062

7. Morgado, JC, Sousa, J., & Pacheco, JA Educational transformations in times of pandemic: from social confinement to curricular isolation. praxis Educational (Brazil), 15, 2020. https://doi.org/10.5212/PraxEduc.v.15.16197.062

8. Nóvoa, A., & Alvim, Y. Nothing is new, but everything has changed: A viewpoint on the future school. Prospects (Published online), 2020. DOI: 10.1007/s11125-020-09487- w

9. OECD, Learning to Change: ICT in Schools, Schooling for Tomorrow, OECD Publishing, Paris, 2001. https://doi.org/10.1787/9789264195714-en.

10. OECD School education during COVID-19: Were teachers and students ready?. Country Notes, 2021. Available at: https://www.oecd.org/education/coronavirus-education- country-notes.htm. Accessed on: November 18, 2021.

11. Pacheco, JA Notes on curriculum diversification/differentiation in Portugal. InterMeio: Journal of the Graduate Program in Education-UFMS, 14 (28), 2008. Available at: https://periodicos.ufms.br/index.php/intm/article/view/2498/1699. Accessed on: November 15, 2021.

12. Pacheco, JA, Morgado, JC, Sousa, J., & Maia, IB Basic education and pandemic. A study on the perceptions of teachers in the Portuguese reality. Revista Iberoamericana de Educación, 86 (1), 187-204, 2021. https://doi.org/10.35362/rie8614346

13. Reich, J. Failure to disrupt: Why technology alone can't transform education. Harvard University Press, 2020.

14. Romero, C. & Ventura, S. Data mining in education. Wiley Interdisciplinary Reviews: Data Mining and Knowledge Discovery, 3 (1), 12-27, 2013.

15. Sahlberg, P.. Does the pandemic help us make education more equitable? Educational Research for Policy and Practice, 20, 11–18, 2021. https://doi.org/10.1007/s10671-020-09284-4

16. Tiede, J., & Grafe, S. The Integration of Media-Related Studies and Competencies into US and German Initial Teacher Education. A Cross-National Analysis of Contemporary Practices and Trends. In Society for Information Technology & Teacher Education International Conference (pp. 1709-1717), 2019. Association for the Advancement of Computing in Education (AACE).

17. Unesco Education: from disruption to recovery, 2021. Available in https://en.unesco.org/covid19/educationresponse/ Access in August, 19, 2021

18. World Bank. Acting Now to Protect the Human Capital of Our Children: The Costs of and Response to COVID-19 Pandemic's Impact on the Education Sector in Latin America and the Caribbean, 2021. Available on https://openknowledge.worldbank.org/handle/10986 /35276?locale-attribute=en. Access in August, 19, 2021

Shaping the Digital Transformation of the Education Ecosystem in Europe
EDEN Digital Learning Europe Proceedings
2022 Annual Conference | Tallinn, 20-22 June, 2022
ISSN: 2707-2819

INCLUSION AND DIVERSITY MANAGEMENT IN ONLINE EDUCATION

Pia Lappalainen, Aalto University

Abstract

Digitally supported collaboration has traditionally been examined mainly through the role of technology. This narrow, technology-focused approach has overlooked the nature of the digital environment as a shared space built on social and affective dimensions influencing individual's efficiency, well-being and quality of life. The remote context has accentuated the related challenges in all spheres of life, including higher education, calling for attention to learner differences and needs. The ultimate challenge derives from inclusion and diversity management pursuits, as student experiences in the online mode range even more widely than in the classroom. As a result, creating and transmitting a sense of equality has become a more pronounced pedagogical challenge than ever. The objective of this commentary is to criticize the technology orientation and argue for stronger socio-affective pedagogical foci. The objective is pursued by 1) reviewing literature on the influences of digitally mediated work modes and 2) proposing dialogical approaches supporting multivocality in heterogeneous groups. The broader intent is to call for inclusion and diversity management as means of safeguarding student well-being in the digital environment.

Keywords: Inclusion, diversity management, university education, online teaching

Introduction

Thanks to digitalization on the one hand, and the pandemic-induced forced online teaching mode on the other, diverse forms and methods of education are multiplying, shaping the education system. Traditionally, digitally supported collaboration has mainly been examined through the role of technology [1], which produces distorted or incomplete notions of the related impacts. Analyses of digital education that are dominated by foci on digital transformation and the related tools and strategies draw attention to pedagogies that support or hinder students' explicit, measurable performance [2].

This narrow, technology-focused approach has, unfortunately, overlooked the nature of the digital environment as a shared space built on social and affective dimensions [3]. A broader approach optimizing the interaction of both technical and social dimensions and examining the interaction of technology, tasks, social structures and people-related factors has been speculated to yield advantages in terms of students' holistic performance and sustained learning outcomes [4]. Besides what students and faculty can do technically, research should take an interest in what they will do and what impacts their preferences and sentiments [5]. Remote work modes in general are associated with undeniable benefits such as increased efficiency, but concerns have been raised e.g. about deteriorated team dynamics, psychological safety, and wellbeing[6].

To promote factors increasing student motivation and well-being in the virtual context, this paper 1) reviews recent literature on the influences of digital work modes on individuals and 2) proposes a multi-disciplinary base of dialogical tools supporting multivocality in student groups. The overall objective of this commentary is to critically assess the current technology orientation in pedagogics to safeguard student well-being. The paper is based on literature on the influences of forces remote work modes during the pandemic.

Emerging trends in university education

Student well-being in the virtual setup

Due to the pandemic-induced barriers to physical contact and teacher presence, many pedagogues have worried about the student experience, putting even more effort to communication through the increasing channels mediated by digital tools. Such efforts have included augmented one-on-one consultation time with each learner, more feedback provided per learner, and more frequent instruction by contacting students via multiple channels. At the same time, studies have yielded alarming findings related to student well-being, or rather, ill-being. A study conducted on a large university student sample showed proportionally more mental health symptoms and a higher prevalence of psychological distress than in the whole adult population: one third of university students suffered from anxiety and depression. Among female students, the prevalence was close to 40%, manifesting a three-fold risk of eating disorders compared to male students. Every three females and every four males lacked a sense of belonging [7].

It has been assumed that the root causes of student ill-being are unrelated to online teaching as such, as the related capabilities and structures were well in place already before the pandemic. The percentage of digital education means,

e.g. pre-recorded sessions, e-exams and digital platforms allowing virtual lectures was growing already prior to the forced remote work era, thanks to investments in the related development through special funding instruments, as digital development was growingly regarded as the future direction [8].

Rather, the corruptors of student well-being derive from several environmental and psychological factors. The intensity and totality of isolation during the pandemic exposed students to loneliness, which partly explains the finding that every three females and every four males lacked a sense of belonging [7]. The pandemic only strengthened trends that have been emerging for years in education and society alike: besides technical and domain-specific expertise, added value is increasingly sought in psycho-social factors.

Concerns with perceived equality

The pandemic-induced dramatic discontinuity has pushed to the surface certain social and psychological trends that risk equality, polarize student experiences, and increase tensions in the student community [9]. The duality shows particularly in times of disruption: some individuals thrive on autonomy and freedom, some suffer from the loneliness and apathy related to physical and temporal isolation. Some appreciate the uninterrupted school day efficiency, some are exhausted by the loss of porosity [10].

The dichotomized learner experiences force faculty to balance between control and trust, between close pedagogical supervision and learner latitude, between freedom and interventions. Teacher attention is divided between those who feel well and those who feel ill, not only physically or ergonomically but in terms of all the five dimensions of student well-being: affective, cognitive, social, academic, and psychosomatic. For example, some personalities may be more apt for digitally-mediated conditions than others, individuals are differently equipped for online collaboration with others, overall life management may be easier for some learners than others, autonomy is experienced in varying ways depending on individual capabilities [11].

As the digital conditions treat students differently as viewed through student perceptions, digital education cannot be planned, supervised or monitored as a uniform experience but rather as circumstances causing clashes in learner experiences. These varying perceptions of the university reality have been associated with concerns about the group-level features that harm the virtual environment: declining creativity, mechanization, psychological unsafety and missing social support [10].

Psychological capital as an emerging pedagogical focus

Psychological capital has established itself as a reservoir accounting for positive behaviors and outcomes [12] on cognition, performance and physical health. It is challenging the earlier focus on efficiency targets and countable end-products and directing pedagogical attention to themes impacting student well-being and sentiments. Ignoring the affective and social realities in student life or the impact of individual learner styles, ineffective self-motivation strategies [13], self-doubt [14], optimism, and self-efficacy [15] might jeopardize study attainment and degree completion, particularly in times of growing uncertainty.

Even though teacher qualifications are typically a minimum requirement in the education sector, the absence of formal qualifications in pedagogy among academics in the engineering community has been recognized and accepted as the norm. This has been aggravated by the general preference in the engineering world to operate primarily on the basis of technical expertise and analytical intelligence, despite such a one-eyed approach possibly being conducive to pedagogical inefficiency in the transmission of generic working life skills.

In the postmodern working life, teamwork has become the norm: presently 60% of employees belong to at least one team [16]. The related interdependency sometimes materializes as tension [17], turning work into emotional labor that elicits subjective feelings and affective responses [18]. These evolutions alone call for a stronger emphasis on students' psycho-social capabilities, on the one hand to enhance the learner experience but on the other, to hone their employability and working life skills.

Dialogical teachership

Fortunately, postmodern pedagogy offers tools and methodologies for holistic, impactful education also in the virtual setup. Dialogical pedagogics, which is a key characteristic of the standardized Finnish teachership, provides means of integrating both efficiency and sustainable impact targets. It rests not only on the teacher's pedagogical tools but also on his/her personality and emotive capabilities [19], connecting to student needs on many levels [20].

The commonly noted philosophy in dialogical teachership is founded on three central elements: perceived caring, psychological safety and teacher immediacy. It draws on partnership, manifesting as low hierarchy between faculty and students [21]. Its core tools include teacher warmth and approachability, and high levels of psychological safety in the classroom [22]. Concretely, this has meant a sense of belonging among the student group without fear of discrimination, exclusion, or ostracism. Psychologically safe student groups are colored by a feeling of mutual appreciation, and permission to be vulnerable and to question and challenge, even the teacher. Table 1 compiles the central elements of teacher immediacy.

Perceived caring	Warmth Empathy and compassion Intensive listening Benevolence Sensitivity
Psychological safety	Sense of belonging Appreciation Challenging Vulnerability Justice and equal treatment
Teacher immediacy	Low hierarchy Approachability Agreeableness Emotional regulation Attentiveness and active responsiveness

Table 1. Elements of dialogical teachership.

Inclusion

Inclusion has traditionally been viewed as norms and conduct opposite to discrimination, i.e. injust or prejudiced treatment of human groups on the basis of e.g. religion, ethnicity, sex or disability. This has served as a critical discussion opening in society, increasing awareness of reprehensible behaviors and fortifying acceptance and tolerance. In addition to industry, where it provided arguments and validated benefits related to equal treatment, it has triggered much progress in the academic world by diversifying faculty and enhancing quality of life in the student community [23]. This evolution provided critical understanding of the uniqueness and individual needs of each student. Although still pronouncing the idea of differences, it was important in adding appreciation of the hidden potential and richness in diversity.

However, diversity programs have still not sufficed to ensure psychological safety among the student body. These formal means, often articulated in the university structures and policy statements, need to find concrete manifestations and practices in the classroom, whether on-site or off-site.

Sources of inclusive strategies

Ultimately, equality, justice and inclusion materialize in interpersonal relationships through genuine multivocality and appreciation [24]. Every human encounter serves as an opportunity to either bolster or corrupt trust, feelings of safety, and sense of mutual respect; this is why university education in communication ought to progress from skilling in reporting, presentations and negotiations towards interaction and influence. The critical means are beyond communicative – they are dialogical and can be derived from many domains.

Table 2 outlines disciplines that serve as potential resource pools when searching for tools and strategies aiding inclusion and diversity management in the classroom, whether on-site or virtual. This listing is tentative, incomplete and a scratch of the surface, serving merely as an opening for pedagogical purposes.

Research domain	Strategy, tool, knowledge or capacity for interaction
Communication [25]	Echoing Clean language Paraphrasing Bakhtian multivocality Open vs closed questions
Interaction [26]	Affective appeals Influence Persuasion Calling Mercy
Work psychology [27]	Emotional intelligence Forms of empathy Social intelligence Systems intelligence Empowerment
Conflict management [28]	Root causes of misunderstanding Conflict management modes: assertion and empathy Evaluation vs restoration Perspective-giving Perspective-taking
Management and leadership [29]	Directive vs non-directive styles Trust vs control Authority vs partnership Motivating and engaging Coaching and serving
Negotiation [30]	Positioning techniques Rational and affective appeals Reframing Rebuttal Anchoring techniques
Process consultation [31]	Agency Self-observation Self- efficacy Biological decoding Post-traumatic growth
Education [32]	Character strengths Teacher immediacy Verbal and nonverbal immediacy behaviors Instructor credibility Affective learning

Table 2. Research domains yielding interaction strategies for inclusion.

The principles, capacities and strategies listed in the right-hand column serve as concrete background knowledge or instruments in situations where mutual understanding is jeopardized due to different backgrounds, life histories, capabilities, personality traits, or skills. They are particularly supportive of bonding when personal rapports are at risk due to misunderstandings, biases, attitudes, transference, or inaccurate interpretations. When remote teaching and the related collaboration is hurdled by technology mediation, these instruments may be found advantageous in fortifying the human connection and sustaining open and genuine dialog.

Discussion

This paper is concerned with student well-being and perceptions of studies carried out at a distance, independently of location and possibly time. Despite consensus on the importance of treating learners as unique individuals whose personal preferences need to be considered, the ultimate question in the virtual learning context still remains: why do some students prosper and thrive, while others become demotivated and lag behind? Individuals' willingness and aptitude to operate remotely is assumed to be impacted both by school day efficiency and quality, which is why discussion of learning arrangements should move beyond digital tools and efficiency towards learner experiences and individual outcomes.

Universities need therefore to gather evidence of the factors impacting individual learner experiences in the virtual context and the best way to gather is by asking! Such a genuine discussion is critical both in order to enhance psychological safety and inclusion in the classroom but also to transmit and model working life skills securing the graduates' employability. To be able to navigate in its complex arenas with growing international and individual diversity, the academic faculty needs to identify practices ensuring compatibility of stakeholder interests in student groups. Safeguarding multivocal, genuine decision-making regarding teaching arrangements requires safer dialogue, not only within faculty but also between faculty and students.

Managing student experiences at the extreme poles of the continuum should not be based on once-size-fits-all ideology. The opposite experiences of students are a reality in digital learning environments and rather than making uniform, standard decisions dictating teaching arrangements all across the education institution, universities ought to provide individual teachers with more latitude to take these decisions course by course.

Remote work practices, including online teaching, have been accused of accentuating societal inequality as they discriminate those whose psycho-social needs are not met in the digital environment [33]. Student experiences are affected by a multitude of factors that are individually derived and that should be appreciated by educators to ensure a motivating and effective remote learning experience. Awareness and knowledge of these factors require genuine dialog with our students, to make sure all aspects and voices have been heard when deciding in a well-substantiated fashion on learning arrangements. The dialogical instruments proposed in this paper serve as instruments for such discussions, but they also provide pedagogical instruments more generally, facilitating teaching and learning in complex, hybrid environments [34].

References

1. Orlikowski, W. (1992). The Duality of Technology: Rethinking the Concept of Technology in Organizations. Organization Science, 3(3), Focused Issue: Management of Technology, 398-427.
2. Golden, T.D. & Gajendran, R.S. (2019). Unpacking the role of a telecommuter's job in their performance: Examining job complexity, problem solving, interdependence, and social support. Journal of Business and Psychology, 34 (1), 55–69.
3. Taris, T. W. & Schaufeli, W. (2015). Individual well-being and performance at work: A conceptual and theoretical overview. In M. Van Veldhoven &R. Peccei (Eds.): Well-being and performance at work: The role of context (pp. 15–34). London: Psychology Press.
4. Martinez-Amador, J. (2016). Remote and on-site knowledge worker productivity and engagement: a comparative study of the effect of virtual intensity and work location preference. Dissertation, Weatherhead School of Management, Case Western Reserve University, Ohio, the USA.
5. Barrick, M. R. & Mount, M. K. (1993). Autonomy as a moderator of the relationships between the Big Five personality dimensions and job performance. Journal of Applied Psychology, 78 (1), 111–118.

6. Bentley, T.A.; Teo, S.T.T.; McLeod, L.; Tan, F.; Bosua, R.; Gloet,
7. M. (2016). The role of organisational support in teleworker wellbeing: A socio-technical systems approach. Applied Ergonomics, 52, 207– 215.
8. Finnish Institute for Health and Welfare. Finnish Student Health and Wellbeing Survey (KOTT), 2021.
9. Charalampous, M; Grant, C.; Tramontano, C.; Michailidis, E. (2018). Systematically reviewing remote e-workers' well-being at work: a multidimensional approach. European Journal of Work and Organizational Psychology, 28 (1), 1-23.
10. Bonacini, L.; Gallo, G.; Scicchitano, S. (2020). Working from home and income inequality: risks of a 'new normal' with COVID-19. Journal of Population Economics, 34, 303–360.
11. Samek L. M. (2021). The impact of teleworking and digital work on workers and society. Policy Department for Economic, Scientific and Quality of Life Policies Directorate-General for Internal Policies. PE 662.904 – April 2021
12. https://www.europarl.europa.eu/RegData/etudes/STUD/2021/662904/I POL_STU(2021)662904_EN.pdf
13. Solis, M. (2016). Moderators of telework effects on the work-family conflict and on worker performance. European Journal of Management and Business Economics, (26) 1, 2017, 21-3.
14. Avey, J., Avolio, B. J., & Luthans, F. (2011). Experimentally analyzing the impact of leader positivity on follower positivity and performance, The Leadership Quarterly, 22 (2), 282-294.
15. Biedron, A. & Pawlak, M. (2016). The interface between research on individual difference variables and teaching practice: The case of cognitive factors and personality. Studies in Second Language Learning and Teaching, 6 (3), 395-422
16. Cameron, J.; Nairn, K.; Higgins, J. (2009). Demystifying Academic Writing: Reflection on Emotions, Know-How and Academic Identify. Journal of Geography in Higher Education, 33 (2), 269–284.
17. Lonka, K.; Chow, A.; Keskinen, J.; Hakkarainen, K; Chow, K; Keskinen, J; Hakkarainen, K; Niclas Sandström, N.; Pyhältö, K. (2014). How to measure PhD. students' conceptions of academic writing - and are they related to well-being? Journal of Writing Research, 5(3), 245- 269.
18. De Dreu, C. and Weingart, L. (2003). Task Versus Relationship Conflict, Team Performance, and Team Member Satisfaction: A Meta- Analysis. Journal of Applied Psychology, 88 (4), 741–749.
19. Deutsch, M. (1983). Conflict Resolution: Theory and Practice. Political Psychology, 4 (3), 431-453.
20. Medina, F., Munduate, L.; Dorado, M. (2005). Types of intragroup conflict and affective reactions. Journal of Managerial Psychology, 20 (3/4), 219-230.
21. Woodall, T.; Hiller, A.; Sheilagh, R. (2014). Making sense of higher education: students as consumers and the value of the university experience. Studies in Higher Education, 39 (1), 48-67.
22. King, P. & Witt, P. (2009). Teacher Immediacy, Confidence Testing, and the Measurement of Cognitive Learning. Communication Education, 58 (1), 110-123.
23. Houser, M.; Frymier, A. (2009). The Role of Student Characteristics and Teacher Behaviors in Students' Learner Empowerment. Communication Education, 58 (1), 35-53.
24. Comstock, J.; Rowell, E.; Bowers, J. (1995). Food for thought: teacher nonverbal immediacy, student learning, and curvilingearity. Communication Education, 44 (3), 251-266.
25. Frymier, A.; Shulman, G.; Houser, M. (1996). The development of a learner empowerment measure. Communication Education, 45 (3), 181-199.
26. Cropanzano, R., Byrne, Z. S., Bobocel, D. R., & Rupp, D. E. (2001). Moral virtues, fairness heuristics, social entities, and other denizens of organizational justice. Journal of Vocational Behavior, 58, 164–209.
27. Galvin, B.; Waldman, D.; Balthazard, P. (2010). Visionary Communication Qualities as Mediators of the Relationship between Narcissism and Attributions of Leader Charisma. Personnel Psychology, 63, 509-537.
28. Claes Nilholm (2021) Research about inclusive education in 2020–How can we improve our theories in order to change practice? European Journal of Special Needs Education, 36 (3), 358-37.

29. Areni, C. & Sparks, J. (2005). Language Power and Persuasion, Psychology & Marketing, 22 (6), 507-525.
30. Jordan, P. J., & Troth, A. (2011). Emotional intelligence and leader member exchange. Leadership & Organizational Development Journal, 3, 260–280.
31. Altmäe, S., Turk, K., and Toomet, O-S. (2013). Thomas- Kilmann's Conflict Management Modes and their relationship to Fiedler's Leadership Styles. Baltic Journal of Management, 8 (1), 45- 65.
32. Arnold, J.; Arad, S.; Rhoades, J.; Drasgow, F. (2000). The empowering leadership questionnaire: the construction and validation of a new scale for measuring leader behaviors. Journal of Organizational Behavior, 21, 249-269.
33. Putnam, L. (2010). A Point in Practice. Communication as Changing the Negotiation Game. Journal of Applied Communication Research 38 (4), 325-335.
34. Bandura, A; Caprara GV; Barbaranelli C; Pastorelli C; Regalia C. (2001). Sociocognitive self-regulatory mechanisms governing transgressive behavior. Journal of Personality and Social Psychology, 80, 125–135.
35. Gardner, R. (2019). Classroom interaction research: The state of the art. Research on Language and Social Interaction, 52 (3), 212–226.
36. Gigauri, I. (2020). Remote Working Concerns During The Covid- 19 Pandemic. International Journal of Social Science and Economic Research, 5, 2803-2818.
37. Wang, Y. & Haggerty, N. (2011). Individual virtual competence and its influence on work outcomes. Journal Of Management Information Systems, 27 (4), 299–334

ISSN: 2707-2819

BEYOND MOOC: AN ANALYSIS OF INFORMAL ONLINE LEARNING UTILIZING OPEN EDUCATIONAL RESOURCES (OER) FOR A DIGITAL & INCLUSIVE SOCIETY

Guy Cohen, Anat Cohen, Tel Aviv University

Abstract

The COVID-19 pandemic and the containment measures that followed have highlighted the importance of equal access to up-and reskilling opportunities for life and work, for workers as well as job seekers. EU Digital Education Action Plan highlights the central role of digital learning in increasing equity and inclusiveness through the wide array of digital technologies, beyond formal education and including lifelong learning. In the digital ecosystem for education, informal online learning plays a key role. Informal learning processes are facilitated through open education, which provides access to unlimited amounts of knowledge for personal or professional development. However, little literature has focused on informal open online learning (IOOL) that occurs in everyday life. Specifically, few studies differentiate between informal learning for professional and personal development, nor between workers and job seekers. While the COVID-19 crisis led to a massive shift towards online courses for training, the current exploratory research uses a broader view of OER use among adults who are not interested in academic credit or professional certification in light of their individual characteristics. During COVID-19's lockdown, a questionnaire was distributed to capture three themes: types of OER used for learning during the crisis; perceived OER usefulness (PU); and changes in OER usage due to the crisis. Among other findings were low utilization of Massive Open Online Courses (MOOCs); a particular preference for social networks among workers with low technology literacy and low English proficiency; and a significant gap in OER usage between personal or professional development among workers. These insights can be used both for the development of effective models of open learning in support of digital transformation in educational institutions as well as for future evaluation.

Keywords: Open Educational Resources (OER), Open Education, Lifelong learning, Informal learning, Adult learning, COVID-19.

Introduction

While the COVID-19 pandemic aggravates the digital skills gap that already existed (EC, 2020b), educational inequality remains a source of concern (Lambert, 2020). Lifelong learning is essential, and yet fewer than two-fifths of European adults participate in learning each year (EC, 2020b). To address these societal challenges, the EU Digital Education Action Plan 2021-2027 (EC, 2020a), backed up by the EU Skills Agenda (EC, 2020b) and the UN Sustainable Development Goals (UN, 2021), outlines equipping all learners with digital skills, especially senior citizens, and those most in need of access to education; and deploying the growing array of digital technologies to improve and extend learning (EC, 2020a).

The use of Open Education Resources (OER) has been described by several studies as promoting a critical, relevant, and equal education (Lane, 2009; Veletsianos & Kimmons, 2012). Massive Open Online Courses (MOOCs) are being promoted as a tool for implementing open education by educational institutions, organizations, and policymakers, who have an increasing role as providers of lifelong learning. Despite these efforts, demographic and socioeconomic factors still influence likelihood of enrolling in online courses (Horrigan, 2016; Lambert, 2020) and dropout rates are high (Soffer & Cohen, 2019). The type and design of technological tools and platforms directly affect the inclusion or exclusion of individuals from learning (EC, 2020a). However, while there has been a lot of research on MOOCs, few studies have challenged the assumption that online courses are the predominant means for delivering educational content to online audiences (Holland, 2019). Furthermore, open education encourages the transition from informal to formal learning settings (Farrow et al., 2015). Although informal online learning is an integral part of our learning ecosystem during which know-how and skills are acquired through everyday experiences, only a limited amount of research has been conducted on this type of learning (Holland, 2019).

COVID-19 had a different effect on job seekers and workers whose jobs remained secure. Due to social distancing restrictions, workers in sectors that were not allowed to remain open and who was unable to work at home have been laid off from their jobs. Based on EU analysis, these jobs are less secure, concentrated in low-income areas, and filled disproportionately by migrants and workers with little education (Sanchez et al., 2020). In line with the EU Digital Education Action Plan's second strategic priority, digital skills and competences are needed to enable digital transformation by equipping workers and job seekers with digital skills, beyond formal education and including lifelong learning (EC, 2020a). Nevertheless, very little research has differentiated between these populations by their informal learning preferences (Holland, 2019).

In addition, learning for the benefit of professional and personal development throughout life is essential to personal fulfilment, economic growth, and innovation. At present, employers are having trouble recruiting skilled workers in some of the economic sectors, including the digital sector, while too few adults are retraining to fill these vacancies (EC, 2020a). Further, there is a need for individuals beyond skilling for a job, such as older people who need new skills as well (EC, 2020b). Accordingly, the first strategic priority of the EU Digital Education Action Plan identifies it as a strategic priority to promote the development of a high-performing digital education ecosystem by addressing technology gaps and developing inclusive organizational capabilities for hybrid learning modes (EC, 2020a). However, not many studies separate informal online learning preferences between professional (ongoing work-related goals) and personal development (Holland, 2019).

Research goal and questions

In the midst of the Covid-19 crisis, there was no alternative but to use digital technologies for educational purposes. During stakeholder consultations organized by the EC, education authorities stressed the importance of mapping, researching, and documenting responses to the crisis (EC, 2020a). While online courses for training have been widely reported (OECD, 2020), this study seeks to gain a deeper understanding of informal online learning through various types of OER during the COVID-19 crisis among adults over the age of 18 who are not interested in academic credit or professional certification. Specifically distinguishing between job seekers and workers, as well as between professional development (PrD) and personal development (PeD). In light of the emergence of distance learning and the resulting escalation of social disparities, this exploratory research can provide some useful insights for future research. According to our research goal and literature review, we formulated three research questions:

1. How does Informal Open Online Learning (IOOL) for personal development during the COVID-19 crisis differ between workers and job seekers?
2. How does Informal Open Online Learning (IOOL) during the COVID-19 crisis differ between professional and personal development among workers?
3. How does Informal Open Online Learning (IOOL) during the COVID-19 crisis differ between groups with varying individual characteristics (Technological literacy, Academic background, Age, English proficiency, Gender)?

Methodology

Research Tool

To avoid any associations with formal educational frameworks and to mitigate the social distance restrictions enforced at the time of the study, like other researchers (e.g. Kaisara & Bwalya, 2021; Krishnapatria, 2020), the questionnaire was distributed via social networks (e.g., Facebook, LinkedIn, and WhatsApp) between mid-April and early May 2020. The first part of the questionnaire collected demographic data: age, academic background, English proficiency level, gender, technological literacy, and employment status due to COVID-19 crisis. This section was based on the Pew Research Center questionnaire (Horrigan, 2016), which examined digital learning. The second part examined IOOL through perceived usefulness (PU) ratings of a closed list of OER types (on a scale from 1 to 10). This section was based on various studies showing that technology adoption is positively impacted by its PU, especially among learners (Abdullah et al., 2016). According to this section, respondents were asked to consider only free resources from a list of OER types, based on a survey that examined usage patterns of formal and informal media, as well as learning environments (Zawacki-Richter et al., 2015). In order to get a more accurate picture, we constructed the third part of the questionnaire as two open-ended questions: To identify the types of OER, we first asked respondents to describe a positive learning experience gained through use of OER during the crisis. Secondly, we asked respondents to describe how their use of OER changed during the given period. Workers were required to answer the last two sections twice, for PeD and PrD (Figure 1).

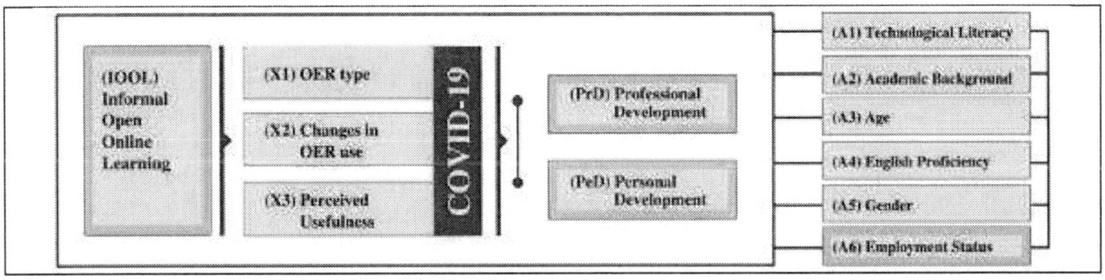

Figure 1. Research model

Data Analysis

Once data collection was complete, we conducted a mixed methods analysis that entailed quantitative alongside qualitative analysis. This article describes one aspect of the research and deals exclusively with the quantitative findings, including those that emerged from the qualitative analysis. As a way to examine IOOL, the analysis included frequencies of (a) different types of OER, (b) changes in OER use, and (c) PU ratings of OER. Further, T-test analyses were performed to compare between workers and job seekers as well as ANOVA tests and two multiple regression analyses to examine the effect of individual differences on PU (PeD and PrD).

Research Population

The study population includes 141 participants: 87% Israelis and 7% residents from other countries (e.g., Austria, Belgium, Germany, Poland), 67% workers and 22% job seekers who lost their jobs during the crisis. Notably, 11% were already unemployed before the crisis, thus, they were not included in the analyses. Additionally, the majority were young women with an academic background and a high level of both technological literacy and English proficiency. No significant differences in gender, age group, academic background, English proficiency level or technological literacy were found between workers and job seekers participants (Table 1).

Table 1: Population demographics

		Workers (N=94)	Job seekers due to COVID-19 crisis (N=31)	Total (N=124)	$\chi 2$
Gender	Women	63.5%	77.4%	66.9%	2.053
N (%)	Men	36.5%	22.6%	33.1%	
Age group	18-29	38.7%	35.5%	37.9%	0.132
N (%)	30-39	34.4%	35.5%	34.7%	
	40-55	17.2%	19.4%	17.7%	
	56-72	9.7%	9.7%	9.7%	
Academic background	Yes	92.5%	90.3%	91.9%	0.145
N (%)	No	7.5%	9.7%	8.1%	
English proficiency level	Low	20.4%	32.3%	23.4%	1.815
N (%)	High	79.6%	67.7%	76.6%	
Technological literacy	Low	19.4%	22.6%	20.2%	0.158
N (%)	Medium	46.2%	45.2%	46.0%	
	High	34.4%	32.3%	33.9%	

Findings

Workers vs. job seekers due to COVID-19

First, in terms of PU, job seekers and workers alike rated videos the highest (out of 24 items). However, job seekers ranked significantly ($t(123)= 2.361$, $p<.05$) social networks' posts ($M= 6.32$, $SD= 3.26$) higher than workers ($M=4.61$, $SD=3.59$). In concurrence, videos sharing in social networks were significantly ($t(123)= 2.01$, $p<.05$) highly ranked by jobseekers ($M=6.3$, $SD=3.23$ vs. $M=5.0$, $SD=3.52$) (Figure 4). Moreover, regarding a positive learning experience, among job seekers (N=31), webinars/video conferences (33.3%) and videos (27.8%), were most frequently reported for personal development, whereas among workers (N=94), videos were most common (38.2%) (Figure 2). With regards to the changes in OER use due to the COVID-19 crisis, the significant change was "OER use has increased", both among job seekers (50%) and workers (45.2%) (Figure 3).

Professional vs. personal development

Among workers, the average PU rating of all resources was significantly ($t(91)= 2.770$, $p<.01$) higher for personal development (M= 4.59, SD= 2.30) than for professional development (M=4.05, SD=2.67). As a confirmation of this statistic, almost half of the employees reported that their use of OER for personal development has increased (45.2%), while regarding professional development, they reported that they had not used OER (35.1%) and their activity had not changed" (44.4%). Additionally, videos received the highest PU average rating, both for personal and professional development, even though a significant difference was found between them ($t(90)=3.89$, $p<.05$) (Figure 4). Furthermore, the use of videoconferences for professional development and personal development was ranked sixth and thirteenth respectively, supporting the report on the increasing use of these applications for professional development (Figure 3). Although these applications received a low rating, it was frequently mentioned as a useful learning resource (32.4% and 14.5% respectively) (Figure 2).

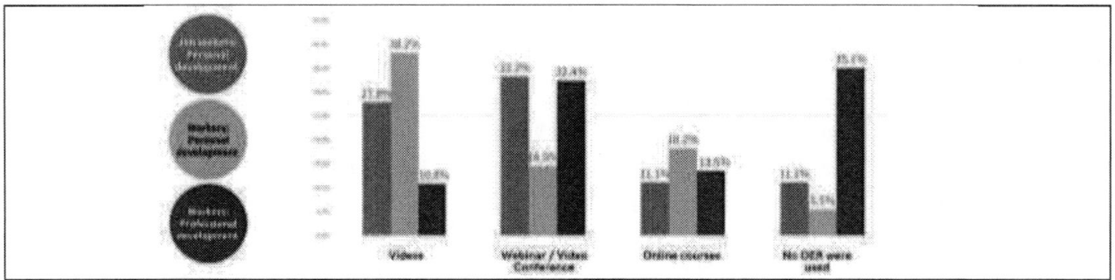

Figure 2. Frequencies of participants with regard to main types of OER used during the COVID-19 crisis

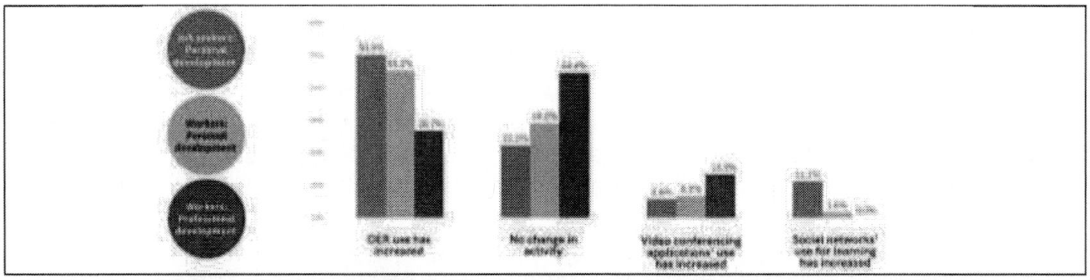

Figure 3. Frequencies of participants with regard to main changes in OER use during the COVID-19 crisis

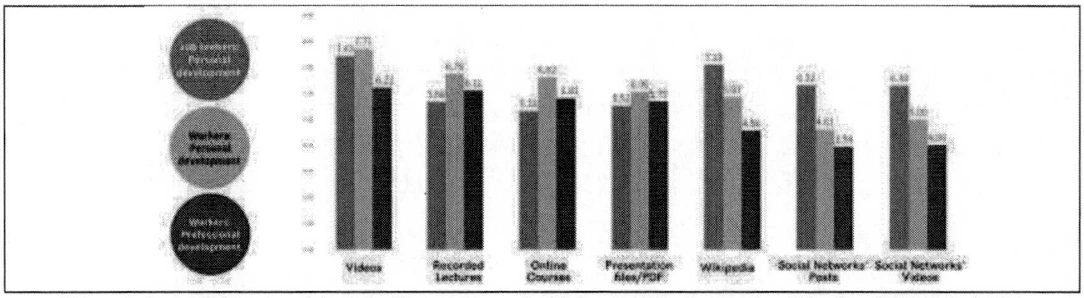

Figure 4. Frequencies of participants with regard to main OER categories by average PU rating (PU rate is 1-10)

Individual characteristics and IOOL

Two multiple linear regressions (PeD: $F(5,134)=5.36$, $p<.001$, $R^2=0.167$; PrD: $F(5,99)=5.89$, $p<.001$) revealed that technological literacy as well as gender are significant predictors of average PU rating for personal as we professional development ($p<0.005$ and $p<0.05$ respectively). Additionally, English proficiency level was found to be a significant predictor of average PU ranking only for professional development ($p<0.05$). These analyses indicate that the average PU rating of all OER types increases with the level of technological literacy, women rate PU higher than men, and employees with high a level of English proficiency rank PU higher than those with a low level (Figure 5).

Moreover, T-test analyses revealed significant differences in PU (t(104)= 3.43, p<.001) between high and low levels of English proficiency (M=4.48, SD=2.30, M=2.65, SD=1.90 respectively), as well as between participants with and without academic backgrounds (M =4.25, SD =2.33, M =2.34, SD =1.65 respectively). With respect to age, Anova analyses revealed significant differences in PU (F(102)=6.466, p<.001) between the oldest and youngest groups (p<.005, M=1.65, SD=1.64, M=4.55, SD=2.46 respectively). Furthermore, participants with low levels of technological literacy and English proficiency discussed increasing their use of social networks as OER type for personal development.

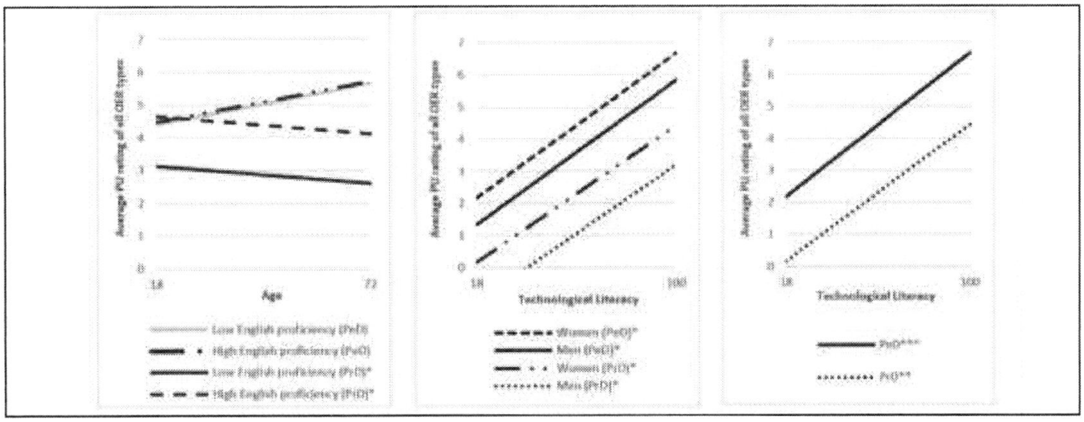

*<.05, **<.01, ***<.001; PeD: F(5,134)=5.367, p<0.001, R2=0.167; PrD: F(5,99)=5.899, p<0.001, R2=0.23

Figure 5. Regression for average perceived usefulness (PeD and PrD) of all OER types

Conclusion and discussion

Workers vs. job seekers due to COVID-19

As a form of Informal Open Online Learning for personal development, watching videos is favored by workers and job seekers. It is consistent with previous studies that have found a preference for clear identification of the learning object's content (Holland, 2019), especially videos (Liao et al., 2019). Furthermore, the COVID-19 crisis led to an increase in the use of OER both by workers and job seekers. Particularly among job seekers with low levels of technological literacy and English proficiency, respondents noted an increased use of social networks for learning. Accordingly, social networks might be a suitable and attractive platform for this audience.

Professional vs. personal development

Despite the low perceived value of videoconferencing, the actual use was substantial, especially for professional development. Evidence to this is the fact that during the crisis, the PU of these applications was low among those who had never used them before (Batastini et al., 2020). The use of these applications appears to alter informal learning activities. However, the question remains whether they will persist in the new normal. In addition, the employee population in this study was less likely to use OER for professional development than for personal development. Furthermore, English proficiency was found to be a significant barrier to OER usage for professional development, which may indicate a lack of resources localized for work-related activities (Cohen et al., 2019; Farrow et al., 2015). Thus, the question arises as to how an educational organization can overcome the barriers of OER implementation for work-related purposes, which are primarily used for personal purposed.

Recommendations and Limitations

The study offers a broader picture of informal learning online through a variety of OER among online adult users who are not seeking academic credit or certification. The wide array of OER is a key tool for increasing equality and inclusiveness, though there is a focus on MOOCs that are characterized by low usage and high dropout rates. In light of these findings, other popular OER to reach target audiences based on their preferences may be worth considering. Furthermore, this study sheds light on the fact that the preference for different OER types differs between workers, job seekers, and individuals with different development goals. Consequently, policymakers and education organizations should consider personalization in this context. It is important to note that the research sample is not large nor representative in terms of volunteering and characteristics, however it gives a glimpse to an unexplored issue. In addition, this study focuses on OER types regardless of content. Thus, therefore, a further and broader examination would provide a more current perspective.

Acknowledgement

This work was supported by the Minducate Science of Learning Research and Innovation Center of the Sagol School of Neuroscience, Tel Aviv University.

References

1. Abdullah, F., Ward, R., & Ahmed, E. (2016). Investigating the influence of the most commonly used external variables of TAM on students' Perceived Ease of Use (PEOU) and Perceived Usefulness (PU) of e- portfolios. Computers in Human Behavior, 63, 75-90. doi: https://doi.org/10.1016/j.chb.2016.05.014
2. Batastini, A. B., Pike, M., Thoen, M. A., Jones, A. C., Davis, R. M., & Escalera, E. (2020). Perceptions and use of videoconferencing in forensic mental health assessments: A survey of evaluators and legal personnel. Psychology, Crime & Law, 26(6), 593-613. doi: https://doi.org/10.1080/1068316X.2019.1708355
3. EC. (2020). Digital Education Action Plan 2021-2027: Resetting education and training for the digital age. Retrieved from: https://eur-lex.europa.eu/legal-content/EN/TXT/HTML/?uri=CELEX:52020DC0624&from=EN
4. EC. (2020). European skills agenda for sustainable competitiveness, social fairness and resilience. Retrieved from: https://eur-lex.europa.eu/legal-content/EN/TXT/HTML/?uri=CELEX:52020DC0274&from=EN
5. Farrow, R., de los Arcos, B., Pitt, R., & Weller, M. (2015). Who are the open learners? A comparative study profiling non-formal users of open educational resources. EURODL (European Journal of Open, Distance and E-Learning), 18(2), 50-74. doi: https://doi.org/10.1515/eurodl-2015-0013
6. Holland, A. A. (2019). Effective principles of informal online learning design: A theory-building metasynthesis of qualitative research. Computers & Education, 128, 214-226. doi: https://doi.org/10.1016/j.compedu.2018.09.026
7. Horrigan, J. B. (2016). Digital Readiness Gaps. Pew Research Center. Retrieved from: https://www.pewresearch.org/internet/2016/09/20/digital-readiness-gaps/
8. Kaisara, G., & Bwalya, K. J. (2021). Investigating the E-Learning Challenges Faced by Students during COVID- 19 in Namibia. International Journal of Higher Education, 10(1), 308-318. doi: https://doi.org/10.5430/ijhe.v10n1p308
9. Krishnapatria, K. (2020). From 'Lockdown'to letdown: Students' perception of e-learning amid the COVID-19 outbreak. ELT in Focus, 3(1), 1-8. doi: https://doi.org/10.35706/eltinfc.v3i1.3694
10. Lambert, S. R. (2020). Do MOOCs contribute to student equity and social inclusion? A systematic review 2014–18. Computers & Education, 145, 103693. doi: https://doi.org/10.1016/j.compedu.2019.103693
11. Lane, A. (2009). The impact of openness on bridging educational digital divides. The International Review of Research in Open and Distance Learning, 10(5). doi: https://doi.org/10.19173/irrodl.v10i5.637
12. Liao, C. W., Chen, C. H., & Shih, S. J. (2019). The interactivity of video and collaboration for learning achievement, intrinsic motivation, cognitive load, and behavior patterns in a digital game-based learning environment. Computers & Education, 133, 43-55. doi: https://doi.org/10.1016/j.compedu.2019.01.013
13. OECD. (2020). The territorial impact of COVID-19: Managing the crisis across levels of government. Retrieved from: http://www.oecd.org/coronavirus/policy-responses/the-territorial-impact-of-covid-19-managing-the-crisis- across-levels-of-government-d3e314e1/
14. Sanchez, D., Parra, N., Ozden, C., & Rijkers, B. (2020). Which Jobs Are Most Vulnerable to COVID-19? What an Analysis of the European Union Reveals. World Bank Research and Policy Briefs. Retrieved from: https://openknowledge.worldbank.org/bitstream/handle/10986/33737/Which-Jobs-Are-Most-Vulnerable-to-COVID-19-What-an-Analysis-of-the-European-Union-Reveals.pdf?sequence=5&isAllowed=y
15. Soffer, T., & Cohen, A. (2019). Students' engagement characteristics predict success and completion of online courses. Journal of Computer Assisted Learning, 35(3), 378-389. doi: https://doi.org/10.1111/jcal.12340
16. UN. (2021). The Sustainable Development Goals Report 2021. New York: United Nations. Retrieved from:

https://unstats.un.org/sdgs/report/2021/The-Sustainable-Development-Goals-Report-2021.pdf

17. Veletsianos, G., & Kimmons, R. (2012). Assumptions and challenges of open scholarship. The International Review of Research in Open and Distance Learning, 13(4), 166-189. doi:https://doi.org/10.19173/irrodl.v13i4.1313
18. Zawacki-Richter, O., Müskens, W., Krause, U., Alturki, U., & Aldraiweesh, A. (2015). Student media usage patterns and non-traditional learning in higher education. International Review of Research in Open and Distributed Learning, 16(2), 136-170. doi: https://doi.org/10.19173/irrodl.v16i2.1979

Shaping the Digital Transformation of the Education Ecosystem in Europe
EDEN Digital Learning Europe Proceedings
2022 Annual Conference | Tallinn, 20-22 June, 2022
ISSN: 2707-2819

TEACHERS – VICTIMS OF CYBERBULLYING

Elena-Ancuța Zăvoianu and Abdelmoula El Hadi, University of Bucharest

Abstract

Cyberbullying is a social phenomenon that takes place with the help of technology that causes suffering to victims. Children being attracted to technology and not having enough knowledge about the safe use of technology devices have become potential victims of this phenomenon. In order to prevent and reduce this phenomenon, most researchers have turned their attention to combating online bullying among teenagers. They lost sight of the fact that cyberbullying does not take into account gender, age or status and neglected teachers.

According to the few studies on online aggression against teachers, the effects of this phenomenon are similar to those experienced by children. This article aims to highlight the need to create a positive school climate that helps teachers, students and parents to communicate assertively and develop harmonious relationships.

Keywords: cyberbullying, students, teachers, parents, aggression

Introduction

Technology has become a part of our lives. It is used in all fields of activity from education to health, as it makes our work easier, helps us to communicate faster, to inform ourselves, to learn, but also to have fun.

Like anything, in addition to these advantages, it also has a number of disadvantages when it is used improperly. Specifically, technology becomes a threat to our well-being (Hoel, Faragher, & Cooper, 2004) when it is used to harass, threaten, ridicule, exclude, or defame others.

The use of technology for these negative purposes is called cyberbullying. This phenomenon is characterized by: use of technology, frequency, intentionality, anonymity and unequal power ratio (Slonje & Smith, 2008; Tokunaga, 2010). Frequency refers to the constant aggression of the victim over several days at any time. Intentionality appeals to the aggressor's express desire to cause suffering to the victim. The anonymous character refers to the difficulty of identifying the perpetrator and punishing him (Macaulay et al., 2018). The anonymous character also creates an unequal power relationship between the victim and the aggressor. These are supported by the development of technology that gives the aggressor the freedom to choose the best device for aggression (phone, tablet, computer, laptop), but also the social networks that easily provide information about everyone to anyone.

Ways and causes of online aggression

The ways of aggression evolve as technology progresses and so we can talk about: messages, phone calls, emails, websites, blogs, sharing video and photo content, etc. (Smith et al., 2006). Thus, they can be classified as aggressions carried out by telephone (messages, calls) and the Internet (e-mail, messaging, content posting on various sites (Smith et al., 2008), masquerade, flaming, exclusion, denigration, harassment and sexting (Willard, 2007). Summarizing all this, we can talk about four types of aggression behaviors (Nocentini et al., 2010): written / verbal texts, visual content, social exclusion and creating fake profiles.

Currently, the factors that influence the phenomenon of cyberbullying are more and more diverse, varying from one case to another. There is no pattern of aggression, as it affects all social groups, regardless of gender or age. General causes that contribute to the development of online aggression include: the accelerated evolution of technology (Cassidy et al., 2013), lack of online security rules, lack of digital literacy of Internet users, anonymity (Sticca & Perren, 2013) and unhealthy school climate (Wong et al., 2014).

The effects of cyberbullying are devastating for all participants in this phenomenon, influencing them physically, mentally, emotionally, socially, educationally and professionally (Bauman et al., 2013; Tanrikulu, 2018). Specifically, we can talk about anxiety, depression, low self-esteem, suicidal ideation (Bauman et al. 2013), anger, frustration (Raskauskas & Stoltz, 2007), weight loss, insomnia, somatization (Jang et al., 2014).), low motivation (Cassidy et al., 2013), low academic or professional performance (De Wet, 2010).Teachers' online aggression

Cyberbullying is frequently identified with children and adolescents and almost not with adults. This is due to the fact that students are seen as vulnerable and defenseless against this phenomenon, while adults are considered to have the necessary skills to manage these aggressions. Unfortunately, in addition to students, another social category is deeply affected, namely teachers. According to research, 3 / 4 teachers are assaulted online (Küçüksüleymanoğlu, 2019).

Cyberbullying is often a continuation of school bullying at home in the online environment. Thus, teachers spending so much time with students and trying to resolve conflicts at school as effectively as possible, have come to turn from witnesses to victims of their own students or parents. In particular, teachers who work with students between the ages of 6 and 14 (Tosun, 2016).

Cyberbullying has become a way for parents and students to take revenge on teachers for those times when they feel upset, disturbed, or wronged. Also, with the COVID-19 pandemic, the interactions between parents, students and teachers took place with the help of technology. This way of informal communication has created opportunities for students and parents to harass teachers (Küçüksüleymanoğlu, 2019).

The most used methods for their aggression are: e-mails, messages, phone calls, letters, defamatory websites (Barker, 2008; May et al., 2010; Kauppi & Pörhölä, 2012). These consist of aggressive, threatening and disrespectful discussions of the teacher that lead to increased stress (Foley, 2014), frustration (McEwen, 2005), loss of confidence in professional skills and even sick leave due to burnout (Küçüksüleymanoğlu, 2019).

Like students, teachers avoid talking about being bullied online. Most of the time, they refuse to talk about their experiences if they feel that they are being bullied because of personal characteristics. Instead, they are more willing to talk about the experience of aggression that they consider to be related to the institution in which they work (Kauppi & Pörhölä, 2012).

In conclusion, cyberbullying is a social phenomenon that can affect anyone at any time. There are no limits regarding the place, time or person. Unfortunately, nowadays, cyberbullying tends to take on increasing proportions and tends to equal the prevalence of cyberbullying among students. In order to reduce cases of cyberbullying among teachers and students, schools must ensure a positive school climate; promote the growth of well-being among teachers and students, but also a genuine and assertive communication between parents and teachers. All this are important, as the well-being of teachers contaminates the well-being of students and their motivation for learning.

References

1. Barker, I. (2008). Are we ready for parents to watch our lessons by webcam? Times Educational Supplement, 4805, 20-21.
2. Bauman S (2013) Cyberbullying: What does research tell us?. Theory Into Practice 52(4), 249–256
3. Bauman, S., Toomey, R. B., & Walker, J. L. (2013). Associations among bullying, cyberbullying, and suicide amongst high school students. Journal of Adolescence, 36, 341-350.
4. Cassidy, W., Faucher, C., & Jackson, M. (2013). Cyberbullying among youth: A comprehensive review of current international research and its implications and application to policy and practice. School Psychology International, 34(6), 575–612.
5. De Wet, C. (2010). Victims of educator-targeted bullying: A qualitative study. South African Journal of Education, 30, 189–201.
6. Foley, C. May, D Blevins, R. K, & Akers, J. (2015). An Exploratory Analysis of Cyber-Harassment of K-12 Teachers by Parents in Public School Settings. Educational Policy.
7. Hoel, H., Faragher, B., & Cooper, C. L. (2004). Bullying is detrimental to health, but all bullying behaviours are not necessarily equally damaging. British Journal of Guidance & Counselling, 32, 367–387.
8. Jang, H., Song, J., & Kim, R. (2014). Does the offline bully-victimization influence cyberbullying behavior among

youths? Application of General Strain Theory. Computers in Human Behavior, 31(1), 85-93.

9. Kauppi, T. & Pörhölä, M. (2012). School teachers bullied by their students: Teachers' attributions and how they share their experiences. Teaching and Teacher Education, 28(7), 1059-1068.

10. Kokkinos, C. M. (2007). Job stressors, personality and burnout in primary school teachers. British Journal of Educational Psychology, 77, 229–243.

11. Küçüksüleymanoğlu, R. (2019). Cyberbullying among secondary school teachers by parents. International Journal of Evaluation and Research in Education, 8(1), 151–157.

12. Macaulay, P. J., Betts, L. R., Stiller, J., & Kellezi, B. (2018). Perceptions and responses towards cyberbullying: A systematic review of teachers in the education system. Aggression and Violent Behavior, 43, 1-12.

13. May, D.C., Johnson, J., Chen, Y., Hutchinson, L., & Ricketts, M. (2010). Exploring parental aggression toward teachers in a public school setting. Current Issues in Education, 13(1), 1- 34.

14. McEwen, E. K. (2005). How to deal with parents who are angry, troubled, afraid, or just plain crazy (2nd ed.). Thousand Oaks, CA: Corwin Press.

15. Nocentini, A., Calmaestra, J., Schultze-Krumbholz, A., Scheithauer, H., Ortega, R., & Menesini, E. (2010). Cyberbullying: Labels, behaviours and definition in three European countries. Journal of Psychologists and Counsellors in Schools, 20(2), 129–142.

16. Slonje, R. & Smith, P. K. (2008). Cyberbullying: Another Main Type of Bullying?. Scandinavian Journal of Psychology, 49(2), 147–154

17. Smith, K., Mahdavi, J., Carvalho, M., Fisher, S., Russell, S., & Tippett, N. (2008). Cyberbullying: its nature and impact in secondary school pupils. The Journal of Child Psychology and Psychiatry, 49 (4), 376-385.

18. Smith, P., Mahdavi, J., Carvalho, M., & Tippett, N. (2006). An Investigation into Cyberbullying, its Forms, Awareness and Impact, and the Relationship Between Age and Gender in Cyberbullying. Research Brief No. RBX03-06. London: DfES.

19. Tokunaga, R. S. (2010). Following you home from school: A critical review and synthesis of research on cyberbullying. Computers in Human Behavior, 26, 277–287.

20. Tosun, N. (2016). Cyberbully and Victim Experiences of Pre-Service Teachers, European Journal of Contemporary Education, 15(1), 136-146.

21. Tosun, N. (2016). Cyberbully and Victim Experiences of Pre-Service Teachers, European Journal of Contemporary Education, 15(1), 136-146.

22. Willard, N. E. (2007). Cyberbullying and cyberthreats: Responding to the challenge of online social aggression, threats, and distress. Champaign, IL: Research Press.

23. Wong, D. S. W., Chan, H. C., & Cheng, C. H. K. (2014). Cyberbullying perpetration and victimization among adolescents in Hong Kong. Children and Youth Services Review, 36, 133-140.

ISSN: 2707-2819

TIME POVERTY AS A MEDIATOR BETWEEN VOLUNTARY ONLINE ENROLLMENT AND COLLEGE OUTCOMES

Claire Wladis, City University of New York

Alyse C. Hachey, The University of Texas At El Paso

Katherine M. Conway, City University of New York

Abstract

This study investigated the phenomenon of time poverty and its relationship with online course enrolment and college outcomes. Data from before the COVID-19 pandemic collected from the City University of New York were analysed, including student surveys and institutional data. Students who enrolled in one or more fully online courses were found to be significantly more time poor than students who did not. Parental status, age, and paid work were found to largely explain this difference between online students and non-online students. Students who took online courses had lower college retention rates and credit accumulation on average. Time poverty partially mediated the relationship between online enrolment and college retention and fully mediated the relationship between online enrolment and credit accumulation, suggesting that it is likely a critical factor, which should be taken into account when measuring online student outcomes. Online course outcomes did not explain any of the differences in college outcomes between students who took courses online versus those who did not, suggesting that other factors which correlate both with online enrolment and outcomes simultaneously (e.g., higher stress, lower quality of time, more health or eldercare responsibilities) likely play a role in college retention for online students.

Keywords: Time Poverty; Postsecondary Outcomes; College Retention; Credit Accumulation; Online Course Enrolment

Motivation for the Study

Online education had become widespread in tertiary education prior to the COVID-19 pandemic, increasing in contrast to the overall negative enrolment trends within higher education overall (Allen & Seaman, 2016). Prior to the pandemic when most instruction moved online, students chose whether to enroll online (Gelles et al., 2020), a feature that has resurfaced as the fully remote instruction of the pandemic has ebbed. Although prior studies have investigated whether online course-taking impacts college outcomes, such research has produced mixed results, so it is unclear whether the relationship is positive, negative, or non-existent (Wladis et al., 2016; Shea & Bidjareno, 2014). Exploring this relationship has become more critical because even after the fully remote instruction of the pandemic has receded, online enrolment has outpaced overall college enrolment (NC-SARA, 2021). Institutions grappling with the implications of this remain uncertain about whether to maintain increased online offerings or revert to more on-campus courses.

This study investigated the relatively unexplored factor of time poverty, which may differentiate students who voluntarily enroll in online courses compared to those who do not. Time poverty is the extent to which students do not have sufficient time for their studies (Wladis et al., 2018). Historically, online students have been more likely to be older, to be parents, and to be employed full time than students who only take on-campus courses (Cavanaugh, & Jacquemin, 2015); all of these characteristics are associated with time poverty. Prior research indicates that students choose to take courses in the online modality because they value and need the flexibility that they offer (Jaggars & Bailey, 2010). Such findings suggest that time (or a lack of it) may be a critical issue for online students. Thus, time poverty may mediate the relationship between online course enrolment and college outcomes. It also may be a potential equity factor distinguishing students who choose to enroll online from those who do not.

Theoretical Framework

Time has been conceptualized as a finite resource (e.g., Giurge et al., 2020), and time poverty has typically been described as lacking sufficient time to maintain physical and mental well-being (Vickery, 1977). Time poverty has been defined in the context of higher education as insufficient time to devote to college work, or to maintain academic well-being (Wladis et al, 2018). We consider time poverty as it relates to demographic and environmental factors that reduce the quantity and quality of time that students have available for their academic studies. Such a lack of time would be expected to simultaneously encourage students to enroll in the online medium and also to increase the likelihood of poorer college outcomes (i.e., college retention and credit accumulation).

Prior studies have found relationships between online enrolment, college outcomes, demographic factors, and environmental factors (McPartlan, et al, 2021). However, the relationship between online enrolment and college outcomes has been inconsistent across studies (Wladis et al., 2016; Shea & Bidjareno, 2014). One reason for the seeming inconsistencies in these relationships is that students choosing online course options often have noticeably different characteristics than those who do not (Cavanaugh, & Jacquemin, 2015), such as work and family responsibilities. Time poverty has been shown to explain college outcomes for student parents (Conway et al, 2021; Wladis et al, 2018), and is also correlated with many of the characteristics of online students; thus, time poverty may explain connections between student characteristics, online enrolment, and college outcomes.

Characteristics such as being female, older, having family responsibilities, or paid work obligations that are more likely within online student populations have also been associated with time poverty. For example, parents (especially mothers) have been found to have greater time poverty than those who are not parents in general (Chatzitheochari & Arber, 2012). The same has been found within higher education contexts, directly explaining differences in academic momentum, as measured by credit accumulation (Wladis et al., 2018). Students parents, particularly mothers, in the U.S. have been found to have greater time poverty and lower quality of the time for their academics (Conway et al., 2021). Additionally, groups such as females, older students, and working students who opt for the online modality to gain flexibility to deal with competing responsibilities have also been found be less engaged in their academics and to do worse in their classes (McPartlan et al., 2021). This may be due to non-academic time demands, such as commuting or caring for dependents. Such findings suggest that online students like these were likely experiencing time poverty which impacted their time available for academic activities.

Method

Students from the City University of New York (CUNY) in the U.S. were surveyed between Fall 2015 and Spring 2017 if they enrolled in a course that had both fully online and face-to-face sections. The analytical sample from this highly diverse student population combined 41,574 survey responses with institutional records. This sample was found to be roughly representative of the larger CUNY population, as is desired for research of this type (Fosnacht et al., 2017). After weighting for the likelihood of survey completion (with propensity scores based on logistic regression), multiple imputation by chained equations in Stata was used to generate 15 imputations (Manly & Wells, 2015) to handle the missing data (median of 3.7% missing for variables with missing data). Courses were classified as online (technically defined as 80% or more instruction online, but in practice typically 100% online) and face-to-face (any courses not classified as online).

Outcomes investigated included college retention (subsequent semester re-enrollment) and credit accumulation during the term. Such measures were chosen because they are a significant predictor of longer-term college outcomes such as transfer or degree completion (DesJardins et al., 2006). The independent variable of interest was time poverty, defined as total reported non-discretionary time; non-discretionary time was operationalized as time spent on paid work, housework (all unpaid work necessary to sustain the household, except childcare), and childcare (Wladis, et al., 2018). This measure was based on surveys of time spent on various activities during a typical week that term. Results report logistic and linear regression models showing the relationship between non- discretionary time and outcomes. Control variables included gender, race/ethnicity, age, G.P.A., median household income of the student's zip code, first-generation college student status, disability status, and whether the student was a first-time freshman. Mediation models allowed further exploration of some of these relationships using the KHB decomposition method (using Stata's khb package). This analysis allowed exploration of the extent to which the relationship between online enrolment (IV) and academic outcomes (DV) could be explained by the mediating variable of time poverty. This relationship was broken into the direct "effect", which measures the proportion of the relationship between the IV and DV which cannot be explained by the mediator, and the indirect "effect", which measures the proportion of this relationship which can be explained by the mediator. Although mediation is often associated with causal analysis, causal inference is not appropriate for this observational study; we thus put the word "effect" in quotation marks to reinforce this, while also reminding the reader that causal inferences are not appropriate based on this study.

Results

Figure 1 shows students' weekly non-discretionary time separately for students who did not take any fully online courses and students who enrolled in one or more fully online courses. The difference is significant and substantial.

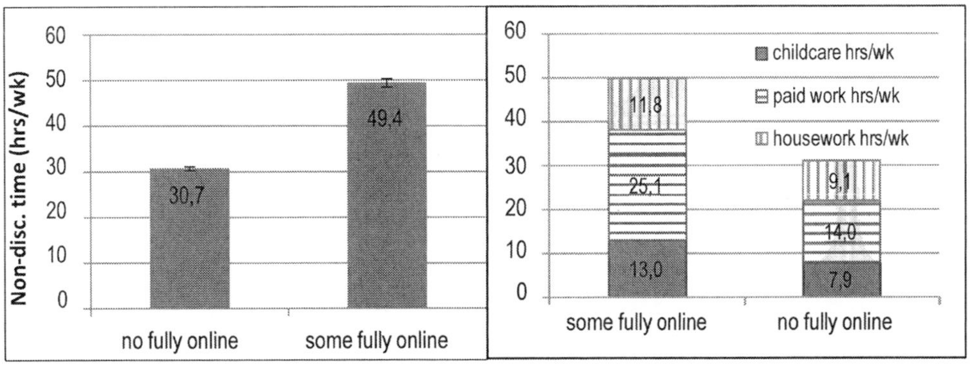

Figure 1a. Non-discretionary Time (Hours/Week) Figure 1b. Mean Hours/Week Spent on Childcare, Paid Work, and Housework by Enrollment Status (From Separate, Weighted, Imputed Regression Models)

Students in the "some fully online" group were significantly more time poor (Figure 1a), with 18.7 more hours/week of non-discretionary time commitments on average than those who did not taken any online courses ($p < 0.001$), a relationship that was reduced but remained after including control variables (11.8 hours/week, $p < 0.001$). This indicates that typical control variables used in research are not sufficient to account for differences in time poverty among online-vs.-face-to-face students. Prior studies, which have not controlled for time poverty, may therefore have significant limitations, particularly since time poverty has been shown to be strongly related to college outcomes for some groups like student parents (Wladis, et al., 2018).

Students who choose to enroll in online courses may be more time poor because they are more likely to work, to have families, and to be older (Cavanaugh, & Jacquemin, 2015). Thus, to better understand patterns in Figure 1a, we broke up non-discretionary time into time spent on housework, paid work, and childcare, and compared subcategory differences between online and non-online students in Figure 1b. Work was the biggest difference, as students in the "some fully online" group spent 80% more time working compared to those not taking online courses. Childcare was the second biggest difference (65% more), and housework showed the least difference (30% more). Considering the relationship between fully online course enrollment, college outcomes, and time poverty, we analyzed the extent to which time poverty mediates the relationship between fully online course enrolment and college retention and credit accumulation, using the KHB method (see Table 1).

Students in fully online courses were roughly 6.2 percentage points less likely to re-enrol the next semester and roughly, 7.9% of this difference was explained by online students' greater time poverty. Time poverty explained a significant portion of retention differences, but other factors also contribute to this retention gap. Such factors could include quality of time, stressors, or measures of time not included in our measure of non-discretionary time such as eldercare or health care. Additionally, when exploring the relationship between fully online course enrolment, credit accumulation, and time poverty in base models, enrolling online it did not predict earning fewer credits (since the direct "effect" was not significant). Rather, online students' increased time poverty entirely explained this difference. Students enrolled fully online earned on average about one half credit less than students who did not enroll in fully online courses, and 98.1% of this difference was explained by their higher time poverty. This difference, though small, could affect time-to-degree. For example, at the mean enrolment intensity, students enrolled only in face-to-face courses would be less than one credit shy of finishing in 11 semesters, whereas students enrolled in at least one online course would need 12 semesters. Time poverty appears to explain almost all credit accumulation differences between those who did and did not take fully online courses.

TIME POVERTY AS A MEDIATOR BETWEEN VOLUNTARY ONLINE ENROLLMENT AND COLLEGE OUTCOMES

	base		full	
College retention	**APE**	**SE**	**APE**	**SE**
online enrolment (ref. gp. not online)				
total "effect"	-6.2pp***	0.2pp	-5.2pp***	0.2pp
direct "effect"	-5.7pp***	0.2pp	-5.0pp***	0.2pp
indirect "effect"	-0.5pp***		-0.2pp***	
Credit accumulation	**Coef.**	**SE**	**Coef.**	**SE**
online enrolment (ref. gp. not online)				
total "effect"	-0.487***	0.029	-0.357***	0.030
direct "effect"	-0.009	0.030	-0.111***	0.030
indirect "effect"	-0.477***	0.009	-0.245***	0.009

Full model includes control variables: gender, ethnicity, age, disability, GPA, income, first generation status pp denotes percentage points

*** $p < 0.001$; ** $p < 0.01$; * $p < 0.05$

Table 1: Time Poverty as a Mediator Between Voluntary Online Enrolment and College Outcomes, Linear Regression Coefficients and Average Partial Effects Reported

Some scholars have suggested that worse college outcomes experienced by online-vs-face-to-face students, when they are observed, are the result of poorer outcomes in online courses (e.g., Xu and Jaggars, 2011). However, in this study, rates of successful course completion were higher for online than face-to-face courses, even as college retention and credit accumulation were lower (in models both with and without controls). Mediation models (not included here because of lack of space) confirmed that course outcomes in online courses do not explain differences in college outcomes for those students who choose to enroll in online courses versus those who do not. While time poverty fully mediated the relationship between online enrolment and credit accumulation, it only partially mediated this relationship for college retention, suggesting that there are other factors (e.g., stressors, quality of time available for study, other demands on time such as healthcare or eldercare not measured in this study) that likely simultaneously increase the likelihood of students enrolling online and dropping out of college.

Limitations

Time measures were retrospective and self-reported, so they may have been impacted by desirability bias or inaccurate time use recollections. Future replication research may seek to use alternate measures of time use (e.g., experience sampling method, Sonnenberg et al., 2012). Also, since our measure of time poverty did not include time spent on eldercare or healthcare, findings may underestimate the time poverty of some groups, and thus the relationship between time poverty and college outcomes. Future research is currently underway to address this limitation. We also note that the relationship between income and time poverty has not been investigated in depth here. This relationship is quite complex: Income and time poverty may be positively related, since as work hours increase, discretionary time decreases; they may also be negatively related, as increased income affords paying for more childcare or other time saving help, increasing discretionary time. Although we have used some income measures as controls, clear conclusions cannot be drawn about whether a student's time poverty is voluntary (e.g., opting for part-time enrolment due to other priorities) or resulting from significant financial need (e.g., lacking resources for childcare). We aim to address this in future research. We note also that local policy likely impacted results: nationally, the U.S. does not provide universal childcare, or sufficient financial aid to cover the financial need of most college students. However, New York City (where this study was conducted) provides more childcare and other public benefits than most other U.S. states and municipalities. Thus, the time poverty relationships in this study may underestimate national trends in the U.S. It would be fruitful for future research to explore the relationship between these trends and local policies and practices.

Conclusion and Implications

Results indicate that students enrolled in at least one fully online course spent 63% more time on childcare; and 80% more time working, compared to students not enrolled online. This is in line with prior research showing online learners are more likely to be parents and tend to be employed for more hours than on-campus students (e.g., Xu and Jaggars, 2011). However, adding new knowledge to the literature, this study measured the costs facing online students in terms of time available for college related to childcare and paid work by quantifying their non-discretionary time.

Online students were retained at lower rates and had lower credit accumulation. Mediation analysis revealed lower rates of retention and credit accumulation among online students could not be explained by outcomes in online courses. Differences in college outcomes thus cannot be explained by students completing online courses less successfully; rather other factors (e.g., time poverty, health issues, stressors, quality of time for college) may encourage students to take online courses while simultaneously making them more likely to drop out or accumulate fewer credits. In this study, time poverty mediated the relationship between online enrolment and college outcomes, partially explaining differences in retention and fully accounting for differences in credit accumulation.

COVID-19 required higher education to pivot dramatically, expanding efforts to develop online courses, which have been systematically, if slowly, happening for several decades at higher education institutions. The emergency remote teaching pivot engendered by the pandemic and the resulting shifts in expectations by students and other stakeholders has required institutions to re-think how courses will be offered in the "new normal" which continues to evolve (Garcia-Morales et al., 2021). Institutions must decide whether to return to pre- pandemic levels of online instruction or to take this opportunity to permanently increase the availability of online offerings. Better understanding who chooses to enroll online and what affects these students' success (both in online courses and in college overall) has thus become even more critical. The results presented here suggest that future discussion, research, and interventions for online students may need to consider time poverty as a factor. For example, given that many online students face time poverty, and given the time costs associated with attending face-to-face classes (e.g., commute, lower flexibility of time [Gherhes et al., 2021]), there may be unrecognized risks to any policies which require or pressure students who prefer (or need) online courses to take them face-to-face instead.

This study also revealed limitations with current supports for online students. Although retention interventions for online students often include technology or academic support, we know of no widespread interventions aiming to reduce time poverty for those who choose to enroll online. However, our results suggest that interventions to improve online student outcomes should consider ways to measure and address time poverty. As an example, supports aimed to reduce hours of paid work (e.g., financial aid that covers living expenses of students' dependents) or to provide free on-campus childcare show promise for future interventions to be tested through causal studies. Also, institutional data readily contains information about online enrolment, which could help institutions identify students who may be particularly time-poor and need further support efforts.

Within the culture of higher education, time is often seen as an individual good free from constraint (Bennett & Burk, 2017). However, this is likely not consistent with many online students' lived realities, where time may be constrained by work and family commitments. Within the students studied, four-fifths of student parents indicated that the childcare available to them was insufficient to allow them time for their studies, and within this student population overall, over three quarters of students who work do so to pay living expenses (CUNY, 2018), so increased childcare and work hours among this population may not be voluntary (i.e., many of these students might opt to spend more time on their studies if they could afford to). Thus, the inequitable distribution of time poverty among college students, and online students in particular, has critical equity implications. Time, like money, is a resource that is inequitably distributed in society, and this may be contributing to differential educational outcomes.

References

1. Allen, I. E., Seaman, J., Poulin, R., & Straut, T. T. (2016). Online report card: Tracking online education in the United States, 1–4. http://onlinelearningsurvey.com/reports/onlinereportcard.pdf
2. Ashby, J., Sadera, W. A., & McNary, S. W. (2011). Comparing student success between developmental math courses offered online, blended, and face-to-face. Journal of Interactive Online Learning, 10(3). https://eric.ed.gov/?id=EJ963670
3. Bennett, A., & Burke, P. J. (2017). Re/conceptualizing time and temporality: an exploration of time in higher education.
4. Discourse: Studies in the Cultural Politics of Education, 39(6), 1–13. https://doi.org/10.1080/01596306.2017.1312285
5. Cavanaugh, J. K., & Jacquemin, S. J. (2015). A large sample comparison of grade based student learning outcomes in online vs. face-to-face courses. Online Learning, 19(2), n2. https://olj.onlinelearningconsortium.org/index.php/olj/article/view/454/138
6. Chatzitheochari, S., & Arber, S. (2012). Class, gender and time poverty: a time-use analysis of British workers' free

time resources. The British journal of sociology, 63(3), 451-471. https://doi.org/10.1111/j.1468- 4446.2012.01419.x

7. Conway, K.M., Wladis, C., & Hachey, A.C. (2021). Time Poverty and Parenthood: Who Has Time for College? AERA Open. https://doi.org/10.1177/23328584211011608
8. CUNY. (2018). 2018 Student Experience Survey: A survey of CUNY undergraduate students [Tableau presentation]. https://public.tableau.com/views/2018StudentExperienceSurvey/CoverPage?:language=en&:display_count=y &:origin=viz_share_link
9. DesJardins, S. L., Ahlburg, D. A., & McCall, B. P. (2006). The effects of interrupted enrollment on graduation from college: Racial, income, and ability differences. Economics of Education Review, 25(6), 575-590. https://doi.org/10.1016/j.econedurev.2005.06.002
10. Fosnacht, K., Sarraf, S., Howe, E., & Peck, L. K. (2017). How important are high response rates for college surveys?. The Review of Higher Education, 40(2), 245-265. https://doi.org/10.1353/rhe.2017.0003
11. Garcia-Morales, V.J., Garrido-Moreno, A. & Martin-Rojas, R. (2021). The transformation of higher education after the COVID disruption: Emerging challenges in an online learning scenario. Frontiers in Psychology. https://doi.org/10.3389/fpsyg.2021.616059
12. Gelles, L.A., Lord, S.M., Hoople, G., Chen, D.A. & Mejia, J.A. (2020). Compassionate flexibility and self-discipline: Student adaptation to emergency remote teaching in an integrated engineering energy course during COVID- 19. Education Sciences, 10(11), 304. https://doi.org/10.3390/educsci10110304
13. Gherhes, V., Stoian, C.E., Farcasiu, M.A., Stanici, M. (2021) E-Learning vs. Face-To-Face Learning: Analyzing Students' Preferences and Behaviors. Sustainability, 13, 4381, 1-15. https:// doi.org/10.3390/su13084381
14. Giurge, L. M., Whillans, A. V. & West, C. (2020). Beyond material poverty: Why time poverty matters for individuals, organizations, and nations. Harvard Business School. https://www.researchgate.net/publication/343405199_Why_time_poverty_matters_for_individuals_organisatio ns_and_nations
15. Jaggars, S., & Bailey, T. R. (2010). Effectiveness of fully online courses for college students: Response to a Department of Education meta-analysis. Community College Research Center. Teachers College, Columbia University. https://doi.org/10.7916/D85M63SM
16. Manly, C. A., & Wells, R. S. (2015). Reporting the use of multiple imputation for missing data in higher education research. Research in Higher Education, 56(4), 397-409. http://doi.org/10.1007/s11162-014-9344-9
17. McPartlan, P., Rutherford, T., Rodriguez, F., Shaffer, J.F. & Holdton, A. (2021). Modality motivation: Selection effects and motivational difference in student who choose to take courses online. The Internet & Higher Education, 49(2021) 100793, 1-14. https://doi.org/10.1016/j.iheduc.2021.100793
18. NC-SARA. (2021). NC-SARA ANNUAL DATA REPORT: Technical Report for Fall 2020 Exclusively Distance Education Enrollment & 2020 Out-of-State Learning Placements. https://nc- sara.org/sites/default/files/files/2021-10/NC-SARA_2020_Data_Report_PUBLISH_19Oct21.pdf
19. Shea, P., & Bidjerano, T. (2014). Does online learning impede degree completion? A national study of community college students. Computers & Education, 75, 103-111. https://doi.org/10.1016/j.compedu.2014.02.009
20. Sonnenberg, B., Riediger, M., Wrzus, C., & Wagner, G. G. (2012). Measuring time use in surveys–concordance of survey and experience sampling measures. Social science research, 41(5), 1037-1052. https://doi.org/10.1016/j.ssresearch.2012.03.013
21. Vickery, C. (1977). The time-poor: A new look at poverty. Journal of Human Resources, 12(1), 27-48. https://doi.org/10.2307/145597
22. Wladis, C., Hachey, A. C., & Conway, K. (2018). No time for college? An investigation of time poverty and parenthood. The Journal of Higher Education, 89(6), 807-831. https://doi.org/10.1080/00221546.2018.1442983
23. Wladis, C.W., Conway, K.M. & Hachey, A.C. (2016). Assessing readiness for online education – Research models for identifying students at risk. Online Learning Journal, 20(3). https://files.eric.ed.gov/fulltext/EJ1113351.pdf
24. Xu, D., & Jaggars, S. S. (2011). The Effectiveness of Distance Education across Virginia's Community Colleges: Evidence from Introductory College-Level Math and English Courses. Educational Evaluation and Policy Analysis, 33(3), 360–377. https://doi.org/10.3102/0162373711413814

ISSN: 2707-2819

IMPROVEMENT IN DIGITAL COMPETENCIES AMONG UNIVERSITAT D'ANDORRA GRADUATES

Montserrat Casalprim Ramonet, Universitat D'andorra, Sant Júlia De Lòria, Andorra

Betlem Sabrià Bernadó, Universitat D'andorra, Sant Júlia De Lòria, Andorra

Josep M. Duart Montoliu, Universitat Oberta De Catalunya, Barcelona

Carlos Madrid Gari, Universitat Oberta De Catalunya, Barcelona

Abstract

The majority of work environments have become increasingly more digitized and this requires that their professionals have a set of skills, knowledge, attitudes, and strategies for using ICTs and digital media to do their work.

In this paper we analyze the impact that an education at the Universitat d'Andorra (UdA) has on improving the digital competencies of the graduates of official studies and postgraduate programs between the years 2000 and 2019.

The results show a clear perception of improvement in all competences related to information technology, after attending the UdA. The factor analysis per- formed using the values for the variables on digital competence prior to initiating studies at UdA presents a single latent factor which confirms that these variables tend to measure digital competence. Performing this same analysis using the values at degree completion, two latent factors are obtained, one that primarily measures the ability to create and manage tools and the other which measures more transversal, less-technical skills.

There is a significant negative correlation at 99%, which indicates there is a higher level of improvement in digital competence for those entering with a lower competence level. This indicator shows there is confidence of achieving an equivalent level of output for all students.

Attending the University of Andorra contributes to the improvement in digital competence among its graduates and to profiles specializing in different skills.

Keywords: Digital Competence, Social Impact, Skills.

Introduction

The educational environment in Andorra

Andorra is a small country with an area of 468.7 Km   located in the Pyrenees, between

France and Spain. It has an estimated population1 of 79,535, of which 48% are of Andorran nationality, 25% of Spanish nationality, 11% of Portuguese nationality and 5% of French nationality. The remainder (11%) represent various other nationalities. There are three public education systems in the country: Andorran, Spanish and French, with all levels completed (primary, secondary and baccalaureate). In addition to this public offering, there is also a private complementary offering with a school from the Spanish education system, at all levels, and a school in the British education system that provides primary and secondary education.

The distribution of students by education system, according to data published by the Department of Statistics (www.estadistica.ad), at the baccalaureate level, in 2020, is 40% in the Andorran system and 30% in each of the other two systems (Spanish and French). In total, there are 1,119 baccalaureate students in the country.

The majority of university students in the country complete their studies at foreign universities, especially in France and Spain.

During the 2019-2020 academic year, there were 733 (46.8%) students at Spanish universities and 129 (8.2%) at French universities, with the remaining 44% of university students enrolled in official studies at the University of Andorra (690 students), according to data provided by the Centre for Sociological Research (CRES).

University degrees in Andorra follow the guidelines established by the European Higher Education Area (EHEA), which are structured into 3 cycles: first-cycle studies (bachelor's), of 180 ECTS (3 years assuming full-time status), second-cycle (master's) of 120 ECTS (2 years assuming full-time status) and a third-cycle program (doctoral). There are also first-cycle specialization degrees (specialized bachelor's), with an additional 60 ECTS at the bachelor level.

The Universitat d'Andorra was created in 1997, and it is the only public university in the country. It has a small and flexible structure, suited to the reality of the country, and can be easily adapted to meet the needs and changes of the society it is designed for. Currently, the official degree programs offered by the University of Andorra include 4 on-site bachelor's degrees (in Business Administration, Education, Nursing and Computer Science), 1 bachelor of specialty (in obstetrical and gynecological nursing), 1 blended-learning master's degree (in Education), and other online courses offered in collaboration with the Universitat Oberta de Catalunya (4 online bachelor's degrees - Communication, Law, Humanities and Catalan Language, and an online master's degree in Law). It also offers an interdisciplinary program and an advanced professional diploma in the administration and finance field.

For the 2020-2021 academic year, the Universitat d'Andorra had a total of 644 students enrolled in official degree programs, of which there were 408 enrolled in first- cycle programs offered on campus.

As for the lifelong learning opportunities at the University of Andorra, these very dynamic and adapted to the needs indicated by the country's professionals and are structured as postgraduate programs, which are aimed primarily towards qualified professionals, and carry a minimum of approximately 10 ECTS, refresher courses, with a shorter duration (between 1 and 10 ECTS) and training courses, which do not award a diploma as they are not evaluated.

The subjects of this study are graduates of official degree programs and postgraduate programs between 2000 and 2019.

The object of study

The Universitat d'Andorra, since it was founded in 1988, has been the leading institution in higher education in Andorra for many years. It promotes a diverse and quality academic offer with the aim of responding to the academic and professional needs of all Andorrans. After more than 30 years of experience, it is time to perform an analysis of the real impact that UdA has on the country's society and economy.

Higher education serves the function of providing training for the working world and for all areas of life of its graduates. It is responsible for the generation, transmission and preservation of knowledge. Students are taught and provided with an environment that enables them to improve their skills on their own (Kivinen & Nurmi, 2007).

According to (Teichler, 2015) universities need to be better informed about the employment and work of their graduates to act in a specific way, subordinate to presumed demands, proactive approaches, etc.

As part of a study aimed at analysing the economic and social impact the Universitat d'Andorra has on the country, a quantitative analysis of graduate profiles has been carried out in a comparative context using a survey of graduates of official degree programs and postgraduate programs between 2000-2019, about the personal, professional or social benefits of having studied at UdA. In this study we focus on analysing the impact that an education at UdA has on improving the digital competencies of its graduates.

Profile of UdA graduates in comparison to graduates of Catalan universities

The average age of UdA graduates (34.9 years) is higher than that of graduates of Catalan Universities (26.1 years, for 2017)(Carnoy et al., 2019), whether we take into account both the graduates of postgraduate programs (with an average of 37.8 years) or only the graduates of official degree programs (31.8).

In regards to combining studies with work, the report by Ariño et al. (2019) indicates that for universities that belong to the Xarxa Vives d'Universitats (XVU) network, 24.8% of students balance their studies with regular paid employment, whereas at the UdA, this percentage is 46.4%. Of these, 37.5% of UdA students and 19.5% of those in the Xarxa Vives d'Universitats work more than 35 hours a week. With these data we can say that the profile of students who have to combine their studies with some type of work is higher at the UdA, which could explain the fact that the average age of their graduates is higher.

The survey carried out for this study shows that 71.9% of UdA graduates who worked did so in a job related to their studies. For postgraduate students, 75.1% are working in a job related to their studies, and for students pursuing an official degree, it is only 40.7%.

Of those who were working, 42% had their education fully funded by their company (most of whom, 72%, have a postgraduate degree) and 22% had it partially funded, in contrast to 36% not having their studies funded by a company. For graduates of official degree programs, the percentage of those who have funding from the company where they work is lower than for postgraduate students, with 32.1% having their studies fully funded by the company, 17.3% partially-funded and 50.6% without any funding from the company.

For postgraduate graduates, the majority obtain some type of funding from the company where they work, with 47.2% having their studies fully funded by the company, 24.3% partially funded and 28.5% without any funding from the company. 94% of graduates are currently working more than 19 hours a week.

As for the sector in which UdA graduates work, most of them are in the Public Administration, Education and Health sector, which are the areas with the most education opportunities offered by the University.

Methodology

The research methodology applied is quantitative. Univariate descriptive statistics were used to obtain the sample profile and measures of central tendency and dispersion and bivariate analysis to obtain correlations of variables related to digital competence.

A factor analysis was also performed with these variables prior to initiating studies and at the end to group them and obtain the latent factors.

Instrument utilized

To assess the extent that the education received at UdA has provided a personal, professional or social benefit to graduates; an online questionnaire was distributed be- tween September and October 2020 to all UdA graduates of official degree programs and postgraduate programs between 2000-2019.

The questionnaire was designed following the guidelines established in international literature, in accordance with previous studies carried out in Catalan universities (Suri- ñach et al., 2017) and following a process of validation by experts, which included three research experts from the country (director of research at the Ministry of Higher Edu- cation and Research, director of the Andorran Higher Education Quality Agency and director of the Centre for Snow and Mountain Studies of Andorra, from the Institut d'Estudis Andorrans) and three international experts (researchers from the Universitat Autònoma de Barcelona and the Universitat Oberta de Catalunya, who had participated in a similar study).

The questions analyzed in this study refer to the changes perceived by graduates in terms of the different aspects of their digital competence, as shown in the question posed in the questionnaire:

Question 12: Thinking about the time before and after you attended UdA, we now ask you to rate on a scale of 1 to 5, with 1 being "beginner level" and 5 "expert level", your user level with respect to the digital competencies presented below.

	Before attending UdA	After attending UdA
1- Finding information, communicating and sharing digital content		
2- Planning tasks in a virtual environment.		
3- Application or software programming.		
4- Working as a team in a virtual environment.		
5- Sharing digital content.		

6- Creating websites, blogs and similar re- sources.		
7- Using data-analysis software (Excel, SPSS, etc.).		
8- Creating digital content in different formats (text, numeric, video, presentation).		
9- Ensuring my security and protecting my online identity and personal information.		
10- Solving technical problems and applying digital solutions to the needs identified.		

Table 1: Questions about digital competency on the questionnaire

Population and sample

The characteristics of the population and the sample for the survey are:

Population: 2,073 graduates, of whom 1,102 (53.16%) have a postgraduate degree and 971 (46.84%) have an official degree.

Sample: 369 survey responses, of which 193 (52.30%) are for postgraduate and 176 (47.7%) are for official degree studies.

Error: 4.6%

The questionnaire was distributed on 24 September 2020 to the entire population. A reminder was made on 2 October, and the survey period officially closed on 12 October. In terms of the degree completed, 46% of the respondents held postgraduate degrees, a figure that is very close to the profile of UdA graduates. Figure 1 shows the relationship between the sample obtained and the total population:

Figure 1: Comparison between the population and the sample

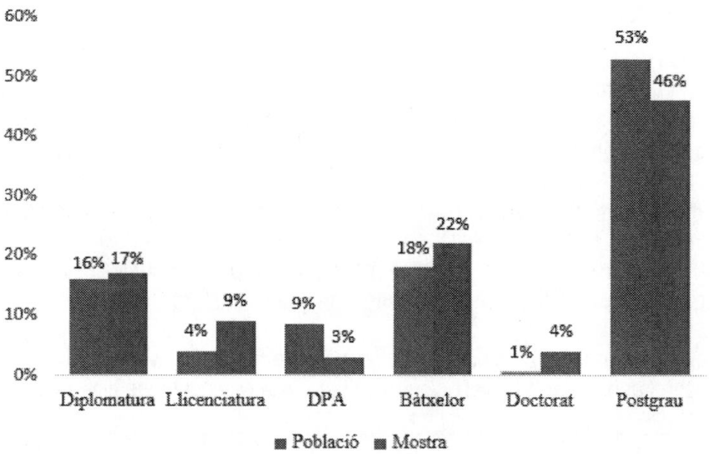

Source: Survey UdA graduates (2000-2019)

With regard to gender, there is a certain imbalance in favor of women, who make up 58% of graduates who responded to the survey. For official degree students, the percentage of women is 56% and for postgraduate students it is 60%.

The average age of UdA graduates in this sample at the time of degree completion is 34.9 years. It is higher than that of graduates of Catalan Universities, 26.1 years for 2017(Carnoy et al., 2019). The average age of participants at the time of the survey is

42.0 years.

Results and conclusions

The results of this survey show a clear perception of improvement in all competences related to information technology, after attending the UdA, as seen in the table below.

Figure 2: Improvement in ITC competencies among UdA graduates between 2000-2019

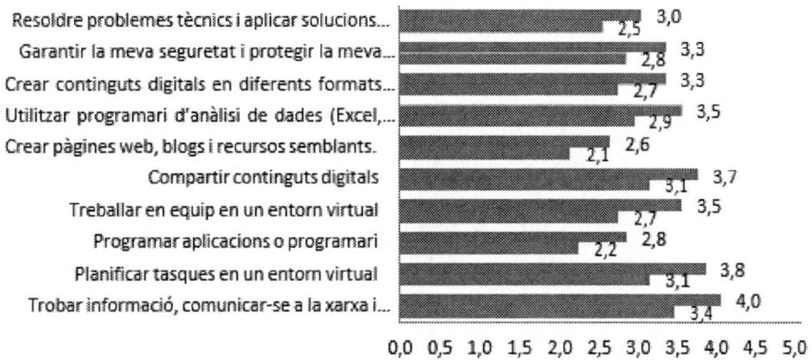

Source: Survey UdA graduates (2000-2019)

The factor analysis of these questions before attending the UdA was performed and a single factor was clearly found (KMO = 0.922). The percentage of variance explained by a single factor is 63%.
The following table shows the values of the component matrix that are quite high, as they are in the range of [0.715, 0.854].
Therefore, this confirms that these variables tend to measure students' digital competence before attending UdA.

1-Finding information, communicating online and sharing digital content	0.719
2- Planning tasks in a virtual environment.	0.803
3- Application or software programming.	0.715
4- Working as a team in a virtual environment.	0.822
5- Sharing digital content.	0.820
6- Creating websites, blogs and similar resources.	0.808
7- Using data-analysis software (Excel, SPSS, etc.).	0.771
8- Creating digital content in different formats (text, numeric, video, presentation).	0.793
9- Ensuring my security and protecting my online identity and personal information.	0.796
10- Solving technical problems and applying digital solutions to the needs identified.	0.854

Table 2: Component matrix from the factor analysis of variables before attending UdA

Conversely, with the results for the same variables that measure digital competence after attending UdA, we note that KMO is high (0.890) and therefore, we can perform the factor analysis.

Explaining 55% of the total variance requires two factors, one explaining 53% and the other 12%.

The following table shows the values of the component matrix that are quite high, as they are in the range of [0.517, 0.847].

	Factor 1	Factor 2
1-Finding information, communicating online and sharing digital content	0.131	0.808
2-Planning tasks in a virtual environment.	0.294	0.847
3-Application or software programming.	0.778	0.202
4-Working as a team in a virtual environment.	0.408	0.697
5-Sharing digital content.	0.284	0.796
6-Creating websites, blogs and similar resources.	0.819	0.248
7-Using data-analysis software (Excel, SPSS, etc.).	0.446	0.549
8-Creating digital content in different formats (text, numeric, video, presentation).	0.741	0.305
9-Ensuring my security and protecting my online identity and personal information.	0.517	0.187
10-Solving technical problems and applying digital solutions to the needs identified.	0.831	0.318

Table 3: Component matrix from the factor analysis of variables after attending UdA

This means that when students graduate, digital competence has two components, one that corresponds to questions: 10, 6, 3, 8 and 9, which primarily measures the ability to create and manage tools, and the other that corresponds to questions: 2, 1, 5, 4 and 7, which measures more transversal, less-technical skills.

Attending the University of Andorra contributes to the improvement in digital competence among its graduates and to profiles specializing in different skills.

The following table shows the increases to these scores:

Table 4: Improvements in user-level of UdA graduates between 2000-2019 in the evaluation of their level of digital competencies

	N	Average value upon attending UdA	Average value upon leaving UdA	Var.	An swers that note an im provement (%)
Finding information and communicating online	35 3	3.40	4.02	+0.6 2	39.8
Planning tasks in a virtual environment	34 5	3.07	3.80	+0.7 3	46.8
Application or soft-ware programming	34 5	2.24	2.83	+0.5 9	32.2
Working as a team in a virtual environment	34 7	2.74	3.50	+0.7 6	43.7
Sharing digital con-tent	33 9	3.10	3.73	+0.6 3	38.6
Creating websites, blogs and similar re-sources	33 9	2.07	2.59	+0.5 2	27
Using data-analysis software (Excel, SPSS, etc.)	33 8	2.88	3.46	+0.5 8	35.9
Creating digital con-tent in different formats	34 2	2.68	3.25	+0.5 7	33
Ensuring my security and protecting	33 9	2.78	3.29	+0.5 1	31.6

online identity and personal Information					
Solving technical problems and applying digital solutions	33 5	2.46	3.01	+0.5 5	34.6

Source: Survey UdA graduates (2000-2019)

The highest perceived improvements in digital competence are in regards to the ability to work as a team in a virtual environment (with an increase of 0.76 points on the scale of 1 to 5), followed by the ability to plan tasks in a virtual environment, where the increase is 0.73 points.

Table 5: Pearson's correlation coefficient (r) for digital competence before attending UdA and its improvement

Digital competency	R
1- Finding information and communicating online	-0.695
2- Planning tasks in a virtual environment	-0.603
3- Application or software programming	-0.237
4- Working as a team in a virtual environment	-0.470
5- Sharing digital content	-0.526
6- Creating websites, blogs and similar resources	-0.163
7- Using data-analysis software (Excel, SPSS, etc.)	-0.416
8- Creating digital content in different formats	-0.342
9- Ensuring my security and protecting identity and personal information	-0.436
10- Solving technical problems and applying digital solutions	-0.340

Source: Survey UdA graduates (2000-2019)

All correlations are significant at 99% because all p-values are less than 0.01.

There is a significant negative correlation at 99%, which indicates there is a higher level of improvement in digital competence for those entering with a lower competence level. This indicator shows there is confidence of achieving an equivalent level of output for all students.

References

1. Departament d'Estadística del Govern d'Andorra www.estadistica.ad, last accessed 2022/04/06.
2. Kivinen, O., & Nurmi, J. (2007). Job Requirements and Competences: Do Qualifications Matter? BT - Careers of University Graduates: Views and Experiences in Comparative Perspectives (U. Teichler (ed.); pp. 131–142). Springer Netherlands. https://doi.org/10.1007/978-1-4020-5926-1_8
3. Teichler, U. (2015). Higher Education and the World of Work: The Perennial Controversial Debate BT - Mass Higher Education Development in East Asia: Strategy, Quality, and Challenges; pp. 269–288. Springer International Publishing. https://doi.org/10.1007/978-3-319-12673-9_16
4. Ariño, A., Llopis, R., Martínez, M., Pons, M., & Prades, A. (2019). Via Universitària: Accés, condicions d'aprenentatge, expectatives i retorns dels estudis universitaris (2017- 2019). Resultats principals, conclusions i propostes. Castelló de la Plana: Xarxa Vives d'Universitats.
5. Suriñach, J., Murillo, J., Vayá, E., Duro, J. A., Segarra, A., Teruel, M., Segarra, P., & Setó, M. D. (2017). Impactes socioeconòmics de les Universitats Públiques i el Sistema Públic de Recerca de Catalunya (p. 303). Associació Catalana d'Universitats Públiques (ACUP). http://www.indicadorsuniversitats.cat/impactes/documents/2016/informe.pdf
6. Carnoy, M., Duart, J. M., Albert, S.-G., & Riccardo, V. (2019). La contribución de la UOC a la sociedad catalana. Informe de investigación. UOC.

Shaping the Digital Transformation of the Education Ecosystem in Europe
EDEN Digital Learning Europe Proceedings
2022 Annual Conference | Tallinn, 20-22 June, 2022
ISSN: 2707-2819

DIGITAL RHETORIC OF TIKTOK

Viktorija Tataurova, Diāna Ivanova, Jekaterina Martinova, Riga Technical University

Abstract

The COVID19 pandemic has reshaped our understanding of education. It has proven that some subjects can be successfully delivered remotely, or partly remotely. However, the presentation of the material to the students should be adapted, as it is difficult to maintain the attention of the learners, to keep them motivated and involved in the studying process with the coursebook-bound tasks only. The teachers should welcome the changes and embrace the opportunities that the digital world has to provide, as the students are accustoming to the changes at a very fast pace and the speed of information perception of the nowadays' students has accelerated greatly. Currently one of the most topical applications among the students is TikTok, a platform encompassing a great number of short, usually one-minute-long educational and entertainment videos. The aim of the present paper is the analysis of TikTok educational videos considering the theory of digital rhetoric. Digital rhetoric is an extension of classical rhetoric, the purpose of which is to entertain, inform and persuade the audience by the means of words and body language. Digital rhetoric refers to the communication happening in the digital environment by the means of multimedia, e.g., text, animation, graphics, virtual reality, audio, and video. For the purposes of the present paper, there have been five TikTok bloggers selected whose content is aimed at teaching English as a foreign language. The content has been analyzed on the various means (including verbal means and multimedia) the presenters use to inform, entertain and persuade the audience. The videos were afterward sent to the students to analyze their perception of the material delivery.

Keywords: TikTok, multimedia learning, social media learning, bite-sized learning, digital rhetoric, rhetorical analysis of digital texts, communication competence

Introduction

According to the Communication Competence theory developed by Hymes, in order to develop communication competence, it is essential that the learners are immersed in the English-speaking environment. However, due to COVID pandemic restrictions, face-to-face learning was substituted with remote learning, which left the English language learners without the possibility of developing their communication competence by means of communication in the English-speaking setting, as the ability of the learners to travel abroad for studies was highly restricted. Nevertheless, when there are restrictions, there are always new possibilities. A number of educators, including English native speakers from all around the world, started using social media platforms to reach the youth with interactive English language classes. The application of the short videos filmed by the native speakers in the second or foreign language classroom allows the educators to immerse the learners in the English-language setting. The purpose of the present research is the analysis of the potential of TikTok as an assistant to English as a second or foreign language teachers in the development of the communicative competence of the learners. The learner evaluation questionnaire of TikTok videos of five successful TikTok English language educators was used to establish that. To assess the rhetorical means the selected TikTok educators employ to reach the audience, the rhetorical analysis of digital texts was utilized by the researchers.

Bite-Sized Learning

The cognitive learning theory research and practice have resulted in the emergence of bite- sized learning (Jacobs et al. 2022). Learning in a cognitive theory is viewed as a process, in which the information is processed by learners who then respond with specific actions (Mayer 2003). These cognitive processes incorporate the rearrangement of mental processes expanding human intelligence, which can be viewed as knowledge (Piaget 2000). Wang and Noe (2010) define knowledge as the mental processing of data and the comprehension of how the tasks should be carried out. Miller (2002) stresses the subjective nature of knowledge which is shaped by the individual's comprehension of information. Jacobs et al. (2022) stress that it is by the means of mental process that the learners absorb information and therefore build and accept knowledge.

The research carried out by Burns (1985), Hattie and Yates (2013) have proved that the attention and recall of the students diminish if they are exposed to long and monotonous tasks and activities. The study carried out by Burns revealed that the first five minutes of studies make a major influence on learning with a later decline. The research made by Hattie and Yates demonstrated that learners memorize information better if they are exposed to multiple short sessions of learning instead of one long session. It is clear that long, uninterrupted sessions and one-way communication are not functional learning strategies in relation to learners who have become passionate users of short video platforms and chat applications (Jacobs et al. 2022).

The study carried out by Mayer and Moreno (2003) explored the means of diminishing the cognitive load in learning. One of the ways of load minimization turned out to be segmenting, which is the time allocated between sequential bite-sized pieces of learning. The method is also called bite-sized learning which is related to just-in-time learning, which promotes casual, learner-initiated knowledge creation and application (Weintraub and Martineau 2002). Just-in-time learning recommends that materials are shorter and concentrated on the particular learning goals (Jacobs et al. 2022). In bite-sized learning, the learning session with numerous learning goals is modified into multiple short sessions that can be easily absorbed and have one main learning goal for each short session (ibid.).

Job and Ogalo (2012) suggest that bite-sized learning has a positive influence on knowledge acquisition by the means of small-scale learning content and the methods of information delivery. Stahl et al (2010) also point out the fact that the application of bite-sized learning results in better information memorization in relation to a presentation of a large piece of information in one session. Gray (2015) asserts that one of the benefits of bite-sized learning is the rise in student involvement.

Just-in-time and bite-sized learning has been used in organizational training and work-related learning (Armstrong and Sadler-Smith 2008). With the application of WhatsApp, the bite- sized learning approach has been highly-welcomed by high school students in formal education and has resulted in the improvement of learning results (So 2016). The research conducted by Manning et al (2021) has shown that the immediate post-test results of the medical residents taught using the bite-sized learning approach turned out to be higher in comparison with a group of students taught by case-based teaching.

Bite-sized learning gives the students the ways how they can control the cognitive load successfully and based on their own will (Jacobs et al. 2022). Due to the fact that mobile technologies are developing so fast, there exist practical and economical means for bite-sized learning (So, 2016). The application of mobile, web, and e-learning education techniques allows for data and knowledge sharing via mobile devices in an opportune and contemporary way (Hayes, 2020). Students are more inclined to apply mobile devices rather than laptops for non-traditional classroom tasks and activities (Dahlstrom et al. 2015). Jacobs et al. (2022) hypothesize that the application of bite-sized learning via mobile devices can be a successful way to approach learners due to the fact that the value and application of smartphones among students have been rising sharply over the last years.

Multimedia learning

Multimedia learning incorporates the conveyance of instructional material to learners with a combination of words and pictures aimed at stimulation of meaningful learning (Mayer 2003). According to the studies carried out by Allan Paivio, the information processing in learners happens through two channels, which are visual and verbal channels.

Baddeley et al. (1998) claim that the amount of information that each channel can process is highly restricted. Mayer (2003) identified that the application of various technologies can be an effective tool in promoting human cognition. Velleman and Moore (1996) state that multimedia learning is most efficient when some activities are automated, therefore, instructors can concentrate on the learner's motivation, involvement, communication, and assessment. The application of social media as an aid to instructors can be one of the ways how this approach can be implemented, as some of the instructional tasks are realized through technologies (Jacobs et al. 2022).

Social media in language learning

Multiple research on the use of social media as an aid to educators in English as a foreign language classroom has proved that social media can help to facilitate English language acquisition. Zam Zam Al Arif (2019) demonstrated that the application of social media in language learning improves the learner's motivation and enthusiasm for communication and language acquisition. Previous research has also suggested that the majority of English as a foreign language learners are of the opinion that the application of social media combined with short videos helps to develop their communicative competence by the means of self- managed learning in combination with the topics suggested by the English teachers (Xiong and Zhou 2018; Otchie and Pedaste 2020).

The most widely used social media platform incorporating short videos aimed at the development of English communicative competence is Facebook (Wongsa and Son, 2020). The research carried out by multiple instructors in Indonesian schools and universities has proved that the application of Facebook in English language teaching has improved the learners' English language proficiency levels in the four language skills, namely speaking, reading, writing, and listening through the rise in the learners' self-assurance and wish to communicate in English on the Internet (see Arfiandhani 2020; Haerazi et al. 2020; Putrawan and Riadi 2020; Syah et al. 2020). Moreover, other social media platforms, including WhatsApp, Instagram, and Twitter have been also proven to increase the learners' interest and motivation to apply English as a communicative tool in the internet community, as well as being viewed as an interesting and creative way of learning as perceived by the learners (see Abdulaziz Al Fadda 2020; Akkara et al. 2020; Madzlan et al. 2020; Montaner 2020; Zhou et al. 2020).

In the last decade, social media platforms, such as Facebook, Instagram, and Twitter have been widely researched and applied in foreign language teaching. The social media platform into which there has been little research is TikTok.

TikTok

TikTok is a social media platform that appeared on the market in September 2016 and steadily grew into one of the leading social sharing platforms. On its webpage, they claim that its mission is to become "the leading destination for short-form mobile video [...], to inspire creativity and bring joy" (TikTok 2022). Yuxin Yang (2020: 4) refers TikTok to a User-generated content platform (UGC), which means the users create the content themselves, and then share it with other users. The videos created by the users on this platform are of various types, involving entertainment content, such as lip-sync, dancing, and gaming, as well as educational content, i.e., historical, sports, food and nutrition, news, healthcare, and language learning. The videos published on the platform usually last up to one minute, and the user may make them more interactive by adding music and/or various effects, such as GIFs, stickers, text, augmented reality, green screens, and split-screen for duets made as a reaction to the videos of other users (Jacobs et al. 2022).

TikTok quickly gained popularity; in January 2021 the number of active users reached 689 million (Mohsin 2021). For instance, it took Instagram six years to reach the same number of active users TikTok has gained in less than two years (ibid.). Currently, the screen time of TikTok users has been far greater than the screen time of the users of the competitors (see Figure 1) (TikTok Statistics, 2021).

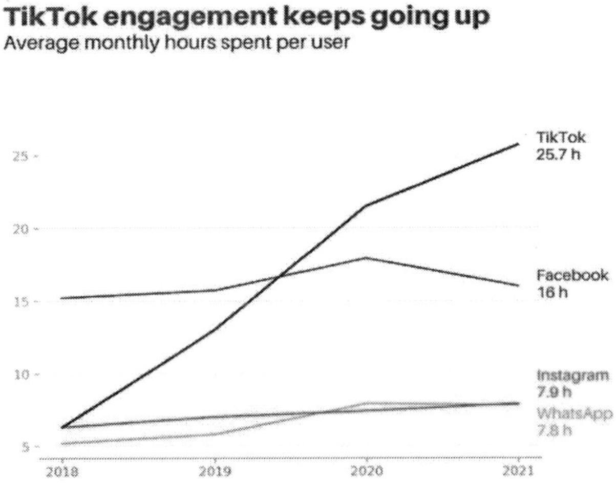

Figure 1. TikTok engagement increase

Potential of TikTok in English language learning

One of the educational functions of social media platforms incorporating short videos is the development of the communicative competence of English as a foreign language learners, specifically of college students constrained by the restrictions of COVID19 pandemics when the learners have less possibility to communicate with the native speakers being unable to travel abroad freely (Arfiandhani 2020). According to Wu (2020), the majority of TikTok users are the youth up to 30 years, also referred to as Generation Z. The average time spent on TikTok by this group of users is 52 minutes a day (ibid.). Syah et al. (2020) suggest that TikTok should be considered an educational tool due to the amount of time the youth spends there. In Indonesian and Indian schools, TikTok has been successfully applied as an educational tool in science education (ibid.). The previous research findings suggest that TikTok has proved to be a platform for knowledge sharing and education in a modern teaching mode increasing the learners' motivation and interest (Xu 2019). Moreover, TikTok can be a source of multiple interactive activities for educators and learners (Xuiwen and Bakar Razali 2021). Science teachers sharing the educational materials on TikTok apply colorful pictures and digital technology to relate the complex science theory with the principles of daily life, which makes the learning material more realistic and effective (Syah et al. 2020). Therefore, the use of TikTok as a learning material can help the youth to increase their learning motivation (Xuiwen and Baker Razali 2021).

Digital rhetoric

According to Bizzel and Herzberg (2000: i), rhetoric is a combination of various overlapping senses, such as the study, strategies, and practice of the art of formal speaking in public; the study and application of written and spoken language in order to inform, persuade and entertain; the theory of the interrelation between language and comprehension; the application and categorization of the figurative and metaphorical senses of the words and expressions. The researchers emphasize that rhetoric is a complicated theory with a long history; therefore, it is more effective to examine the various definitions of it, which have been accumulated over time, and to try to comprehend why each of the definitions appeared and how it changes the field instead of just defining the concept once and forever.

Digital rhetoric is an extension of classical rhetoric, which, according to Aristotle (1991: 37) is "the art of finding out the available means of persuasion" for a specific argument. Aristotle then elaborates on how humans could use a theory to find out the argument, which would be the most effective for public consideration and verdict. Buchanan (1989: 93) specified that "rhetoric is both the practice of persuasive communication and a formal art of studying such communication"; and the capacity of rhetoric's appeal to persuasion lies in the fact that is expressed as an "art of shaping society, changing the course of individuals and communities, and setting patterns for new action".

Initially, rhetoric incorporated the methods an individual could apply to create an effective persuasive argument; these methods were made more comprehensible and systematized by Aristotle in the 4th century

BCE (Eyman 2018: 14). Classical rhetoric only considered the three key types of speech, or oration: legal, political, and ceremonial (ibid.). In building an effective argument, the orator could employ three ways of expression: logos (logical reasoning), pathos (appeal to emotions), and ethos (building the credibility of the speaker) (ibid.). In Aristotle's canon of classical rhetoric, there are five steps in the process of developing an argument:

Invention	finding the most persuasive ways to present information and formulate the argument
Arrangement	the organization of the speech
Style	the use of appropriate and forceful language
Memory	using mnemonic devices so you don't forget your lovely style and arrangement
Delivery	presenting the speech effectively (including projection and appropriate gestures)

Table 1. Aristotle's canon of classical rhetoric (Eyman 2018: 14)

As regards contemporary approaches to the theory of rhetoric, the definitions proposed by various scholars are as follows. Richards (1930) claims that rhetoric is the theory of communication and comprehension. Burke (1966) suggests that rhetoric is the theory of human interaction with specific objectives, or motives and outcomes. The researcher also adds that one of the purposes of rhetoric is joining people holding similar beliefs as groups. Bizzell and Herzberg (2000: 14) in their definition of rhetoric closely associate rhetoric with meaning, as meaning is influenced by the communicative event and context, not just the language itself. Comprehension and confidence are the results of persuasion, the goal of which is to make the controversial issue seem reasonable, to transfer one's belief into the assumption; and it is the power of rhetoric to display these ideological acts (ibid.).

So what are the distinguishing features of digital rhetoric? Lanham (1992: 221) begins his classification of digital rhetoric with the relation between the communication happening with the help of computers and rhetoric: "in practice, the computer often turns out to be a rhetorical device as well as a logical one, that it derives its aesthetic from philosophy's great historical opposite in Western thought and education, the world of rhetoric". The first theorists of digital rhetoric concentrated on hypertext which was viewed in contrast to print text and investigated the outcomes of joining e-documents in the digital environment (Eyman 2018: 25). Gary Heba (1997: 22) proposes the following definition of 'HyperRhetoric': "a form of communication that continually invents and reinvents itself through an ongoing negotiation among users, developers, electronic content, and its presentation in a multimedia environment". Doug Brent in his work "Rhetorics of the Web" (1997) has claimed that the concept of 'New Rhetoric' has become larger than its original meaning of a convincing argument aimed at affecting the audience and making them take the orator's position.

Communication, dialogue, and common construction of knowledge have become the inherent parts of the concept of the new rhetoric (ibid.). Later, James Zappen (2005: 320) highlights that the studies of digital media present some of the main features of interaction in the digital environment and some of the accompanying struggles. The features may serve both as affordances and restraints and therefore may provide an explanation of how the new media assist and facilitate the transformation of the classical rhetoric of persuasion into the digital rhetoric that supports 'self-expression, participation and creative collaboration' (ibid.). The researcher presents a short review and combination of work that he views as being responsible for the formation of digital rhetoric as a theory, concentrating on four main aspects:

- The application of rhetorical strategies in the creation and analysis of digital texts.
- The establishment of the features, restrictions, and affordances of new media.
- The emergence of the digital self.
- The possibility of formation of social communities (ibid.).

The constituent parts presented in the framework above constitute the major part of work done by researchers whose field of work is related to digital rhetoric (Eyman 2018: 29).

The following ideas were presented by Warnick (2007: 13) in relation to rhetorical elements in the digital environment:

Rhetorical forms in online media also include coproduced media discourse, online political campaigns and parody, epideictic discourse in online memorials, and other forms of appeal. Often these are hybrid discourses involving information and aesthetic elements as well as rhetoric, but one of their aims will be more or less explicit appeal to purported audiences in specific communication contexts.

What are digital texts?

First of all, there needs to be a definition of a digital text. Karen Palmer (n.d.) in her 'Diving into Rhetoric' suggests that a general definition of a digital text might be an 'electronic version of a written text'. A more elaborated definition was developed by Gerard Ford (as cited in Palmer, n.d.). The researcher claims that a digital text is a data set characterized by the presence of multiple modes of data, including hyperlinks, embedded images, and video, commenting and annotation options, and other interactive features. These definitions present digital texts as printed text published on the digital platform (Palmer, n.d.). For the purposes of this research, a definition that refers digital texts to all forms of digital media will be employed:

A weather app on a smartphone, a racing game on a video game console and an ultrasound imaging device in a hospital are all digital media products. They are successful because they are engaging, easy to use (even fun in the case of games), and deliver results. Digital Media is a blend of technology and content... (Centre for Digital Media)

As Karen Palmer (n.d.) claims, digital media employs various technologies, including blogs, forums, video, audio, webpages, games, and photoshopped images to build an argument; the communication is not solely limited to words in the digital environment. Before the images and videos began to be employed for rhetorical reasons about a century ago, only written and spoken texts were used in rhetoric. A couple of decades ago, digital media has been introduced with memes, social media platforms, and applications that could be easily transformed, appear or vanish the next day (ibid.).

Modern technologies provide various ways of introducing information, thoughts, and ideas (ibid.). As modern technologies became more accessible, the audience may reach the information, thoughts, and ideas easily in the digital environment (ibid.). However, because of the digital divide, some people cannot reach this information and become part of a discussion in the digital world (ibid.).

Rhetorical analysis of digital texts

The present research will employ the framework of rhetorical analysis designed by Karen Palmer (n.d.) in her online book 'Diving into Rhetoric'.

The first step in this framework is referred to as 'Read the text'. The author suggests reading and summarizing the text as the first step to take. The author notes that digital texts may involve some additional surfaces for the reason that they usually involve some interactivity. The researcher refers to her online textbook which contains not only the text but also incorporated videos, images, and hyperlinks as a basic example of digital text (ibid.).

The second step is called 'Define the Rhetorical Situation'. Here, the author suggests beginning by defining who the speaker is. As it was previously suggested by Barthes (as cited in Palmer, n.d.), the author of a text is the origin of the text, while the reader is the text's destination. Karen Palmer then comments on this claim by stating that nowadays it might be difficult to find the original source of information. The second aspect that should be defined is occasion, which is the context and refers to the reason why the digital text was created, e.g., following a specific event, or a modern trend. The researcher might be interested in whether the website where the digital text was published is recently launched or has existed for a long time, and what is the topic or problem tackled in the digital text. The third aspect to define is the audience. Karen Palmer accentuates that establishing and reaching the audience of the digital text is much more complex than establishing the audience of the print or spoken text, as the audience of digital text is usually much more diverse, involving people of different genders and age groups. The author emphasizes that in certain cases a specific text does not have any particular audience (e.g., developed by the so-called 'trolls'). Sometimes, in order to find out who is the audience of the text, such as a YouTube video, the researcher might investigate the profile of the user and the information section below the video to locate the intended audience, and research the comment section to see the real audience of the video. The following aspect that should be considered here is the purpose for which the author is publishing the digital text. The possible reasons why the specific text appeared on the web might be: to earn money, assemble a community, promote a political belief, employ volunteers, establish the charter of an organization, overwhelm the users with data, attract business associates, or the combination of some. The last aspect characterized here is the style. The researcher first needs to establish the format in which the information in the digital text appears, e.g., website, meme, social media page and the reasons why the author has decided to present the information in this way, the advantages and disadvantages of conveying the message in this way and the guidelines which exist in this type of media (ibid.).

The third step is referred to as '*Identify Rhetorical Strategies*'. Karen Palmer insists that the researcher should remember here that there might be multiple reasons why an author has created a specific digital text, therefore the video might include different layers of rhetorical devices and strategies. The researcher also suggests surveying the attempts made to make the audience a part of the presenter's ethos. In order to establish these, the following features should be considered: the features the digital text uses to create a community, the reason why each aspect of the text has been selected, and the degree to which the text features meet the rhetorical purposes of the text. The researcher states that a well-designed digital text will take advantage of the medium to make the best use of its rhetorical potential in relation to the intended audience. The author also adds here that the design characteristics of the digital text should be considered, such as the layout, use of colors, text, fonts, and use of white space (ibid.).

The last step is called '*Connect the Text to the Rhetorical Decisions*', where the researcher should establish whether the rhetorical purposes of the text suit the rhetorical means selected to deliver the message (ibid.)

Methodology

For the purposes of the present research, five TikTok presenters with 488 k – 3.7 million subscribers were selected. All the selected presenters are native speakers of English.

First, the videos were analyzed on 12 elements (i.e. summary, speaker, occasion, audience, purpose, style, ethos, pathos, logos, kairos, rhetorical devices, and effectiveness) proposed by Karen Palmer (n.d.) in her rhetorical analysis of digital texts.

Afterward, the video evaluation questionnaire was distributed to the students electronically via Google Forms. The questionnaire involved only closed-ended questions, was aimed at the evaluation of the videos filmed by the selected TikTok presenters, and consisted of the questions aimed at the assessment of the speaker, style, and content, and the establishment of social media the learners use for the English language development. 23 first-year students of Riga Technical University participated in the questionnaire.

The evaluation of TikTok videos performed by the learners in the evaluation questionnaire was then compared to the results of the rhetorical analysis of the videos.

Digital rhetoric of TikTok

The first part of the practical research concerned the analysis of TikTok videos of five presenters on 12 elements proposed by Karen Palmer (n.d.) in her framework of rhetorical analysis of digital texts. The results are presented in the tables below:

	Presenter No 1	Presenter No 2	Presenter No 3
Summary	The videos are taken from the classes of the speaker. The speaker uses the whiteboard and concentrates on one subject in a short TikTok (e.g., a difference between effect and affect, back up and backup). In most of the videos, she communicates with the audience, which is her students sitting in the classroom.	The videos usually involve the speaker himself describing the issue in question and the text appearing on the screen. In some TikTok videos, the speaker appears with his daughter.	The videos usually involve the speaker herself discussing the issue; the text is simultaneously appearing on the screen. This way of presenting the information on TikTok is called the 'talking head'. In one video, the screen was divided in two, and the speaker appeared in conversation with another TikTok presenter, which simulated a real-life conversation on the topic of pregnancy.
Speaker	The speaker is an award- winning educator who is teaching seventh- and eighth-graders. Her profile is mainly concentrated on grammar teaching. She is herself passionate about literature.	The speaker is a teacher of economics and business studies. Previously, he taught linguistics in South Korea where he had been living for 11 years.	The speaker is an English language coach who has established her online school for learning English.
Occasion	The videos are concentrated on the problematic aspects of grammar, spelling, and punctuation.	The profile is mainly concentrated on the advanced vocabulary. The speaker also makes the language and grammatical quizzes.	The main topics covered in the TikTok videos of this presenter are phrasal verbs, real-life expressions, conversation practice, and pronunciation.
Audience	It is supposed that the intended audience of the speaker is the native speakers, middle- or high- school students who are struggling with some of the most common issues in written language.	Judging from the fact that the videos involve subtitles and the speed of the information delivery, it is suggested that the intended audience of the presenter is non-native speakers. However, some of the content might also seem interesting to native speakers. For instance, the language quiz where the audience needs to guess which language the writing comes from, punctuation, and historical and geographical content.	The audience of the presenter are non-native speakers of English with some background knowledge as the speed of the material presentation is relatively slow; however, the information presented might also be useful for intermediate and upper-intermediate learners.
Purpose	In very simple language, the speaker is trying to explain some of the most troublesome aspects of writing so that the learners do not experience any worries related to the discussed issues anymore. The speaker is also trying to promote her social media page so that there are more subscribers, as in some TikTok videos the user employs embedded text with the advice to follow her for more grammar lessons.	Judging by the variety of content presented in the speaker's profile, the speaker seems to aim at a very diverse audience of non-native and native speakers. At some point, the speaker also shows the videos of his family to create trust with the audience. Whereas it is believed that the aim of this presenter is to attract as many subscribers as possible with various backgrounds and diverse interests.	The videos of this presenter are relatively short discussing one issue that might be troublesome for English language learners. From time to time, the presenter is referring to her application and online school in the videos, therefore, it is assumed that the main purpose of this TikTok profile is to attract more learners to her online courses.

Style	The speaker uses the whiteboard as she is concentrating on written language, where the visually presented information is better absorbed. However, in some cases, the format of writing on the whiteboard is not very user-friendly for TikTok users, as sometimes the whole whiteboard is not visible as the embedded text, hashtags, gifs, and other TikTok elements take a part of the screen.	The style of this speaker might be claimed as being relaxed. Sometimes, he appears in front of the camera with not brushed hair and a cup of coffee and is referring in the video to this fact, claiming that it is early morning. However, TikTok videos are well-designed, offering historical and geographical insight into the issues. The tasks are of various nature as well, gap-filling, multiple- choice, descriptive, etc.	The speaker's head is usually taking up most of the screen. She is describing the issues in a very short, concrete, and precise manner without much humor involved. The voice of the speaker is usually supported by the appearing text and some smileys.
Ethos	In order to create trust with her audience, the speaker uses her students who film her and seem to be very enthusiastic about her classes as they are actively participating trying to find the right answers to the questions.	The relaxed atmosphere in the videos and the videos offering an insight into the presenter's personal life are the means the user employs to create trust.	The links to the speaker's online language school are expected to create trust with the audience, as the online school is full of positive comments regarding the presenter, such as 'the best teacher'; 'a very warm and friendly teacher', 'a good listener'.
Pathos	The speaker uses real-life examples and humor to build an emotional connection with the audience; the language used for communication is informal so as to create a more friendly environment. The user also uses the embedded stickers (e.g., we love this, now we know) with the inclusive pronoun 'we'.	The speaker uses humor, his family portrayal, and examples from his life to build an emotional connection with the audience. The speaker is referring to the issues the audience wishes him to explain to create an impression of a reachable presenter.	The speaker employs duet conversation practice where the viewer is expected to virtually participate in a conversation with her. Sometimes, she also provides her own judgment of some issues to make them more personal.
Logos	The example sentences are supported with the grammatical rules.	The geographical, historical, and political insight on some linguistic concepts is used to support the arguments.	The expressions and phrasal verbs are supported by real-life examples. The advice given on how to immediately feel confident when speaking English (e.g., breathing, smiling, and slowing down at times) is instantly portrayed by the speaker herself.
Kairos	The videos are supposed to be of the appropriate length in relation to the intended audience, which is native speakers. The length of the videos varies depending on the difficulty of the topic of the discussion.	The videos are of the appropriate length for discussing the issue in question with the varying length of the videos depending on the topic. Sometimes the speaker gave the audience some time to think about the issue/ question and warned them about timing.	Some videos are of the appropriate length for TikTok in relation to the intended audience; the others seem to be too long (e.g., a video intended for demonstrating the right pronunciation of espresso lasts 31 seconds).

Rhetorical devices	Personification – the speaker attributes human characteristics to the words she discusses. The use of the inclusive pronoun we – 'we did it'. The constant use of the pronoun 'you' – 'you know'; 'you did'.	Allegory – the speaker uses real-life examples to portray the issue in question (e.g., for portraying a gender pay gap he used the example of him and his wife). Irony – is used very often as well.	Hyperbole – to make the message clearer, the speaker exaggerates in some places, often to an unrealistic degree.
Effectiveness	Judging by the number of followers on TikTok – 3.6 million, and the number of views on certain TikToks – up to 54.7 million, it is supposed that the speaker has reached the intended audience with the rhetorical choices used.	The user has 1.2 million followers on TikTok with the number of views of certain TikTok videos reaching up to 262.8k. The user is believed to have reached his intended audience with worthy and diverse content.	The speaker has 488 k subscribers on TikTok, with some TikTok videos reaching up to one million views. The main goal of the speaker is believed to be promoting her online school and it is expected that the speaker reaches her goal; however, sometimes it seems that videos lack her personality.

Table 2. Video analysis. Part 1

	Presenter No 4	**Presenter No 5**
Summary	The videos show the speaker's head communicating with the audience and the text appearing on the screen. The speaker does not employ any gestures and shows little emotion about the topic.	The videos show the speaker writing on the whiteboard. The main topic discussed in the videos is pronunciation. The speaker seems to be very enthusiastic about the topic.
Speaker	The speaker comes from Ireland and specializes in teaching adults wishing to improve their fluency in English.	The speaker comes from Wisconsin, US. She has been teaching English for 18 years in public school.
Occasion	The aim of TikTok videos by this speaker is to present the vocabulary, pronunciation, and grammatical points to the audience by the means of conversation practice, speaking activities, drills, and games.	The speaker says that she started making TikTok videos at the beginning of COVID restrictions when she was sitting in isolation and had nothing to do. The videos concentrate on the pronunciation and word form topics.
Audience	The speaker himself tells that his intended audience is the adults wishing to improve their fluency in English and to speak like native speakers. The learners from the elementary up to upper-intermediate level may find the videos valuable as those involve the content of various difficulties starting from numbers, animals, vegetables, and possessive pronouns up to kitchen appliances and advanced level idioms.	The intended audience is English as a second language learner with some English language background, as the speaker speaks quite fast, and employs advanced expressions. The pronunciation issues discussed in the video may be relevant to intermediate – upper-intermediate level learners. The intended audience of the speaker is believed to be the youth due to a humorous and friendly way of information delivery.

Purpose	It is believed that the main aim of this profile is to attract more subscribers, as well as to attract learners to his courses as the speaker directly refers to his one-on-one classes in his TikTok videos. Most of the content is aimed at beginner- intermediate-level learners.	The speaker herself says that making videos is fun, but it has also become her job, as, as she said, she continuously thinks about what she can make the next video about. She owns her merchandise and sells the products of her brand on Amazon. Judging from the way she presents the information, which is very enthusiastic and the information in her bio, in her TikTok profile, where a user will find the link to her merchandise, it is suggested that the presenter enjoys making the videos; however, the profile is also intended at selling products and attracting subscribers.
Style	The style of these TikTok videos is considerably cold; the presenter at some points even seems unemotional about the topic.	The videos are filmed in a humorous manner. The speaker is very emotional, gesturing all the time, emphasizing some issues with her voice.
Ethos	The speaker's character as a native speaker from Ireland is expected to create trust with the audience.	The speaker speaks about herself in the videos and adds examples from her own life.
Pathos	The speaker involves the audience in the virtual conversation by the means of giving them time to guess the names of some objects or numbers in English or participating in a virtual dialogue with the speaker.	The speaker uses humor a lot in her videos. She is constantly answering the questions posed by the users in the comments section which makes her seem reachable. She tells about some news in her life which makes the videos very personal and creates a connection between the speaker and the audience.
Logos	The words and expressions are supported by real-life examples.	Each video is supported by real-life examples, she also offers the etymology of the words.
Kairos	The videos are short and up to the point.	The videos are very well-structured in terms of timing. As concerns the vocabulary videos; it starts with a short introduction; then the audience is presented with the senses and the examples sentences, and there is always a final example sentence that either combines the studied words or presents the word in context.

Rhetorical devices	Apophasis – the speaker says that he is 'passionate about helping his students reach their learning goals' without showing any emotion.	Personification – English is treated as a living object in her speech (e.g., 'Oh, come on, English') Rhyme – 'winner-winner – chicken dinner' Hypophora – she is often asking rhetorical questions and then answers them herself. Hyperbole – the speaker exaggerates some issues to make the issue clearer to the audience. Repetition – 'you have come to another edition of which one does not belong. So, which one does not belong?' Irony – the speaker employs irony in every video. Parallelism – she uses parallel constructions for emphasis (e.g., But I love rolls! Yes, me too, I like cinnamon rolls, I like sourdough rolls').
Effectiveness	The speaker has 3.7 million subscribers on TikTok, with one of his videos even reaching 56.5 million views. The numbers suggest that the speaker successfully reaches his goal of attracting followers to his social media profile. The video where he promotes his one-on-one classes has reached 270k views which suggests that he meets the goal of attracting the learners to his classes as well. Although at some point it seems that the speaker is not enthusiastic about the topic, the videos involve valuable educational content with diversified tasks.	The speaker has 786.2 k subscribers on TikTok, with up to 230.6 k views per one TikTok. It is believed that the speaker successfully meets her goals with her TikTok profile, as those are to have fun, attract followers, and sell merchandise. The videos are very funny, natural, and relevant to non-native speakers of English. The speaker is very enthusiastic about what she is doing and is a very good promoter judging from the number of rhetorical techniques she employs in the videos.

Table 3. Video analysis. Part 2

Evaluative questionnaire of TikTok videos

The second part concerned the evaluative questionnaire completed by the students of Riga Technical University to establish the potential of TikTok as an assistant to educators in second or foreign language learning, the social media platforms the students use for language learning, and their preferences in regard to the selected TikTok presenters.

The first question was employed to establish the demographic situation and asked the respondents to indicate the age gap they are referred to. The results have shown that most of the respondents - 65% are referred to the age gap of 18-22 years. Only 13% of the respondents, or 3 people are older than 30 years (See the Figure below for the results).

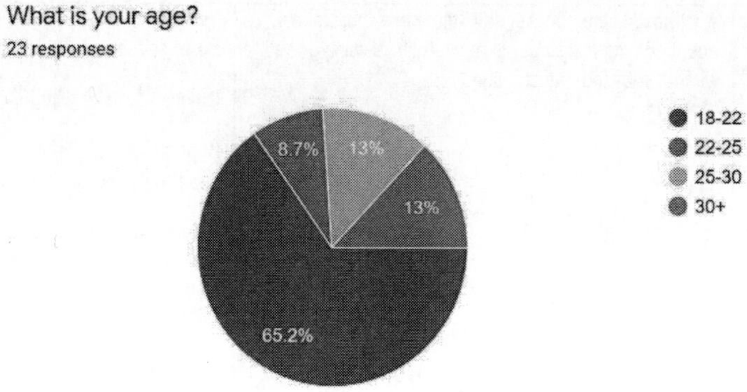

Figure 2. The demographic situation of the respondents

The second question was aimed at the establishment of whether the respondents use social media platforms for educational purposes and which platforms are employed. The results (see Figure 3 for results) suggest that five learners or 21% of the respondents do not use any social media for educational purposes. The social media platforms used by the learners for language learning were YouTube (which was mentioned by seven respondents), TikTok and Instagram (were indicated by six learners), Facebook (which was claimed as being used by five students), and one learner stated that he or she uses LinkedIn for educational purposes.

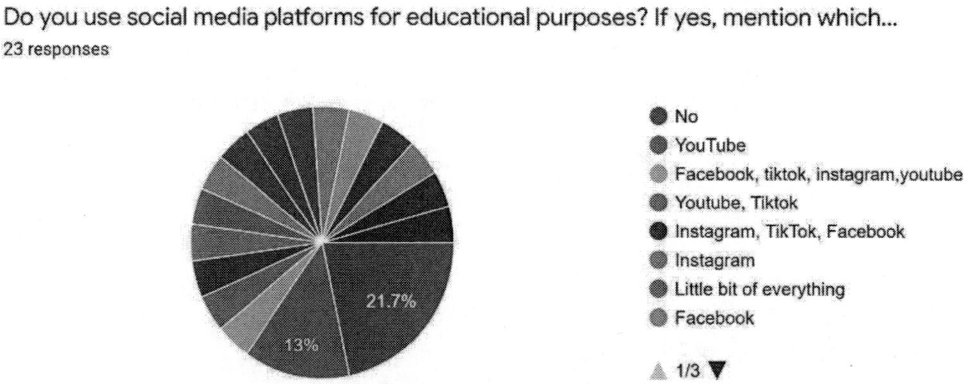

Figure 3. Social media platforms used for educational purposes

The following question was intended to establish for which reasons the respondents use TikTok. It was found out that eight respondents or almost 35% do not use TikTok at all. 10 people or 43.5% suggested that they use TikTok for both educational and entertainment purposes, and five participants or 21.7% claimed that they use TikTok solely for entertainment purposes. None of the respondents indicated that they use the platform solely for educational reasons (see Figure 4 for results).

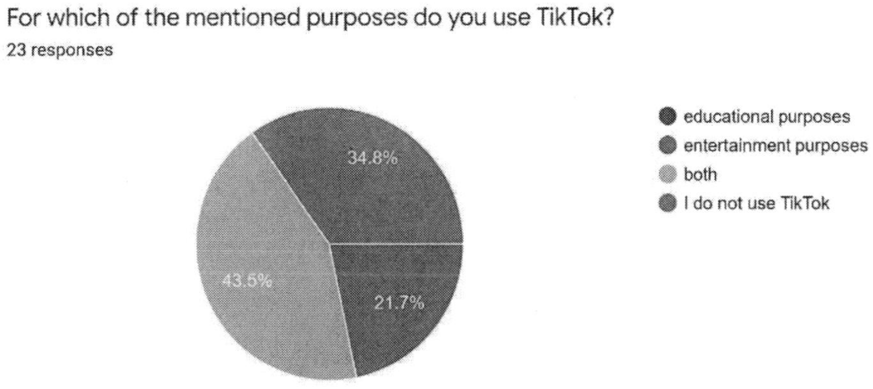

Figure 4. The reasons why the respondents use TikTok

The following question was aimed at those who selected that they do not use TikTok at all in the previous question. The respondents were supposed to mark which social media do they use for educational purposes from the ones listed. It turned out that the majority use WhatsApp (three respondents), and Instagram was marked as being used by two students. The rest have selected YouTube, LinkedIn, Telegram, and Facebook, which were all indicated by one learner (see Figure 5 for results).

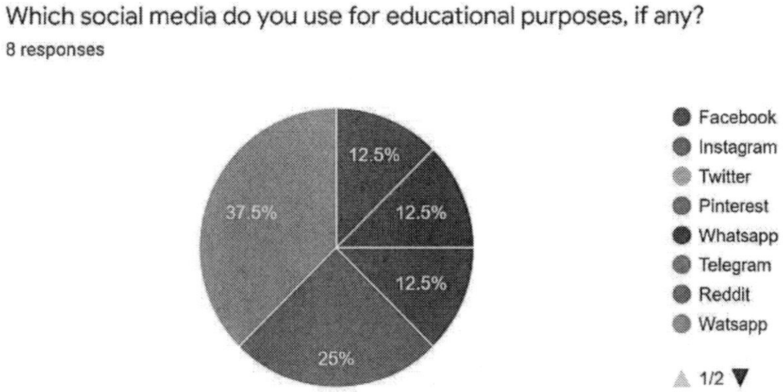

Figure 5. Social media used for educational purposes by the respondents who do not utilize TikTok

The following group of questions was intended for the evaluation of TikTok videos filmed by Presenter No 1. As regards the analysis of the presenter, the majority of the learners or 70% suggested that the presenter is confident and enthusiastic, more than half of the respondents, or 52.2% described her as being professional, and 47.8% claimed that the presenter is interested, passionate and confident. Concerning the style, it was described as fluent, articulate, and eloquent (by 10, nine, and eight learners respectively). Five students suggested that it was smooth and formal. When being asked whether this style is the best to get the information across, the opinions of the learners were divided between yes (marked by 50% of the respondents), no (selected by 40.9%), and other options provided by the learners, which were 'yes and no', and 'it depends on the subject'. The content of TikTok videos was characterized as being informative and interesting (marked by eight and seven learners respectively). Two students have classified it as being chaotic and interactive. When asked to evaluate the TikTok videos on a scale from 1 to 10, most of the students, or eight people assigned it a grade of 8 points; five learners gave it a grade of 7 points (see Figure 6 for results). The mean grade assigned to this TikTok presenter is 6.65 points.

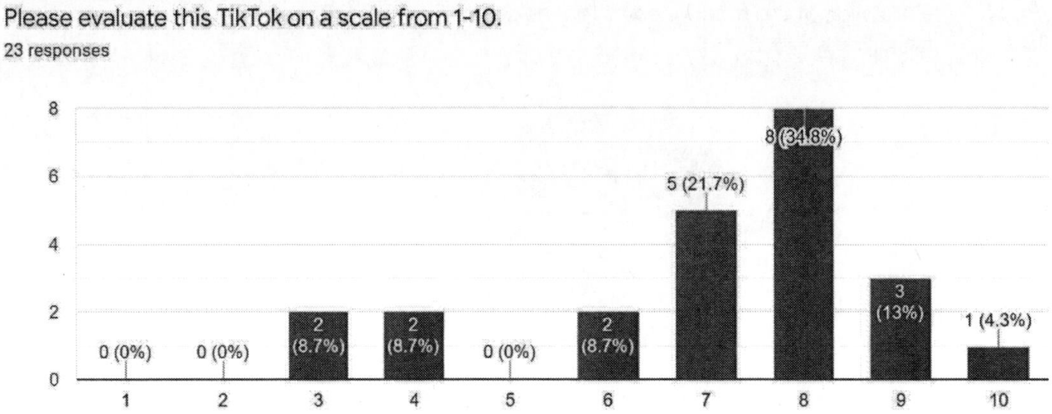

Figure 6. Presenter No 1 evaluation

The next presenter whose TikTok videos were evaluated was Presenter No 2. As concerns the presenter himself, the majority of the respondents evaluated him as being interested, confident, experienced, and professional (marked by 15, 14, 13, and 12 learners respectively). 10 people or 43.5% suggested that the presenter is enthusiastic, while nine students characterized him as being a trustworthy and passionate speaker. What concerns the style of TikTok videos, it was classified as being eloquent by more than half of the respondents, or 12 learners. 43.5% suggested that the style is fluent; 30.4% characterized it as being smooth and persuasive, and 26.1% stated that the style is articulate. In the following question, 86.4% claimed that this style is the best to get the information across, while three people disagreed with the claim. The content of this TikTok was described as being informative (marked by nine learners), interesting (selected by five students), meaningful, and concrete (which were identified by three respondents). When asked to evaluate this TikTok presenter on a scale from 1 to 10, 34.8% of the respondents assessed the performance with eight points, five people assigned nine points, and four learners seven (see Figure 7 for results). The mean grade assigned to this TikTok presenter is 8.04.

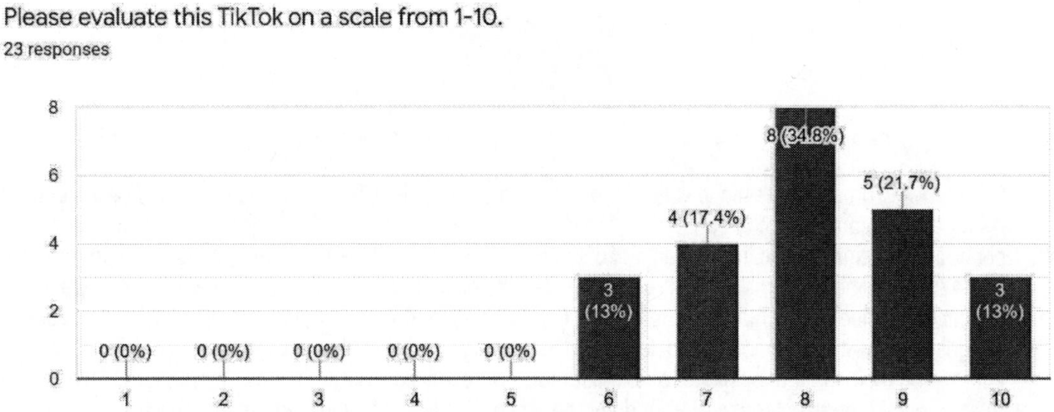

Figure 7. Presenter No 2 evaluation

The following presenter whose TikTok videos were evaluated by the students is Presenter No

The presenter was evaluated as being experienced and professional by the majority of the respondents (13 and 12 learners respectively). Moreover, 10 students assessed the presenter as being confident and interested; seven viewed her as trustworthy and passionate. However, two participants suggested that the presenter was unprofessional, impassionate, and unenthusiastic, one found her untrustworthy. As regards the style of the videos, it was characterized as being fluent (suggested by 11 respondents), articulate (marked by nine learners), smooth (indicated by eight students), persuasive and eloquent (which was selected by seven participants). 61.9% of the respondents believed that this style is the best to get the information across, while 28.6% disagreed with the statement. One person stated in the other section that the style is too narrative, the other claimed that it is a good style for beginners. The content of the videos was described as informative by seven respondents; six learners claimed that it was monotonous and five classified it as interesting. The options meaningful, boring, trivial, chaotic, and interactive were selected by one of the participants. In the question devoted to the evaluation of this TikTok, a major part of the respondents assessed it with eight points (six students selected this option), nine points (chosen by five learners), and seven points (specified by four participants) (see Figure 8 for results). The mean grade assigned to this TikTok presenter is 7.3 points.

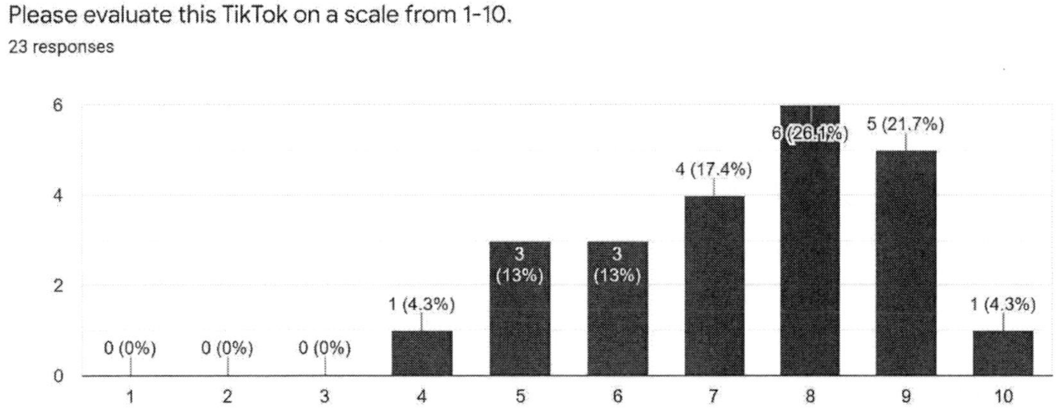

Figure 8. Presenter No 3 evaluation

The next speaker whose TikTok videos' evaluation was performed by the students in the questionnaire was Presenter No 4. In the first question, the students selected the following adjectives to describe the presenter: professional (which was selected by 10 respondents), experienced (which was indicated by eight students), trustworthy and interested (both were chosen by seven learners), and confident (which was specified by six participants).

Nevertheless, five learners have found this speaker impassionate and unenthusiastic and three described him as uninterested. As regards the style of the videos, it was viewed as being articulate by eight respondents, smooth and fluent by seven learners, formal by six students; and four people described it as vague, eloquent, and persuasive. More than half of the respondents, or 63.6% did not believe that this style is the best to get the information across, whereas the rest agreed with the statement. The content of the videos was claimed as being monotonous, boring, informative, interesting, dry and concrete (selected by nine, four, four, three, two, and one respondent respectively). Most of the respondents evaluated the TikTok videos filmed by this presenter with a grade of five, seven, and six points (six, five, and four learners respectively) (see Figure 9 for results). The mean grade assigned to this TikTok presenter's videos is 6.52.

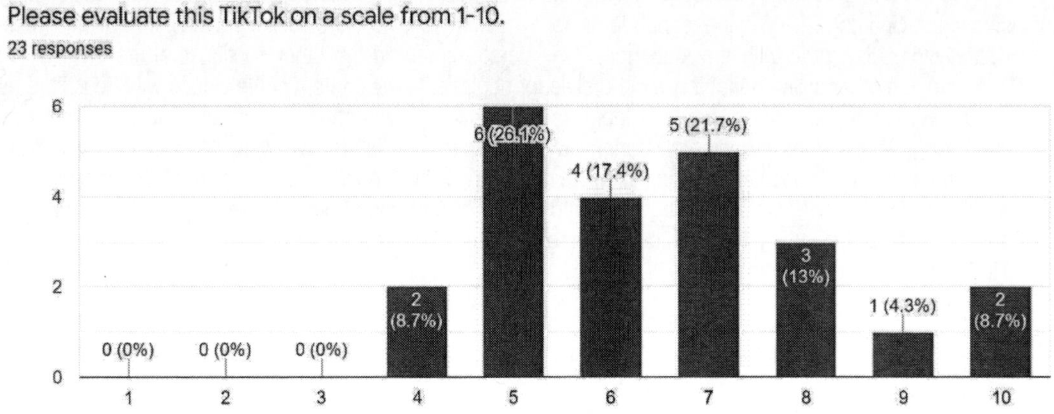

Figure 9. Presenter No 4 evaluation

The last TikTok presenter the videos of whom the students evaluated in the questionnaire was Presenter No 5. More than half of the respondents viewed this presenter as being interested and enthusiastic (the options were selected by 16 people), experienced (which was chosen by 15 respondents), and passionate (14 learners selected this option). The other evaluative adjectives selected by the respondents to describe the presenter were: confident, trustworthy, and professional (chosen by 10, nine, and eight learners respectively). The adjectives selected by the majority of the respondents to describe the style of the videos are fluent, persuasive, smooth, and eloquent (marked by 12, 10, nine, and nine respondents respectively). 90.9% believed that it is the best style to get the information across, two people did not agree with this statement. The following are the adjectives that the respondents chose to assess the content of these videos: interesting, informative, chaotic, and interactive (indicated by 16, three, two, and one people respectively). A major part of the learners marked the videos with a grade of eight, seven, nine, or ten (which were selected by eight, six, three, and three students respectively) (see Figure 10 for results). The mean grade assigned to the videos filmed by this TikTok presenter is 7.48 points.

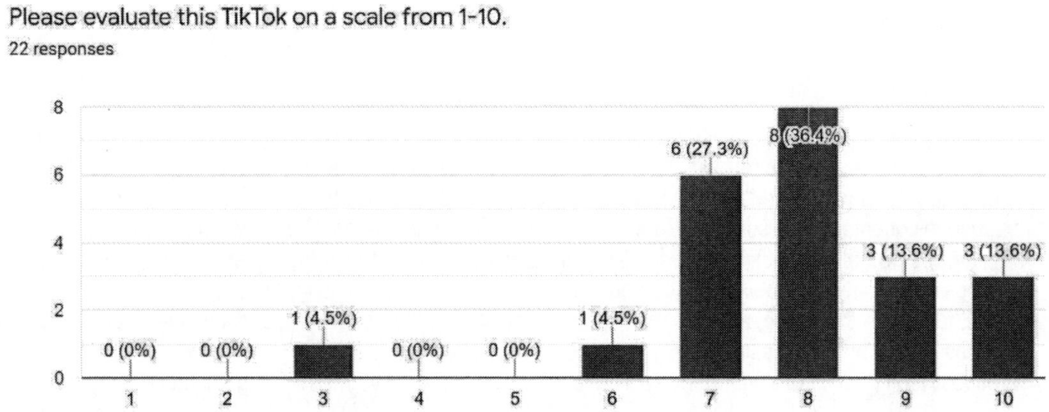

Figure 10. Presenter No 5 evaluation

The last question concerned the respondents' opinion on whether TikTok has a future in language learning and teaching. Most of the respondents or almost 70% responded in the affirmative; 26.1% selected the option 'maybe' and one person supposed that TikTok does not have any potential in language teaching and learning (see Figure 11 for results).

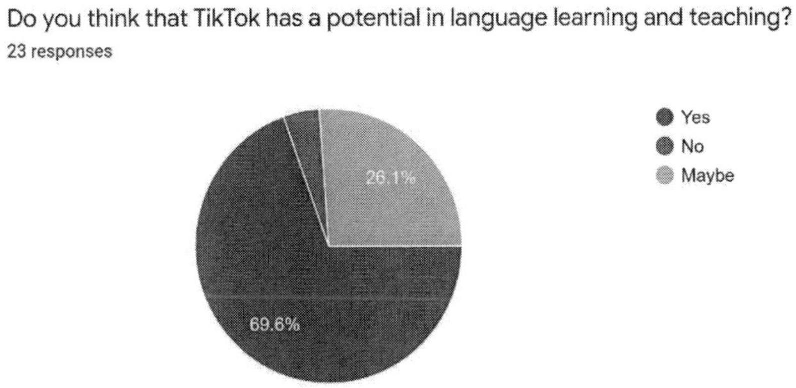

Figure 11. Potential of TikTok in language learning and teaching

Conclusions

The theoretical research has suggested that learners in the digital era absorb information better when they are presented with short sessions concentrated on one learning objective in contrast with the long, uninterrupted, monotonous sessions with multiple learning objectives. Numerous studies have also proved that the application of multimedia in second or foreign language learning improves student motivation, interest, and learning results.

Digital rhetoric refers to the study of communication happening in the digital world, the theory of how knowledge is constructed in the digital environment, and how Internet users shape this knowledge using the vast variety of the new rhetorical means available in the digital setting. The rhetorical analysis of digital texts embodies the analysis of the visual and oral rhetorical means the user employs to reach the rhetorical aims set, which may be of various nature, such as to entertain, inform, educate, sell, attract, create awareness, or persuade the audience.

As regards the rhetorical analysis of the videos filmed by five TikTok presenters employed by the researchers and the students in the evaluation questionnaire, it revealed that TikTok presenter whose videos were the most highly evaluated by the students was Presenter No 2. The presenter uses irony very often in his videos, the style of information delivery can be described as being the most relaxed and open, the speaker offers the largest variety of educational content from the selected speakers, gives an insight into his personal life, employs the real-life examples and the content produced by the speaker is aimed at the diverse intended audience of various background knowledge and interest. The second speaker in terms of assessment was Presenter No 5. Of the selected speakers, the videos of this presenter employ the greatest number of rhetorical strategies used, one of which is irony. The speaker also shares the news from her personal life, gestures a lot, and is very enthusiastic about the topics. The speaker who received third place in terms of assessment was Presenter No 3. The presenter's style of information delivery is an example of the so-called 'talking head', which is a user-friendly method for TikTok users. The speaker shares her opinion about some concepts discussed to make them less theoretical and mimics some concepts to better get the message across. The fourth place in terms of assessment took Presenter No 1. The reason why the speaker has been evaluated worse than some of the others might be the fact that the content is not specifically created for TikTok as these are just the recorded classes, the images, text, GIFs, and smileys appearing on the screen made some of the text written on the whiteboard not visible, as well as the idea that the intended audience of the speaker is the native speakers; therefore, the speed of the information delivery was quite fast. The last speaker in terms of assessment is Presenter No 2. Although the speaker's intended audience is of various background knowledge and the types of tasks are of diverse nature, the main reason why the major part of the learners liked the content produced by this speaker less than the one produced by the others was the fact that the learners have found the speaker's style monotonous and lacking his personal self.

Overall, it may be concluded that the ideas that the learners in the digital age value the most in online educators are humor, the diversity of the content, the variety of the material presentation techniques, the insight into personal life, and real-life examples.

References:

1. Abdulaziz Al Fadda, H. (2020). Determining How Social Media Affects Learning English: An Investigation of Mobile Applications Instagram and Snap Chat in TESOL Classroom. *Arab World English Journal*, 11(1): 3–11. DOI: 10.24093/awej/vol11no1.1
2. Akkara, S., Anumula, V. S., & Mallampalli, M. S. (2020). Impact of whatsapp interaction on IMPROVING L2 speaking skills. *International Journal of Emerging Technologies in Learning (iJET)*, 15(3): 250-262. DOI: 10.3991/ijet.v15i03.11534
3. Arfiandhani, P. (2020). Utilizing Facebook Groups in Teaching English as Foreign Language: Indonesian EFL Teachers' Voices. *International Journal of Language Teaching and Education*, 4(1): 53–60. DOI:10.22437/ijolte.v4i1.10197
4. Aristotle. (1991). *On rhetoric: A theory of civic discourse.* Trans. George Kennedy. New York: Oxford University Press.
5. Armstrong, S. J. & Sadler-Smith, E. (2008). Learning on demand, at your own pace, in rapid bite-sized chunks: the future shape of management development?. *Academy of Management Learning & Education*, 7(4): 571-586.
6. Baddeley, A., Gathercole, S. & Papagno, C. (1998). The phonological loop as a language learning device. *Psychological review*, 105(1): 158.
7. Bizzell, P. & Herzberg, B. (2000). *The rhetorical tradition: Readings from classical times to the present (2nd ed.).* Boston: Bedford/St. Martin's.
8. Brent, D. (1997). Rhetorics of the web: Implications for teachers of literacy. *Kairos: A Journal of Rhetoric, Technology, and Pedagogy*, 2(1): http://kairos.technorhetoric.net/2.1/features/brent/bridge.html
9. Buchanan, R. (1989). Declaration by design: Rhetoric, argument, and demonstration in design practice. In Victor Margolin (Ed.), *Design discourse: History, theory, criticism* (91–109). Chicago: University of Chicago Press.
10. Burke, K. J. (1966). *Language as symbolic action: Essays on life, literature, and method.* Berkley: University of California Press.
11. Burns, R. (1985). Information Impact and Factors Affecting Recall. Presented at the *Annual National Conference on Teaching Excellence and Conference of Administrators*, Austin, USA
12. Centre for Digital Media (n.d.) What is Digital Media? Available from: https://thecdm.ca/program/digital-media [Accessed on June 14, 2022].
13. Dahlstrom, E., Brooks, D. C., Grajek, S. & Reeves, J. (2015). *ECAR Study of Students and Information Technology.* Research report. Louisville, CO: ECAR, December 2015
14. Eyman, D. (2018). *Digital Rhetoric. Theory, Method, Practice.* USA: University of Michigan.
15. Gray, C. (2015). *Designing online education for work based learners: Refining bite sized learning* (Doctoral dissertation, Abertay University).
16. Haerazi, H., Utama, I. M., & Hidayatullah, H. (2020). Mobile Applications to Improve English writing skills viewed from critical thinking ability for pre-service teachers. *International Journal of Interactive Mobile Technologies (iJIM)*, 14(7): 58– 64. DOI:10.3991/ijim.v14i07.11900
17. Hattie, J., & Yates, G. C. (2013). *Visible learning and the science of how we learn.* Routledge: London.
18. Hayes, C., Stott, K., Lamb, K. J., & Hurst, G. A. (2020). "Making Every Second Count": Utilizing TikTok and Systems Thinking to Facilitate Scientific Public Engagement and Contextualization of Chemistry at Home. *Journal of Chemical Education*, 97(10).
19. Heba, G. (1997). Hyperrhetoric: Multimedia, literacy, and the future of composition.
20. *Computers and Composition*, 14: 19–44
21. Hymes, D., Lyons, J., & Kermode, F. (1972). A review of Lyons, Noam Chomsky. *Noam Chomsky: Critical Assessments. Language*, 48(2): 416–427. DOI:10.2307/412143

22. Jacobs, A., Pan, Y. & Ho, Y. (2022). More than just engaging? TikTok as an effective learning tool. *The 27th Academy for Information Systems International Conference (UKAIS 2022)*. USA: California State University.

23. Job, M. A., & Ogalo, H. S. (2012). Micro learning as innovative process of knowledge strategy. *International journal of scientific & technology research*, 1(11): 92-96.

24. Lanham, R. (1992). Digital rhetoric: Theory, practice, and property. In Myron Tuman (Ed.), *Literacy online: The promise (and peril) of reading and writing with computers* (221–43). Pittsburgh, PA: University of Pittsburgh Press.

25. Madzlan, N. A., Seng, G. H., & Kesevan, H. V. (2020). Use of video blogs in Alleviating public speaking anxiety Among ESL learners. Journal of Education and E-Learning Research, 7(1): 93-99. DOI:10.20448/journal.509.2020.71.93.99

26. Manning, K. D., Spicer, J. O., Golub, L., Akbashev, M., & Klein, R. (2021). The micro revolution: effect of Bite-Sized Teaching (BST) on learner engagement and learning in postgraduate medical education. BMC medical education, 21(1), 1-11.

27. Mayer, R. E. (2003). The promise of multimedia learning: using the same instructional design methods across different media. Learning and instruction, 13(2), 125-139.

28. Mayer, R. E., & Moreno, R. (2003). Nine ways to reduce cognitive load in multimedia learning. Educational psychologist, 38(1), 43-52.

29. Miller, F.J. (2002), "I= 0-(Information has no intrinsic meaning)", Information Research, 8(1).

30. Montaner, S. (2020). EFL written competence through Twitter in mobile version in compulsory secondary education. Global Journal of Foreign Language Teaching, 10(2): 101-110. DOI:10.18844/gjflt.v10i2.4665

31. Otchie, W. O. & Pedaste, M. (2020). Using Social Media for Learning in High Schools: A Systematic Literature Review. European Journal of Educational Research, 9(2): 12–16. DOI:10.12973/eu-jer.9.2.889

32. Palmer, K. (n.d.) Diving into Rhetoric. Available from: https://divingintorhetoric.pressbooks.com/chapter/rhetorical-analysis-of-digital-texts/ [Accessed on June 14, 2022].

33. Piaget, J. (2000), Piaget's theory of cognitive development, Childhood Cognitive Development: The Essential Readings, 33–47.

34. Putrawan, G. E. & Riadi, B. (2020) English as a foreign LANGUAGE (efl) Learners' predominant language use for Online informal learning activities through smartphones in Indonesian Context. Universal Journal of Educational Research, 8(2): 695-699. DOI:10.13189/ujer.2020.080243

35. Richards, I. A. (1930). Practical criticism: A study of literary judgment. London: Kegan Paul, Trench, Tubner & Co.

36. So, S. (2016). Mobile instant messaging support for teaching and learning in higher education. The Internet and Higher Education, 31, 32-42.

37. Stahl, S. M., Davis, R. L., Kim, D. H., Lowe, N. G., Carlson, R. E., Fountain, K., & Grady, M. M. (2010). Play it again: The master psychopharmacology program as an example of interval learning in bite-sized portions. CNS spectrums, 15(8), 491-504.

38. Syah, R. J., Nurjanah, S., & Mayu, V. P. A. (2020). Tikio (TikTok App Educational Video) Based on the Character Education of Newton's Laws Concepts Preferred to Learning for Generation Z. Pancaran Pendidikan, 9(4): 132-143. DOI:10.25037/pancaran.v9i4.325

39. TikTok (2022). About TikTok. Retrieved from: https://www.tiktok.com/about?lang=en [Available on June 6, 2022].

40. TikTok Statistics (2021). Retrieved from: https://wallaroomedia.com/blog/social- media/tiktok-statistics/#:~:text=Total%20App%20Downloads%20%E2%80%93%20The%20TikTo k,TikTok%20had%2062%20million%20downloads. [Available on June 9, 2022].

41. Velleman, P. F., & Moore, D. S. (1996). Multimedia for teaching statistics: Promises and pitfalls. The American Statistician, 50(3), 217-225.

42. Wang, S. and Noe, R.A. (2010). Knowledge sharing: A review and directions for future research. Human Resource Management Review, 20(2): 115–131.

43. Warnick, B. (2007). Rhetoric online: Persuasion and politics on the World Wide Web. New York: Peter Lang.

44. Weintraub, R. S., & Martineau, J. W. (2002). The just-in-time imperative. Training & Development Journal, 51-57.

45. Wongsa, M. & Son, J. (2020). Enhancing Thai secondary school Students' English speaking skills, attitudes and motivation with drama-based activities and Facebook. Innovation in Language Learning and Teaching, 15(2): 103-194. DOI:10.1080/17501229.2020.1853134

46. Wu, L. (2020). Comparative analysis of Video stories and user behaviors on WeChat And TikTok. Proceedings of the 2020 3rd International Conference on Humanities Education and Social Sciences (ICHESS 2020), 13(2): 113-124. DOI:10.2991/assehr.k.201214.518

47. Xiong, Y., & Zhou, Y. (2018). Understanding East Asian Graduate Students' Socio- cultural and Psychological Adjustment in a U.S. Midwestern University. Journal of International Students, 8(2): 769–794. DOI:10.32674/jis.v8i2.103

48. Xuiwen, Z. & Bakar Razali, A. (2021). An Overview of the Utilization of TikTok to Improve Oral English Communication Competence among EFL Undergraduate Students. Universal Journal of Educational Research, 9(7): 1439-1451.

49. Xu, L., Yan, X., & Zhang, Z. (2019). Research on the causes of the "TikTok" app becoming popular and the existing problems. Journal of Advanced Management Science, 7(2): 59-63. DOI:10.18178/joams.7.2.59-63

50. Yuxin Yang (2020). Understanding Young Adults' TikTok Usage. Unpublished Undergraduate Thesis. USA: Louisiana State University.

51. Zam Zam Al Arif, T. (2019). The Use of Social Media For English Language Learning: An Exploratory Study of EFL University Students. Metathesis: Journal of English Language, Literature, and Teaching, 3(2): 224–233. DOI:10.31002/metathesis.v3i2.1921

52. Zappen, J. P. (2005). Digital rhetoric: Toward an integrated theory. Technical Communication Quarterly, 14(3): 319–25.

53. Zhou, L., Xi, Y., & Lochtman, K. (2020). The relationship between second language competence and willingness to communicate: The moderating effect of foreign Language Anxiety. Journal of Multilingual and Multicultural Development, 43(11): 1-15. DOI:10.1080/01434632.2020.1801697

Shaping the Digital Transformation of the Education Ecosystem in Europe
EDEN Digital Learning Europe Proceedings
2022 Annual Conference | Tallinn, 20-22 June, 2022
ISSN: 2707-2819

REFLECTION OF EXPERIENTIAL LEARNING IN DUAL STUDY PROGRAMMES – A MODEL

Nicole Geier, Laura Eigbrecht, Ulf-Daniel Ehlers,

DHBW Karlsruhe, Baden-Wuerttemberg Cooperative State University

Abstract

The article presents a conceptual reflection model including intentional and spontaneous points of reflection in work-integrated (dual) study programs. Based on the reflection cycles of David Kolb (1975), Graham Gibbs (1988) and Donald Schön (1983), it models the process that learners go through when reflecting on key experiences in their theoretical and practical study phases. The aim is to identify learning experiences within these two learning spaces throughout the whole student life cycle that help students to develop learner agency, reflective competence, and Future Skills to establish personal action theories, which form the basis of their ability to design personal life courses and work environments and master general societal challenges. Students will collect the reflection of these learning experiences in an e-portfolio and thus create their individual Future Skills passes.

Keywords: Reflection Model, E-Portfolio, Experiential Learning.

Introduction

The integration of work-based learning and practical phases in study programs has been gaining popularity over the last years, which becomes obvious from the fact that for instance dual study programs in Germany gained 260 % of students between 2014 and 2019. The number of study programmes increased from 512 to 1.622 (Bundesinstitut für Berufsbildung [BIBB], 2020, p. 12). Still, one of the biggest challenges to overcome is to fully exploit the potential that the interlink between theory and practice holds for the competence development of students (Deuer & Wild, 2018). A reasonable amount of practical phases during the study programme is not sufficient to achieve the qualification goal of the duality (Fasshauer & Anselmann, 2021, 17f.), which is to support students in developing scientifically sound professional action competence (Beaugrand et al., 2017, p. 19) to make them capable of mastering complex and rapidly changing situations (Seifried et al., 2021). The dovetailing of the two learning spaces is a key factor in generating benefits compared to "classic" degree programs. The inclusion of professional/practical (learning) experiences in the theoretical studies and vice versa is essential (Wissenschaftsrat, 2013). This results in three special features of dual study programs compared to "classic" ones without practical phases:

- Different action-guiding maxims in the learning locations: The university focuses on fulfilling the educational mission. The partner organisations usually pursue primarily economic interests (with the exception of social institutions with a service mission) (Beaugrand et al., 2017).
- Double logic of action: Professional action is based on the two aspects of
- (1) scientific competence in order to understand the logic of theoretical constructs and procedures and (2) hermeneutic competence in order to be able to fathom and successfully manage the contradictions inherent in practice and special "cases" in everyday professional life (Beaugrand et al., 2017 according to Oevermann 1981; Darmann-Finck et al., 2013), because "[t]he action in practice is characterised by situational complexity, heterogeneity and a residue of uncertainty" (Jahncke-Lattek, 2010, p. 19).
- Different forms of knowledge: Dual degree programmes combine the orientation towards scientific knowledge and knowledge of action in equal measure, which is why experiences of practice must not only be perceived and accepted, but must be explored through a scientific and reflexive approach (Beaugrand et al., 2017; Brodsky et al., 2021).

Under these conditions, the integration of opportunities for transfer-oriented, self- directed, reflexive learning into the curricula and the associated didactic forms of action represent both a special opportunity and a challenge (Kupfer et al., 2014; Meyer, 2012). The connection between the two learning locations must not exist exclusively through the students as "boundary crossers" (cf. "connectivity approach" by Aprea et al., 2020), but requires a common understanding of the higher education institution and the partner organisations about how they can jointly support the students' competence learning in both locations (Fasshauer & Anselmann, 2021, p. 20). For the concrete implementation, practice reflections at the beginning of each theory phase (Beaugrand et al., 2017, 35f.), regular feedback discussions with teachers and trainers, and the more concrete integration of reflection reports into the practice phases are recommended (Brodsky et al., 2021, pp. 133–136).

Therefore, this article presents an option to bring these recommendations into reality and aims at providing a discussion basis for integrating (future) skill development through reflection into work-integrated study programs. In the following section 2, we present the DIRK Dual project currently run at Baden-Wuerttemberg Cooperative State University (DHBW) in which we conceive a reflection and e-portfolio concept. In section 3, we describe the theoretical basics of experiential learning and reflection on which we build our reflection model for the dual study program – the core topic of this article. This model, which is explained in section 4, is intended to support reflection processes in dual study programs. We conclude by a brief summary of the model's key facts in section 5.

The DIRK Dual project at Baden-Wuerttemberg Cooperative State University: Developing a digital reflection tool for competence development in dual studies

Within the DIRK Dual (Digital reflection tool for competence development in dual studies) initiative, we develop a concept that aims at developing the first digital portfolio-based tool for self-directed competence development based on reflecting the interlink between theory and practice phases within the dual study programme.

Aim of the project

DIRK Dual is being developed at the DHBW to support the interlink of theory and practice phases for students in dual study programs to promote their competence development. The digital tool will complement the currently rather activity-focused documentation the students' practical phases to promote cyclical, reflective learning throughout the whole student lifecycle and to open it up for coaching and peer learning processes. For this aim, the tool must be developed in harmony with the needs and usability demands of all stakeholders involved, i. e. students, teachers and program directors, instructors/trainers at the cooperating organizations. Consequently, the tools and materials are being developed in close cooperation with students and dual practice partners.

Current state of the project

Based on a participatory design thinking workshop involving students, practice partners and university teachers, a model of reflection for competence development in dual study programs has been developed. It includes the needs of and challenges faced by the different stakeholder groups, which we identified in the workshop. This is the fundament for designing the first prototype materials that will become part of the DIRK Dual e-portfolio concept. Students and practice partners already tested and evaluated the first prototypes on different aspects such as usability, design and if they actually support reflection practices in the dual study experience. Currently, these are being integrated in an organizational/process model in co-creation with all stakeholders. The next step will be to specify the technical implementation of the e-portfolio tool and start the first pilot phase at the end of 2022.

Theoretical basics of experiential learning and reflection

The goal is to support students in developing learner agency, which metaphorically means students sit in the driver seat for their own learning journey. They need to become actively involved in designing their learning paths, including goals and the steps to reach them, in formal, informal, and non-formal learning contexts (Schoon, 2018). "Agency implies self-determination, the ability to make one's own choices, to select and create the developmental environment and create new values" (Schoon, 2018, p. 5). Especially meaningful interactions with other people and collaboration within a community help to foster the development of learner agency (Larsen-Freeman et al., 2021), which is why experiential learning and reflection are suitable ways of enabling the growth of learner agency.

The high potential of experiential learning lies primarily in the fact that it supports competence development by focusing on the development of possibilities for action and goes beyond the mere acquisition of knowledge (Fuchs & Rogmann, 2012 according to Chur 2004). It is "a didactic model based on the assumption that only a direct, practical engagement with a learning object enables a learner to learn effectively and meaningfully. In this model, learning presupposes a concrete experience with a real character outside artificial learning environments"[4] (Stangl, 2022). Accordingly, it is also particularly suitable for the development of Future Skills (FS).

David Kolb's four-stage learning cycle highlights reflective practice as an instrument whereby learners draw conclusions from experiences and then derive ideas from them. The intention is to transfer the learnings to new experiences, completing the learning cycle. Kolb's model aims both at using own experiences and at actively involving learners in the learning process in order to achieve personal development (Kolb & Kolb, 2018). Experience in this context does not mean simple, everyday experiences, but individually significant "deep experiences", which are characterized, for example, as circumstances that strongly irritate one's own world, such as when one is "stuck" with a problem (Kolb & Kolb, 2018, p. 9). For everyday university life, this means that teachers should create learning opportunities in which corresponding experiences can be made, e.g. through excursions, role plays or experiments. In the dual study program, the practical phases, among others, are suitable for this. A detailed explanation of the reflection model is given in Kolb & Kolb, 2018.

Building on Kolb's reflection cycle, Gibbs' reflection model emerged, which supports reflection on experiences by asking clearly formulated questions, involving a bias-free description, feelings/emotions, an evaluation and analysis of the learner's actions, a conclusion, and designing an action plan (Gibbs, 1988).

Another well-known approach is Donald Schön's Reflective Practitioner approach. It distinguishes between reflection-in-action and reflection-on-action with the aim of helping learners become aware of their tacit knowledge and learn from their practical experiences (Finlay, 2008, p. 3). Reflection-on-action is anchored in the active phase, the phase of doing. It encourages the development of one's own capacity for reflection during a performance of action in a concrete practical situation. This is helpful when unforeseen events and/or obstacles to action occur within the action situation. The aim is to reflect on the action while the situation is still being experienced, i.e. ad-hoc, and to consider, if necessary try out and re-evaluate alternative action concepts. Reflection on the action looks at the action retrospectively and starts with considerations of how the experience can be further developed. Schön acknowledges the importance of reflection "to find out how our knowledge in the action might have contributed to an unexpected result" (Schön, 1983, p. 26) and to develop individual concepts for future action practice.

In terms of learning through reflection, Kolb's four-stage cycle is the relevant model on which a reflection model for dual studies can be based. Gibbs has supplemented this basis with questions that support learners in the reflection process by being more concretely formulated than the four steps in Kolb's cycle. Schön frames these two concepts to a certain extent by not only addressing the reflection of individual experiences or their contribution to development as a whole, but also by questioning the learners' action strategies as an additional dimension in order to support them in developing their own theory of action. All three models explain the power of reflection for the development of learner agency, i.e., self-regulated, motivated, participatory and engaged learning. Therefore, these models build the foundation for experiential learning and reflection in the e-portfolio approach for dual study programs.

Construction of a conceptional model for reflection in dual study programs

For the alternating dual study program as practiced at DHBW, we have developed a three-levelled conceptional model for reflecting experiential learning in dual study programs that draws on the reflection models of Kolb, Gibbs and Schön and includes various intentional and spontaneous points of reflection, which are supported by guiding instruments and documented in an e-portfolio.

[4] Translated by the authors

Level 1 (Fig. 1): The idea is to empower students to go through a continuous progression in building learner agency and developing FS through the continuous reflection of experiences (enlarging spiral). For that purpose, we use Kolb's and Gibbs' models, but extend the conceptual framework by Schön's idea to not only see reflection as a skill, but rather support the learners in developing their own theory of action, accompanying them on their way to becoming reflective practitioners. This level is relevant to show learners that their actions are based on certain basic assumptions and that these can both manifest in patterns and change over time. In this process, reflection serves as a fundamental learning principle that enriches the learning of theoretical knowledge in a complementary way and is interlinked with it. In terms of learning theory, the practical phase as a specific feature of the dual study program is a special space of experiential learning, which enables the development of action competences through reflection on professional actions par excellence. In order to operationalize the theoretical models of Kolb and Schön, we developed a pattern for reflection around intentional points of reflection (IPORs) and spontaneous ones (SPORs) that are

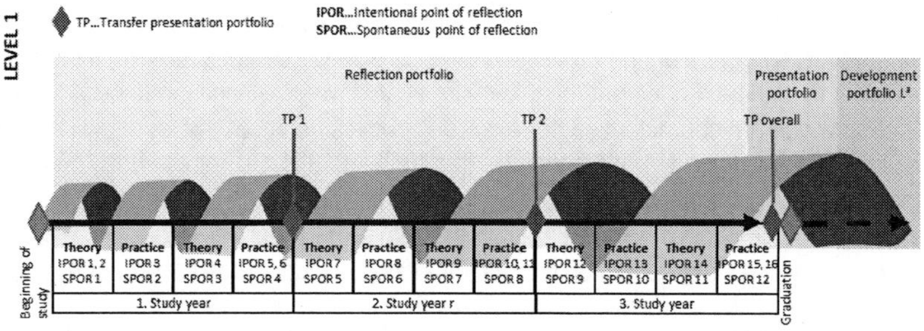

Fig. 1. First level of a conception model for reflection in dual study programs

documented as artefacts in a reflection portfolio. At the end of each study year, students reflect on their previous IPORs and SPORs and select key experiences, which are then transferred to their presentation portfolio (blue rhombs) (classification according to the e-portfolio typology of Baumgartner, 2012).

Level 2 (Fig. 2): It shows an exemplary academic year with theory and practice phases, in which there are various IPORs and SPORs. At each of these IPORs and SPORs, learners apply Kolb's reflection steps. The intention is to provide guidance for a minimum number of IPORs and SPORs during each study year. Program directors and/or dual partners are responsible for the concrete design of IPORs suitable for the respective study program and learners are responsible for planning and choosing relevant SPORs. The examples in figure two refer to the program Business Administration Service Management - Media, Sales and Communication at DHBW Heilbronn.

Level 3 (Fig. 3): For these reflection processes, we have developed a set of tools guiding learners through the process. At the beginning, students are supposed to at-tend a FS workshop where they learn about basics of competence development and have the opportunity to self-assess their FS. The goal of the workshop is that every student projects their career and personal life, identifying relevant skills they want to develop in the course of their study. These development goals and respective steps to reach them will be documented in a personal action/development plan (field a). This plan will be used as a reference for all IPORs and SPORs that are supported by tools/instruments (field b) and documented in the reflection portfolio (field c), for the coaching/mentoring talks and peer feedback (field d) as well as thresholds where key experiences are reflected again (field e) and transferred to the presentation portfolio (field f). Specific tools we are developing at the moment are for instance a FS self-assessment matrix, guidelines for video-based self-reflection, and a guideline for peer- feedback on reflection documentations.

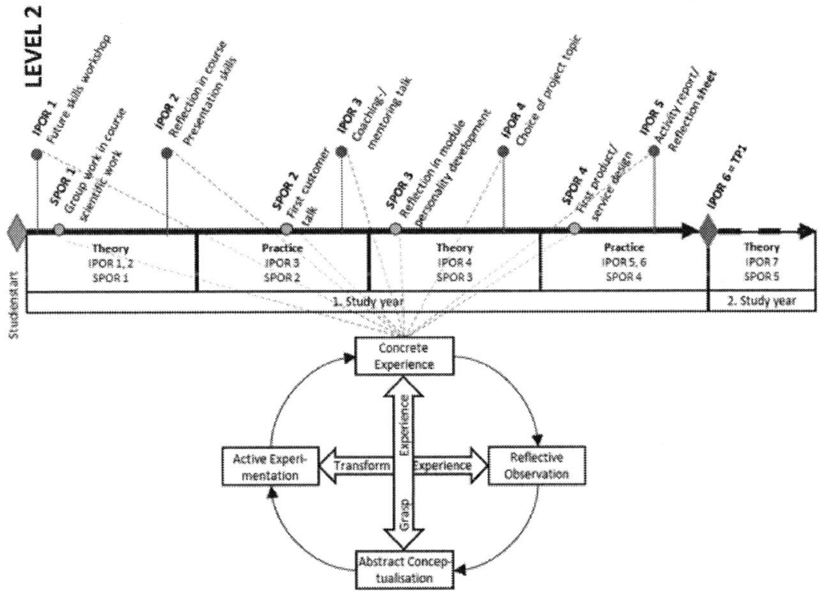

Fig. 2. Second level of a conception model for reflection in dual study programmes

Summary and conclusion

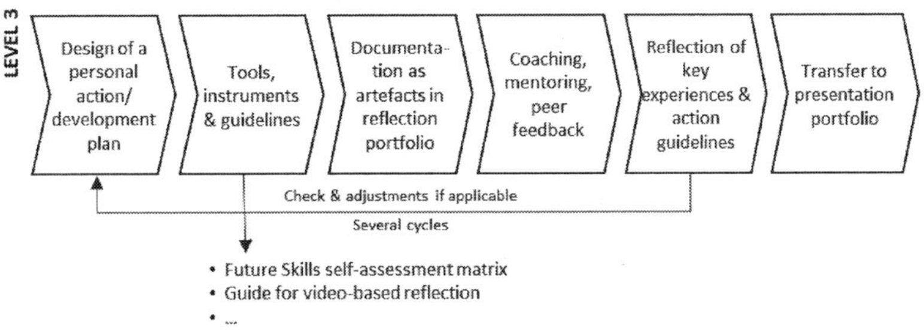

Fig. 2. Third level of a conception model for reflection in dual study programs

Dual study programs hold a great potential for competence development based on experiential and work-based learning, but to fully exploit this, it is necessary to create a true and strong interlink between the two learning spaces theory and practice and empower students to become self-directed learners. The reflection of key experiences, which positively or negatively irritate the learner's environment, is essential to reach this goal. Therefore, learners could follow the reflection steps of Kolb (2018) and Gibbs (1988). These are also used as a basis for the design of a conception mod-el for reflection of experiences that serves to the characteristics of dual study programs. Furthermore, the basics of Schön's reflective practitioner are integrated in order to not only focus on reflection as a skill but to embrace the importance that learners reflect on their basic action guidelines with the goal of developing individual theories of action manifested in their values and principles.

For this aim, the conception model consists of three levels. Level one shows the overall e-portfolio concept for experiential and reflective learning during a three-year dual study program with the goal of enlarging the students' capability of reflective practice and Future Skills development. It also shows the combination of three port-folio types (according to Baumgartner): reflection portfolio, presentation portfolio, and development portfolio. Level two depicts several intentional and spontaneous points of reflection for the example of a business management bachelor degree and show that at each reflection point, students follow the four steps of Kolb's learning cycle. Level three explains the connection to specific tools and instruments and models the process of transferring experiences into reflections, reflections into artefacts, and artefacts into the visualization of the personal (competence) development process presented in a presentation portfolio.

While each experience can be individually assessed through reflection and made fruitful for action competence development, larger individual development projects in the context of one's own professional development lend themselves to being understood as one's own professional development with the approach of the Reflective Practitioner. Studying thus becomes a series of reflection processes that are added to the development of knowledge and skills as a learning process and relate these to one's own actions in practice situations. All reflection events, both IPORs and SPORs, should be documented as artefacts in a portfolio, which can be implemented as a reflection, development and presentation portfolio. By compiling the artefacts in collections (i.e. in the portfolio), the development of action competences and professionalisation processes can be made visible.

References

1. Aprea, C., Sappa, V., & Tenberg, R. (Eds.). (2020). Zeitschrift für Berufs- und Wirtschaftspädagogik - Beihefte: Vol. 29. Konnektivität und lernortintegrierte Kompetenzentwicklung in der beruflichen Bildung. Franz Steiner Verlag. https://ebookcentral.proquest.com/lib/kxp/detail.action?docID=6228788
2. Baumgartner, P. (2012). Eine Taxonomie für E-Portfolios: - Teil II des BMWF-Abschlussberichts "E-Portfolio an Hochschulen": GZ 51.700/0064-VII/10/2006. Krems.
3. Beaugrand, A., Latteck, Ä.-D., Mertin, M., & Rolf, A. (2017). Lehr- und Lernmethoden im dualen Studium: Wissenstransfer zwischen Theorie und Praxis (1. Auflage). Verlag W. Kohlhammer.
4. Brodsky, A., Seifried, J., & Sailmann, G. (2021). Wege zu einer akademischen Beruflichkeit - Lernen am Arbeitsplatz in zwei dualen Studiengängen. In J. Seifried, G. Sailmann, & A. Brodsky (Eds.), Praxispotenziale im dualen Studium: Lernen am Arbeitsplatz als Element akademischer Qualifizierung (pp. 65–146). wbv.
5. Bundesinstitut für Berufsbildung. (2020). Duales Studium in Zahlen 2019: Trends und Analysen (AusbildungPlus). https://www.bibb.de/dokumente/pdf/06072020_AiZ_dualesStudium-2019.pdf
6. Darmann-Finck, I., Böhnke, U., & Straß, K. (Eds.). (2013). Mabuse-Verlag Wissenschaft: Vol. 111. Fallrekonstruktives Lernen: Ein Beitrag zur Professionalisierung in den Berufsfeldern Pflege und Gesundheit (2. Aufl.). Mabuse-Verl.
7. Deuer, E., & Wild, S. (2018). Theorie-Praxis-Beziehung im Kontext des dualen Studiums – Erwartungen und Wahrnehmungen aus der Perspektive der dual Studierenden: Arbeitspapier (Hochschulforschung an der DHBW). Stuttgart. https://www.dhbw.de/fileadmin/user_upload/Dokumente/Schrifterzeugnisse/3482_DHBW_AP12_2018_3_web.pdf
8. Fasshauer, U., & Anselmann, S. (2021). Akademische Beruflichkeit in dualen Studiengängen - Entwicklungspfade aus der Berufsbildung. In J. Seifried, G. Sailmann, & A. Brodsky (Eds.), Praxispotenziale im dualen Studium: Lernen am Arbeitsplatz als Element akademischer Qualifizierung (pp. 11–28). wbv.
9. Finlay, L. (2008). Reflecting on 'Reflective practice' (Discussion Papers for the Practice-based Professional Learning Centre for Excellence in Teaching and Learning (PBPL CETL) No. 52). https://oro.open.ac.uk/68945/1/Finlay-%282008%29-Reflecting-on-reflective-practice-PBPL-paper-52.pdf
10. Fuchs, W., & Rogmann, J. (2012). Erfahrungsbasiertes Lernen - Ein Modell für eine theoriegeleitete Vermittlung von Schlüsselkompetenzen in psychologischen Studiengängen und dessen Implikationen für die psychologiedidaktische Praxis. In M. Krämer, J. Barenberg, & S. Dutke (Eds.), Psychologie: Vol. 12. Psychologiedidaktik und Evaluation IX // Psychologiedidaktik und Evaluation (pp. 205–212). Shaker.
11. Gibbs, G. (1988). Learning by Doing: A guide to teaching and learning methods. Repro-duced 2013 by the Oxford Centre for Staff and Learning Development. Further Education Unit. https://thoughtsmostlyaboutlearning.files.wordpress.com/2015/12/learning-by-doing-graham-gibbs.pdf
12. Jahncke-Lattek, Ä.-D. (2010). Intuition als Bestandteil pflegerischen Handelns in der ambulanten Pflege - Entstehungskontexte und Merkmale intuitiven Handelns (urn:nbn:de:gbv:46-diss000118293) [Dissertation]. Universität Bremen. https://media.suub.uni-bremen.de/handle/elib/2782
13. Kolb, A., & Kolb, D. (2018). Eight important things to know about the Experiential Learning Cycle. Australian Educational Leader, 40(3), 8–14.

14. Kupfer, F., Kolter, C., & Köhlmann-Eckel, C. (2014). Analyse und Systematisierung dualer Studiengänge an Hochschulen: Abschlussbericht. https://www.bibb.de/dienst/dapro/daprodocs/pdf/eb_33302.pdf
15. Larsen-Freeman, D., Driver, P., Gao, X., & Mercer, S. (2021). Learner Agency: Maximiz-ing Learner Potential. https://fdslive.oup.com/www.oup.com/elt/general_content/global/expert/oup-expert-learner-agency.pdf?cc=de&selLanguage=en&mode=hub
16. Meyer, R. (2012). Professionsorientierte Beruflichkeit? Theoretische und konzeptionelle Überlegungen zur Öffnung der Hochschulen als Lernorte der beruflichen Bildung. Bwp@ Berufs- Und Wirtschaftspädagogik - Online, 23, 1–17. http://www.bwpat.de/ausgabe23/meyer_bwpat23.pdf
17. Schön, D. A. (1983). The reflective practitioner: how professionals think in action. Basic Books.
18. Schoon, I. (2018). Conceptualising Learner Agency: A Socio-Ecological Developmental Approach (LLAKES Research Paper No. 64). https://www.llakes.ac.uk/wp-content/uploads/2021/03/LLAKES-Research-Paper-64-Schoon-I.pdf
19. Seifried, J., Sailmann, G., & Brodsky, A. (Eds.). (2021). Praxispotenziale im dualen Studium: Lernen am Arbeitsplatz als Element akademischer Qualifizierung. wbv.
20. Stangl, W. (2022). Erfahrungsbasiertes Lernen. https://lexikon.stangl.eu/14476/erfahrungsbasiertes-lernen
21. Wissenschaftsrat. (2013). Empfehlungen zur Entwicklung des dualen Studiums: Positionspapier. Mainz.

Shaping the Digital Transformation of the Education Ecosystem in Europe
EDEN Digital Learning Europe Proceedings
2022 Annual Conference | Tallinn, 20-22 June, 2022
ISSN: 2707-2819

EDUCATIONAL DESIGN FOR DIGITAL LEARNING WITH MYSCRIPTING

Claude Müller and Jennifer Erlemann, Zurich University of Applied Sciences

Abstract

Designing teaching and learning is both a planning-conceptual and an operative design process, and one that is very close to the concept of design as it is used in other disciplines. This paper discusses design principles for digital learning and describes how digital learning can be designed with the educational design tool myScripting[5] based on the ADDIE process model. The tool suggests context-dependent activities, analyses the design continuously, and provides valuable indications for further development. Role-specific outputs and interfaces to learning management systems (LMS) facilitate the implementation of the scripts. In addition, the collaborative functions support teaching in teams as well as in-depth reflection on educational designs.

Keywords: Educational Design, Digital Learning, Educational Technology

Educational Design Process

More and more educational institutions are considering replacing some face-to-face teaching with blended or online learning. Research shows that such flexible study formats can improve access to education without compromising learning outcomes, but the effectiveness of blended and online learning depends largely on the quality of implementation (Müller & Mildenberger, 2021). The conception of teaching and learning is, therefore, not a process that can be automated but rather a planning-conceptual as well as an operative design process. In order to achieve specific learning outcomes in a particular educational context, teachers must make decisions that are analytical as well as creative. This is remarkably similar to the concept of design thinking used in other disciplines (Graham, 2019; Laurillard, 2013).

Design tools and processes offer valuable support, particularly when teachers have to develop educational designs for previously unknown contexts such as blended learning or online learning. A commonly used process model for systematically planning, implementing and reviewing technology-enhanced teaching and learning is the ADDIE model (Analysis, Design, Development, Implementation, Evaluation). In this model, each phase builds on the results of the previous development step.

In the analysis, all necessary information for the subsequent design phase of a learning offer is elaborated. This analysis examines what the educational context looks like and whether there is a need for training at all (needs analysis), who the target group is (target group analysis), the competencies that are to be developed (task and content analysis) and, related to this, what learning outcomes are aimed for. This is to avoid developing a learning offer without taking into account the needs and prerequisites of the learners. In addition, resources must also be analyzed. A teaching design might be suitable for a certain context, but that result might still not be practicable due to the time structures (e.g., the number of lessons in certain intervals) or infrastructure available (room characteristics, incl. ICT equipment). The design phase is dedicated to the conceptual planning of the learning offer. In this phase the learning objectives and content are structured, and suitable teaching strategies are identified. Then, in a circular scripting process, the educational design is adjusted to four aspects: content delivery, activation, interaction and assessment. Next, in the development phase, the various learning resources are produced and assembled into a learning environment and then, in the implementation phase, the digital learning environment is implemented in practice. Finally, in the evaluation phase, the learning environment is critically reviewed, and appropriate adjustments are defined

for the next design and development process. The following principles are of central importance for the

[5] The online tool *myScripting* can be used free of charge at the URL [www.anonymous]

educational design process:

- Backward design: First, the learning outcomes, i.e., the competencies that the participants should acquire by completion of the learning offer ("Beginning with the end in mind"), are defined. The learning organization and content structure, as well as the educational design (scripting) are then developed on the basis of the learning outcomes.

- Constructive alignment: The design of the digital learning offer is aligned with the learning outcomes, i.e. the learning environment should promote and assess the competencies that are targeted (Biggs, 1999).
- Agile design process: The development and implementation of a digital learning offer is not a process that can be automated, but is rather a circular process with iterative feedback loops that is both planning conceptual and operational.

The design process with myScripting is based on the ADDIE model. In the first step, the temporal and spatial organization of the learning offer (horizontal), as well as the structure of the content (vertical), are determined based on the analyses (see Table 1). Then, in a circular design process, the aspects of content delivery, activation, interaction and assessment are defined. The design may be guided by a specific teaching strategy (such as direct instruction or problem-based learning).

With *myScripting*, the digital learning offer is conceptually developed. The goal is a detailed blueprint for the subsequent media production and the building of the course on a learning platform. The focus of *myScripting* is, therefore, on the design phase in the development of digital learning opportunities. Nevertheless, the preceding and subsequent ADDIE steps are also supported in *myScripting*:

- *Analysis*: The results of the analysis are documented in *myScripting* under the fields of prerequisites (e.g., regarding target audience), learning outcomes, content and assessment. In addition, the analysis determines the basic script settings such as planned workload, target platform and assessment system.
- *Development & Implementation*: For the production of the digital learning offer, the developed script can be exported into LMS. Role-specific outputs for the teaching and learning process can be generated from the scripts. For teachers, *myScripting* develops a chronological lesson plan with optional additional information for class management (table view), and for learners a syllabus is available. These outputs are in Word format and can be further edited.
- *Evaluation*: Once developed, learning offers can be reviewed directly in *myScripting*. For the individual learning phases, topics and the entire script can be specified and assigned a development status.

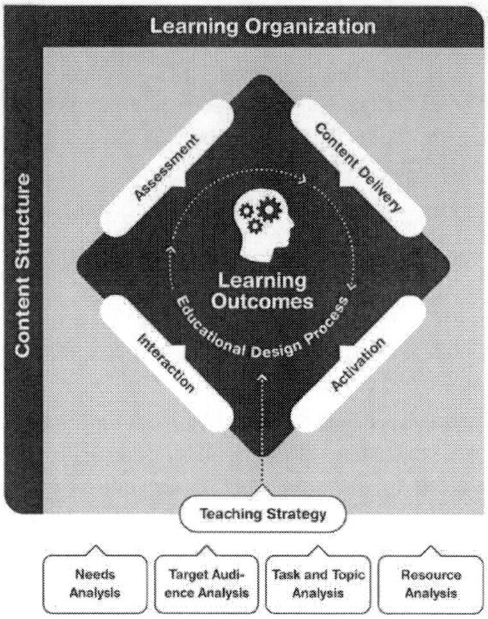

Fig. 3. Educational Design with myScripting.

Learning Organization and Content Structure

Based on the analyses and the learning outcomes developed, the temporal and spatial learning organization and the content structure of the digital learning offer can then be determined.

Learning Organization

Various forms of learning modalities are conceivable depending on the target group, the competencies to be acquired, and the available infrastructure. If the learners are, for example, geographically dispersed and not very flexible in terms of time, the learning offer can be primarily offered asynchronously and online. If they are flexible in terms of time and place, if a modern infrastructure is available (for example, with labs), and if skills are promoted, a synchronous learning organization in the available physical classrooms (onsite) may make more sense. Table 1 shows the possibilities of learning modalities that result from the dimensions of time and space.

Time / *Space*	*Synchronous*	*Asynchronous*
Onsite	Physical presence event (e.g., in classrooms, in the field)	Onsite self-study (e.g., in the learning center, lab, library)
Online	Virtual presence event (with video conferencing system)	Online self-study (with electronic learning resources or learning platform)

Table 1. Learning Modalities.

With today's technical infrastructure, it is also possible to offer face-to-face courses simultaneously onsite and online (also referred to as hybrid learning). Often these synchronous courses are also recorded so that they can then be used for asynchronous learning (Hyflex courses). The following factors have an influence on the structural characteristics of the learning organization in addition to the learning outcomes, which are the guiding factors for all structure characteristics (see Table 2).

Learning modality features	Influencing factors
Proportion of asynchronous/synchronous learning	Availability and needs of learners, desired learning culture
Proportion of online to onsite learning	Availability and needs of learners, required and available learning infrastructure (e.g., lab facilities), desired learning culture
Workload	Prescribed workload (formal education) or reasonable workload (informal education), content structure
Length of learning units	Availability and needs of learners, learning culture
Control (self-paced or instructor-paced)	Availability and needs of learners, resources of instructors, desired learning culture

Table 2. Influencing Factors for Learning Modality Features.

In myScripting, an initial structure of the intended learning phases is created on the basis of the above decisions (see Fig. 2). For this purpose, the learning phases face-to-face physical and face-to-face online for synchronous learning or self-study for asynchronous learning are available. In the course of the design process, the learning phases can be continuously adapted.

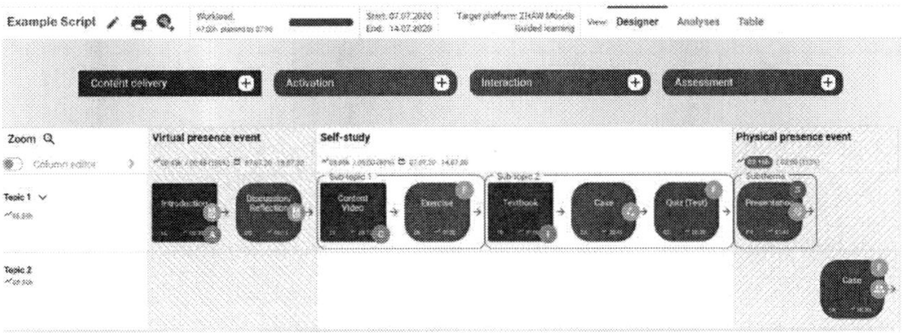

Fig. 4. Learning Organization and Content Structure in the Designer in myScripting.

Content Structure

In the task and topic analysis, the contents to be acquired in a course are identified, and in the definition of the learning outcomes the related levels of abstraction (overview or in-depth) and the targeted cognitive demand levels are defined. Due to the limited capacity of the working memory, novices in particular are usually unable to process complex content and its interrelationships simultaneously (Sweller, 1994). Therefore, the content has to be prioritized and reduced and, if necessary, simplified (didactic reduction), divided into segments (segmentation) and put into chronological order (sequencing).

A frequently used approach for structuring content is the learning hierarchy. In this approach, the content that is a prerequisite for learning the content that builds on it is dealt with first. However, there are various other principles that can be used to segment and sequence content, such as the inductive or deductive approach or the process principle in skills courses (see also Reigeluth, 1999). In the case of very complex content with a high number of interacting elements, the intrinsic load can also be reduced by dividing the elaboration process into sub steps with isolated elements. After the partial elements have been elaborated, they are combined into the whole in a further step (see also 4C/ID-Modell Van Merriënboer & Kirschner, 2017).

The content structure is mapped vertically in myScripting with topics and sub-topics (see Fig. 2). For each topic, the learning process is depicted with the activities in one row. Sub-topics can be represented by grouping activities.

Educational Design

Recent research on digital learning has analyzed aspects of online and blended learning in scientific reviews based on surveys of learners and teachers. The following factors have been found to be particularly effective for digital learning:

- Adequate course structure and guidance for learners
- Activating learning tasks
- Stimulating interactions and social presence of the teachers
- Timely feedback on learning process and outcomes

Activation, in particular, is crucial in the design of digital learning because starting from the learning content, the design of digital learning often focuses on the creation of content delivery, for example, by means of instructional texts and videos. However, content delivery in itself does not imply a pedagogically designed learning environment, or as Merrill (2018, p. 2) puts it: "Information alone is not instruction." In addition to learning resources, learners also need adequate activation: this is what enables learners to transform the information they have absorbed into knowledge and skills, and facilitates the application of learned knowledge and skills in new and real situations. Therefore, the teacher's task is to design goal-oriented and attractive learning so that learners engage in the learning offer (Kahu, 2013) and achieve the learning goals. The ICAP model (Chi & Wylie, 2014) addresses learners' varying levels of engagement with learning resources and assumes that the more intensively learners engage and interact with learning content, the more successful learning will be.

	Passive	Active	Constructive	Interactive
Lecture 	Listen carefully to a lecture	Repeat or rehearse; copy solution steps; make notes	Reflect aloud; draw concept map; ask questions	Argument, defend a position
Text 	Read text passages silently or aloud attentively	Underline or highlight text passages	Explain the text yourself; summarize in your own words	Ask questions of understanding and discuss/clarify with a peer
Video 	Watch video carefully	Pause, play, speed up, rewind video	Explain video content and compare it with previous knowledge or other materials	Explore contents with peers, discuss similarities and differences

Table 3. Activities in the ICAP-Model (according to Chi & Wylie, 2014).

Engagement can be stimulated through assignments on how to use the learning resources. Learners often have little experience with virtual interaction, and need concrete guidance on how to organize and design online interaction and collaboration (Vogel et al., 2017). Useful assignments are, for example, conducting forum discussions (with contributions and feedback), working collaboratively on texts or videos with the annotation function (or other approaches such as producing them with a wiki), explaining learning content to each other (for example, in the context of a jigsaw/group puzzle), or giving each other feedback on learning outcomes or projects. Although often implemented, writing summaries, underlining and marking have been shown to be not particularly effective (Dunlosky et al., 2013). It is better for learners to recall their knowledge and write it down in their own words or explain it to each other, review worked examples, or answer sample exam questions (see also the compilation of learning strategies in Fiorella & Mayer, 2015).

The biggest difference between onsite classroom teaching and online learning is the interaction, which changes with the temporal and spatial distance. For example, synchronous phases are difficult in MOOCs or courses for in-house training with a global group of participants due to the different learning times. It is, therefore, even more important in asynchronous learning environments to integrate opportunities for interaction, such as forum discussions or peer feedback, or to organize learning in smaller groups (e.g., forming learning groups) to promote the sense of social inclusion in a learning community.

In myScripting, the educational design is carried out in the designer. The topics are arranged vertically and structure the script in terms of content; the learning phases are arranged horizontally and structure it in terms of time. The planning consists of specifying how the individual topics are didactically implemented over time. To do this, users choose from predefined activities. Since myScripting was developed especially for digital learning courses, the activities correspond as closely as possible to the tools in LMS. If none of the listed LMSs and corresponding activity sets is used, "Other" can also be selected, which contains a set of activities that is available in all common LMSs. For each of these activities, information is provided on the teaching function as well as on the technical implementation. The activities are assigned to the groups of content delivery, activation, interaction and assessment based on the primary function of an activity; however, activities can often have several functions: a forum, for example, is activating and used for interaction, and the contributions can also be evaluated in the sense of assessment. For this reason, the activities of activation, interaction and assessment are colored light blue to distinguish them from the dark blue content delivery activities.

During the design process, the designed script can be continuously evaluated and reflected upon in the analysis view in myScripting (see Fig. 3). The following analyses are available for this evaluation:

- *Workload*: comparison of the planned and designed workload.
- *Flexible learning*: comparison of workload for asynchronous vs synchronous learning
- *Activities*: comparison of workload for content delivery activities vs activation/interaction/assessment activities
- *Assessment*: number of activities with formative or summative assessment
- *Peer learning*: number of activities with peers (in small/large groups)
- *ICAP learning tasks*: number of learning tasks according to the ICAP model
- *Learning Outcomes*: Number and workload of topics, subtopics and activities that promote the different learning outcomes.

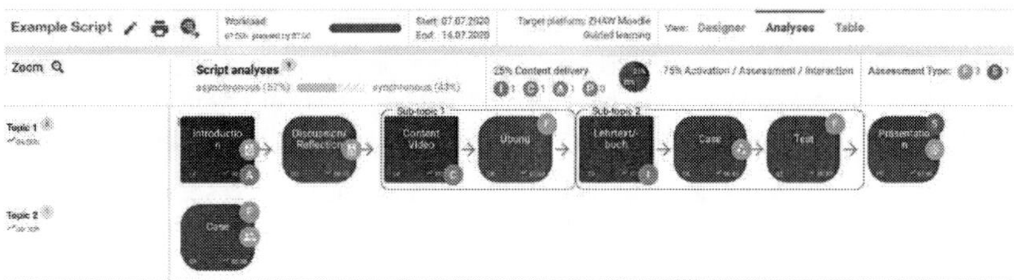

Fig. 5. Analysis View in myScripting.

The educational design should be coordinated in such a way that there is congruence between learning outcomes, learning environment and assessment in the sense of constructive alignment: the digital learning offer should promote the competencies being aimed for and assessed. Digital learning environments enable new learning approaches and processes (e.g., by means of simulations or adaptive learning processes). It is therefore important to design digital learning environments that extend and change conventional learning (according to Puentedura's [6]SAMR) and do not merely reproduce conventional classroom teaching.

Conclusion

The didactic design process presented here shows how the educational design tool myScripting can be used to develop educational designs for digital learning systematically. The tool suggests context-dependent activities for a teaching setting, which can be assigned to topics and learning phases. In addition, design templates are available for central teaching strategies such as flipped classroom, problem-based learning or direct instruction. The various views allow the teacher to maintain an overview during the design process,

[6] http://www.hippasus.com/resources/tte/

and role-specific outputs of the teaching and learning process can be created for teachers or students. Thus, myScripting enables the design of context-specific, diverse learning environments, such as blended learning courses with specific LMSs or online courses for MOOC platforms. In addition, the collaborative functions support teaching in teams and in-depth reflection on lesson designs.

References

1. Biggs, J. B. (1999). Teaching for Quality Learning in University. Society for Research in Higher Education and Open University Press.
2. Chi, M. T., & Wylie, R. (2014). The ICAP framework: Linking cognitive engagement to active learning outcomes. Educational psychologist, 49(4), 219-243. https://doi.org/10.1080/00461520.2014.965823
3. Dunlosky, J., Rawson, K. A., Marsh, E. J., Nathan, M. J., & Willingham, D. T. (2013). Improving students' learning with effective learning techniques: Promising directions from cognitive and educational psychology. Psychological Science in the Public Interest, 14(1), 4-58. https://doi.org/https://doi.org/10.1177/1529100612453266
4. Fiorella, L., & Mayer, R. E. (2015). Learning as a generative activity. Cambridge University Press. https://doi.org/https://doi.org/10.1017/CBO9781107707085
5. Graham, C. R. (2019). Current research in blended learning. In M. G. Moore & W. C. Diehl (Eds.), Handbook of distance education (4th ed., pp. 173-188). Routledge.
6. Kahu, E. R. (2013). Framing student engagement in higher education. Studies in Higher Education, 38(5), 758-773. https://doi.org/10.1080/03075079.2011.598505
7. Laurillard, D. (2013). Teaching as a design science: Building pedagogical patterns for learning and technology. Routledge.
8. Merrill, M. D. (2018). Using the first principles of instruction to make instruction effective, efficient, and engaging. In R. E. West (Ed.), Foundations of Learning and Instructional Design Technology: The Past, Present, and Future of Learning and Instructional Design Technology. EdTech Books. https://edtechbooks.org/lidtfoundations/using_the_first_principles_of_instruction
9. Müller, C., & Mildenberger, T. (2021). Facilitating flexible learning by replacing classroom time with an online learning environment: A systematic review of blended learning in higher education. Educational Research Review, 34, 100394. https://doi.org/https://doi.org/10.1016/j.edurev.2021.100394
10. Reigeluth, C. M. (1999). The elaboration theory: Guidance for scope and sequence decisions. In C. M. Reigeluth (Ed.), Instructional-design theories and models: A new paradigm of instructional theory (Vol. 2, pp. 425-453). Lawrence Erlbaum Associates Publisher.
11. Sweller, J. (1994). Cognitive load theory, learning difficulty, and instructional design. Learning and Instruction, 4(4), 295-312.
12. Van Merriënboer, J. J., & Kirschner, P. A. (2017). Ten steps to complex learning: A systematic approach to four-component instructional design. Routledge.
13. Vogel, F., Wecker, C., Kollar, I., & Fischer, F. (2017). Socio-cognitive scaffolding with computer-supported collaboration scripts: A meta-analysis. Educational Psychology Review, 29(3), 477-511.

European Distance and E-Learning Network (EDEN)
Budapest University of Technology & Economics
H-1111 Budapest, Egry J. u.1.
Hungary

ISBN 978-1-7138-8972-4

CURRAN ASSOCIATES INC.
proceedings.com

Transportation Network Modeling 2018

Transportation Research Record: Journal of the Transportation Research Board Volume 2672, Issue 48

SAGE Publishing